The Babi and Baha'i religions

THE BABI AND BAHAʾI RELIGIONS

FROM MESSIANIC SHIʿISM TO A WORLD RELIGION

PETER SMITH

Department of Humanities, Mahidol University, Thailand
and
Department of Sociology, University of Lancaster

The right of the University of Cambridge to print and sell all manner of books was granted by Henry VIII in 1534. The University has printed and published continuously since 1584.

distributed by
GEORGE RONALD, PUBLISHER
on behalf of
CAMBRIDGE UNIVERSITY PRESS

Cambridge
London New York New Rochelle
Melbourne Sydney

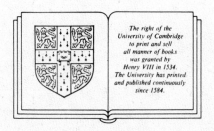

Published by the Press Syndicate of the University of Cambridge
The Pitt Building, Trumpington Street, Cambridge CB2 1RP
32 East 57th Street, New York, NY 10022, USA
10 Stamford Road, Oakleigh, Melbourne 3166, Australia

First published 1987

Printed in Great Britain at the University Press, Cambridge

British Library cataloguing in publication data
Smith, Peter
The Babi and the Baha'i religion: from
Messianic Shi'ism to a world religion.
1. Babism – History 2. Bahai Faith –
History
I. Title
297'.88'09 BP340

Library of Congress cataloguing in publication data
Smith, Peter, 1947 Nov. 27–
The Babi and the Baha'i religions.
Bibliography.
Includes index.
1. Bahai Faith – History. 2. Babism – History.
I. Title.
BP330.S65 1987 297'.88 87-16781

ISBN 0 521 30128 9 hard covers
ISBN 0 521 31755 x paperback

SE

To my mother, Wyn Smith,
and to the memory of my father,
Edward Peatfield Smith (1913–82)

Man is so intelligent that he feels impelled to invent theories to account for what happens in the world. Unfortunately, he is not quite intelligent enough, in most cases, to find correct explanations.

Aldous Huxley
Texts and Pretexts

CONTENTS

PART II: THE BAHAʾI FAITH IN THE EAST, *c.* 1866–1921

PART III: THE BAHAʾI FAITH AS A WORLD RELIGION

ILLUSTRATIONS

All illustrations are reproduced by permission of the Audio-Visual Department at the Bahaʾi World Centre, Haifa.

TABLES

FIGURES

MAPS

TRANSLITERATION

I have employed a modified version of the system of transliteration employed within the Baha'i community, diverging from that system in order to distinguish more clearly separate Arabic and Persian usages, and in much greater Anglicization of oriental terms and place names in common Western usage or of frequent occurrence.

ACKNOWLEDGEMENTS

Western scholarly interest in the Babi and Baha'i religions flourished first in the period from the 1880s to the 1910s, notably in the work of Mirza Kazem-Beg, E.G. Browne, A.L.M. Nicolas, V. Rosen and A. Tumanskii. There then followed a lengthy period of scholarly neglect which came to an end only in the 1970s. Within the Baha'i community, the writings of H.M. Balyuzi and the formation of the Canadian Association for Baha'i Studies (in 1974) contributed significantly to this revival of interest. Within the academic community, interest was primarily reflected by an increasing number of doctoral dissertations. Whilst from the 1920s up to 1970 fewer than a dozen dissertations had been produced, since that date there have been at least twenty. We now at last have a substantial scholarly base for a general academic survey such as the present work.

Let me acknowledge my debts of gratitude. This book had its genesis during my years at the University of Lancaster, first as a graduate student in the Department of Sociology, and later as a research fellow. To the members of that Department and also to those of the Department of Religious Studies at Lancaster, I owe my introduction to academic life and debate. More specifically, the two Departments jointly sponsored a series of Baha'i Studies Seminars, held under my convenorship (1977–80), which contributed both to the present work, and to the development of Baha'i Studies as a venture in co-operative scholarship. In terms of that venture, my thanks are due to all the participants at those Lancaster seminars, and also to the organizers and participants at the Los Angeles Baha'i History Conferences, which from 1983 on were their successors. My particular thanks must go to Juan Cole, Stephen Lambden, Anthony Lee, Denis MacEoin and Moojan Momen for their years of friendship and argument about Baha'i Studies.

I must thank the many individuals who have at one time or other commented on various drafts of this work, or on the doctoral dissertation for which much of the research was originally done. These include Nicholas Abercrombie, John Hughes, Bryan Turner, and Michalina

Vaughan at Lancaster; Eileen Barker from the London School of Economics; and for the present (final) draft, Denis MacEoin, Moojan Momen, Sammireh Smith, and, at Cambridge University Press, Elizabeth Wetton.

I must also thank Sylvia Stackhouse, Mavis Conolly and Shirley Govindasamy for their invaluable secretarial work; archivist Roger Dahl for his co-operation during my extended visit to the American National Bahaʾi Archives at Wilmette, Illinois; the staffs at the National Bahaʾi Centres of Canada and the United Kingdom, and at the Bahaʾi World Centre in Haifa for facilitating my access to library materials; the Department of the Secretariat and the Department of Statistics at the Bahaʾi World Centre for their responses to my various queries; and the International Bahaʾi Audio-Visual Centre for the photographs which illustrate this book. Above all, my thanks are due to my parents, my wife and my children for their support over the long years of research. As is customary, I should record the particularly immeasurable nature of my indebtedness to my wife, and the complete innocence of any of the above for such errors as may still linger in the pages which follow.

Let me close these remarks by noting two aspects of my work on this book. Firstly, whilst I am primarily a sociologist of religion by training, what is here presented is basically a work of history. I see no anomaly in this fact, for I would argue that sociologists need also to be historians. Nevertheless, the reader will note that although sociological ideas are implicit in many sections of this book, formal sociological analysis has been excluded. Secondly, in writing about a minority religion, some brief confession of faith is perhaps required, if only to rebut potential allegations of bias. Let it be said, then, that without claiming to have attained some mystical state of sociological value freedom, I have sought to write without conscious bias and with a general sense of questioning the taken-for-granted assumptions which form part of my background as a Bahaʾi.

Bangkok
January 1986

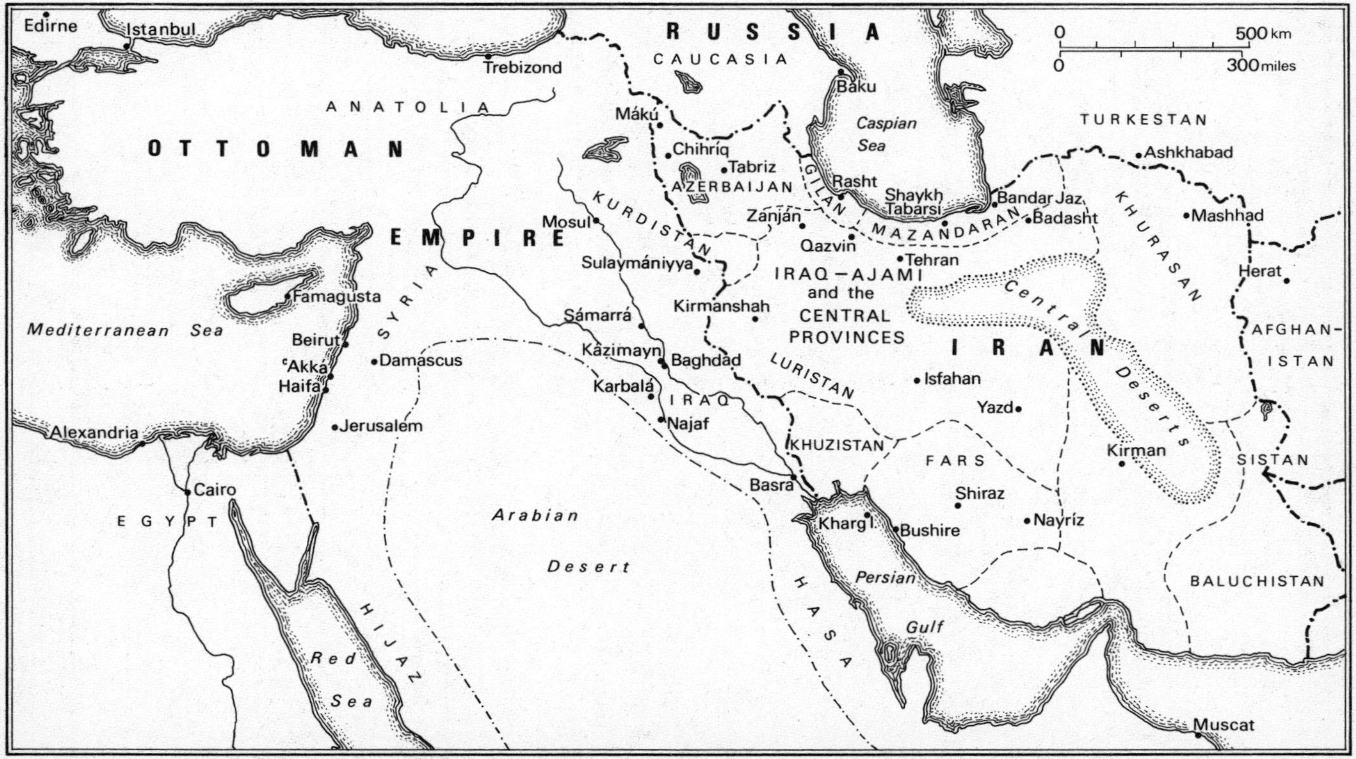

Map 1. Iran and the Ottoman Empire in the mid-nineteenth century. The international boundaries to the east of Iran were not defined or demarcated until the late nineteenth century. Iran's internal provincial boundaries were frequently changed

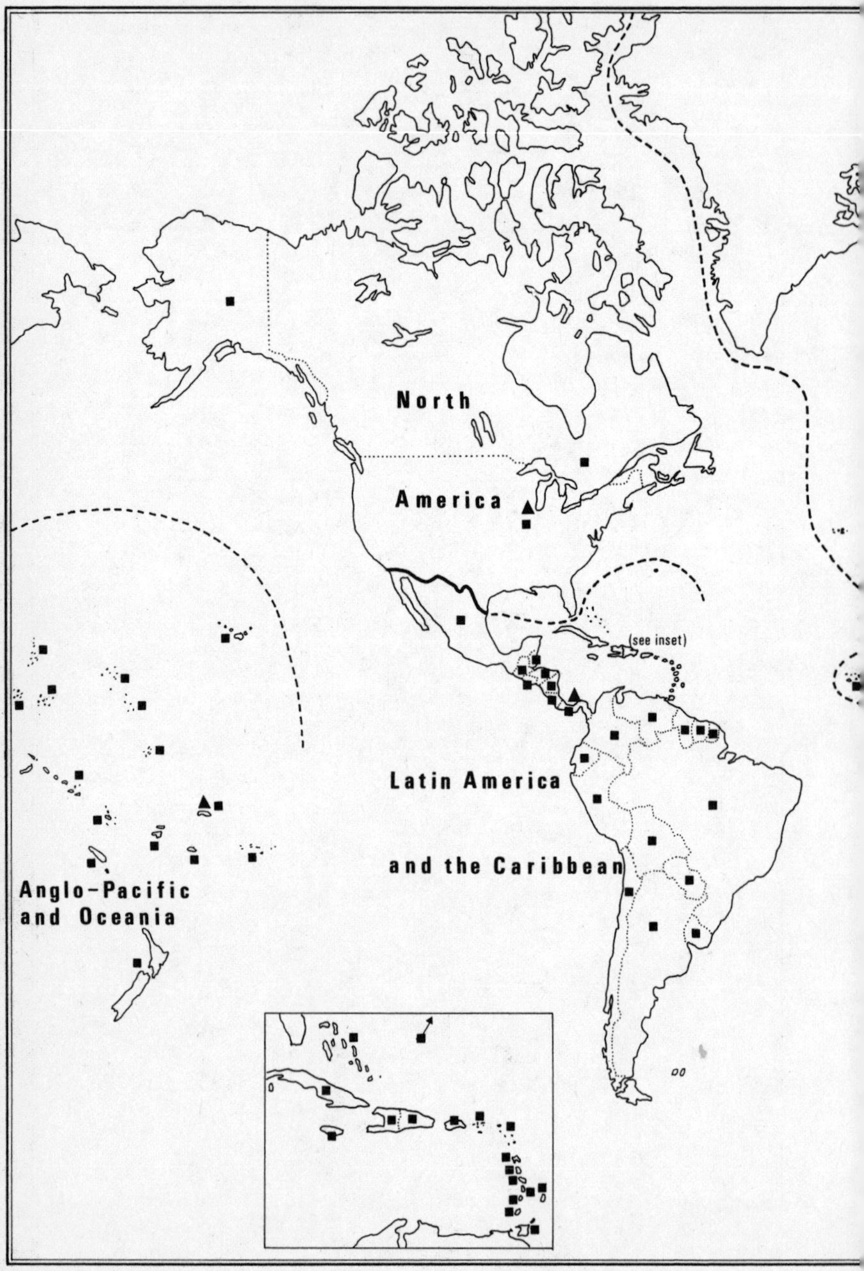

Map 2. Global expansion of the Baha'i Faith (April 1985)

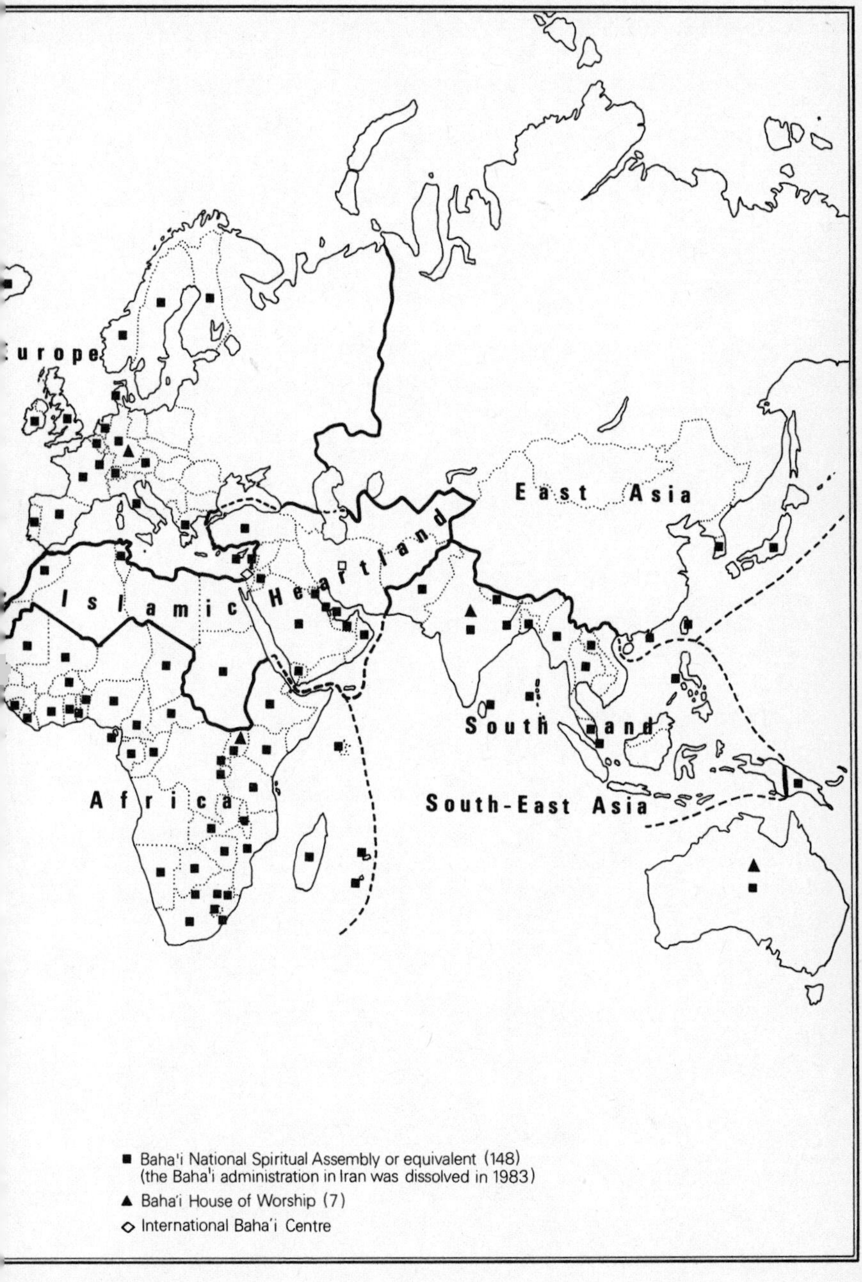
urope
East Asia
Islamic Heartland
Africa
South and
South-East Asia
■ Baha'i National Spiritual Assembly or equivalent (148)
(the Baha'i administration in Iran was dissolved in 1983)
▲ Baha'i House of Worship (7)
◇ International Baha'i Centre

INTRODUCTION

The Baha'i Faith is today a world-wide religious movement of considerable scope and dynamism. Established in most of the countries of the world, the Faith has attracted adherents from a multitude of religious and racial backgrounds, amply demonstrating the validity of its claims to universality. Teaching that their founder is the latest in a succession of messengers from God, and that his mission is the unification of all humanity in a divinely ordained Most Great Peace, the Baha'is have embarked on co-ordinated plans to expand and consolidate their community. Working to establish a Kingdom of God on Earth, they believe that the religious prophecies of all past religions are being fulfilled. Stressing the linkage between the spiritual transformation of the individual and that of society as a whole, the Baha'is propound and seek to embody teachings and principles which embrace many aspects of human life besides the specifically 'religious'. For Baha'is, the advocacy of sexual and racial equality, or of universal compulsory education, is as much part of their religious practice as is prayer or fasting or the challenges of individual morality.

Religious movements are rarely static entities. In the case of the Baha'i Faith, its short but eventful history has witnessed considerable transformation from its origins in the earlier Babi movement. The Babi religion had emerged in mid-nineteenth-century Iran as a powerful expression of the messianic expectations of Shi'i Islam. In 1844, its youthful founder, Sayyid 'Alí Muḥammad Shírází (1819–50), known as the Báb, had laid claim to be the promised one of Islam. His followers soon established a nation-wide movement which explicitly challenged the authority of the Shi'i religious leaders, who moved rapidly to oppose the movement. Aspiring to establish a theocratic state, the Babis also came into conflict with the Iranian government. The movement was then bloodily extirpated (1848–52) and the Báb himself executed. Out of the ashes of Babism, Baha'ism emerged. In the 1860s, one of the Báb's followers, Mirzá Ḥusayn 'Alí Núrí (1817–92), known as Bahá'u'lláh, attracted to himself the devotion of most of the Babi remnant. Claiming to be the promised one of all religions, Bahá'u'lláh promulgated a religion which stood in marked contrast to that of the Babis. In place of the militancy and religious exclusivity of the Babis, the Baha'is were enjoined to adopt an irenic attitude of religious tolerance and political quietism. In place of the messianic theocracy which the Babis had believed would soon be established in Iran, the Baha'is were advised to direct their hopes towards the future establishment of the Most Great Peace, a possibly distant vision of world-wide harmony and universal government. The theme of social reconstruction augmented the millennial vision.

When Bahá'u'lláh died in 1892, an exile in Ottoman Palestine since 1868, his eldest son, ʿAbdu'l-Bahá ʿAbbás (1844–1921), assumed the leadership of the movement as his father's appointed successor. Under his guidance, the Baha'i movement became established in the West. Although the new Western Baha'i communities were small by comparison with those of the East, they exerted an increasingly significant influence on the overall development of the religion as it assumed an ever more international flavour. This was particularly the case when ʿAbdu'l-Bahá's successor, his grandson Shoghi Effendi Rabbání (1897–1957), undertook to replace the movement's earlier charismatic leadership with a more routinized form of administration. Subsequently, after a brief interregnum (1957—63), an elected nine-member Universal House of Justice assumed supreme authority. Extending the series of systematic plans for the propagation of the movement which had been instituted by Shoghi Effendi, the Universal House of Justice has led the Baha'is through a period of increasing expansion and international recognition. As a consequence, the social and religious basis of the Baha'i Faith has increasingly gravitated away from the land of its birth. Whatever may be the future of the Iranian Baha'i community – now beleaguered in a wave of savage persecution – the future of the Baha'i religion is no longer inextricably linked to its fortunes in Iran. The majority of Baha'is are not Iranians, and however vivid they may find the narratives of the origins of their religion, the social and religious context of that genesis must inevitably now be an alien one to them.

This present study has been written with the intention both of describing the original and changing context of the Babi and Baha'i religions, and of providing an account of the overall development of the two movements. To this end, I employ the concept of 'motif' to describe the various dominant religious concerns which have characterized the Babi and

Baha'i religions.[1] As employed here, motifs represent fundamental patterns of religious experience which interact and change in the overall development of a religious movement. In the case of the Babi and Baha'i religions eight such motifs are identified: the regard for authoritative and charismatic leadership (the *polar* motif); the concern with structuring society according to the provisions of a holy law (*legalism*); *millenarian* expectation; the desire to engage in *social reform*; the belief in hidden salvatory knowledge (*esotericism*); the belief in the universality of God's guidance and grace to mankind (*universalism*); the belief that religious knowledge should be compatible with the rationality of the modern world (*liberalism*); and the interlinked Shi'i themes of religious martyrdom and of militant and sacrificial struggle (*holy war*). Two of these motifs – legalism and the regard for authoritative leadership – may be traced through their successive changes from Shi'ism to contemporary Baha'ism. Others are more circumscribed, with the Babi emphasis on millenarian expectation, esotericism and martyrdom continuing traditional Shi'i concerns, but later undergoing radical transformation, and standing in marked contrast to the liberalism, universalism and social reformism of modern Baha'i. These changing motifs may be seen as part of a general process of transformation, whereby what was essentially a messianic Shi'i sect has developed into a world religion.

The book is divided into three parts each with the same general pattern. Part I describes the emergence of Babism (Chapter 1), the movement's dominant religious concerns (Chapter 2), and its role and characteristics as a socio-religious movement in Iran (Chapter 3). Part II examines the emergence of the Baha'i Faith in the East (Chapter 4), its dominant religious concerns (Chapter 5), and the development of the religion in the changing context of Qajar Iran (Chapter 6). Part III deals with the transformation of Baha'i into a world religion, from its initial establishment in the West (Chapter 7), through the establishment of its administration (Chapter 8) and modern dominant concerns (Chapter 9), to its global expansion (Chapter 10). I also offer a few concluding comments in which some of the possibilities of Baha'i development are outlined.

PART I: BABISM

1
THE BABI MOVEMENT

IRAN AND SHI^{c}ISM

The Babi religion developed in the context of mid-nineteenth-century Iranian Shi^{c}ism. Although rapidly diverging from Shi^{c}i orthodoxy and making claim to be the bearers of a new religion, the early Babis continued to live largely within the conceptual universe of Shi^{c}ism.

Iran

Three times the size of France, the land that is now Iran has only intermittently existed as a single political entity. Divided by mountains and by vast tracts of semi-desert, its component parts do not comprise a readily integrated or defensible whole. Subject to recurrent political instability and the centrifugal forces of localism and of ethnic and religious diversity, unification has been imperial rather than national in its inspiration. Under the Safavids (reigned 1501–1722), the effective founders of modern Iran, a rudimentary 'national' consciousness emerged, only to be shattered at the beginning of the eighteenth century by dynastic collapse and renewed political fragmentation. Over seventy years of recurrent war and devastation ensued, a period which was brought to a brutal end at the turn of the nineteenth century by the re-establishment of a unitary state under the tribal leaders of the Qajars (reigned 1796–1925).[1]

Twelver Shi^{c}ism

The establishment of the Safavid dynasty in 1501 had been accompanied by the establishment of Imámí or Ithná-^{c}asharí (Twelver) Shi^{c}ism as the

Iranian state religion. Although only gradually adopted as the predominant religion of the Iranians, Twelver Shiʿism came to form the basis for an effective religious nationalism, marking off the mass of the Iranians from their Ottoman and Central Asian neighbours, who were predominantly members of the Sunni branch of Islam.

The origins of Twelver Shiʿism go back to the succession disputes that followed the death of the Prophet Muhammad in AD 632. As the ideals of the early Islamic theocracy were quickly eroded, many pious Muslims had turned to the hope that some member of the Prophet's own family would supplant the rule of the Umayyad caliphs who had established their rule in AD 661, after the murder of the caliph ʿAlí ibn Abí-Ṭálib, Muhammad's cousin, son-in-law, and close associate. Pious hope combined with political discontent to fuel a series of popular rebellions which eventually led to the overthrow of the Umayyads (747–50), but which failed to establish a theocratic paradise. Those who still hoped that some member of the Prophet's family would one day establish a just and godly rulership over the Muslim peoples increasingly cohered into a number of rival religious sects. These sectarians were now known as the *Shíʿa*, the 'partisans' of ʿAlí and his descendants, different sects identifying different ʿAlids as the putative just ruler.

Those Shiʿis who came to be known as Twelvers identified a series of twelve *Imáms*, beginning with ʿAlí and continuing through the line of descent from his wife Fáṭima, Muhammad's daughter. These Imams came to be regarded as inerrant and immaculate, the only real and rightful rulers of the Islamic community, who sustained and interpreted the faith in succession to the prophetic revelation of Muhammad. The line of Imams ended in AH 260 (AD 873) with the death of the Eleventh Imam and the mysterious disappearance of his supposed son, the Twelfth Imam. Hidden from the eyes of all but his special representatives or 'gates' (*abwáb*, sing. *báb*), the Twelfth Imam lived in concealment (*ghayba*) for a while (873–940), until the fourth gate died and the greater concealment or 'occultation' began. During this occultation, the Hidden Imam functioned as 'the *axia mundi*, the invisible ruler of the universe',[2] sustaining his *Shíʿa* in the realm of the spirit. He would return at the end of time as the Imam Mahdi, the divinely guided redeemer of the iniquitous world.

The ulama and dissent

In centralized Islamic societies, learning and education were traditionally dominated by religious concerns. Those who became learned were distinguished as members of a religiously defined status group, the *ᶜulamá*. Distinctive robes and turbans were worn as signs of this status. The ulama were not a homogeneous grouping, however. Whilst many subsisted as jurisconsults, teachers, preachers and charity administrators, in Iranian Shiᶜism at least, there was no clearly defined clerical career. With the exception of some Sufi leaders, recognition as a member of the ulama derived from attendance at one of the *madrasas* (seminaries), which constituted the only advanced institutes of learning. Through patronage and a few years study students might gain appointment as village or neighbourhood mullas, as teachers at the lowly Quranic schools, or as minor religious functionaries. To rise to the ranks of the higher ulama required further years of study and the acquisition of a reputation for religious learning. Unlike the Ottoman Empire and Egypt, Qajar Iran had no distinct hierarchy of state-sponsored judicial and educational posts. Thus, whilst a few of the higher ulama had stipendiary posts as Friday prayer leaders at the larger mosques (*Imám-Jumᶜihs*) or as titular heads of the local ulama (*Shaykhuʾl-Islárns*), most were independent jurisconsults and teachers who earned their livelihoods from a variety of fees and bequests, and in some cases from land-ownership and trade. The leading ulama also collected and disbursed the religious taxes and controlled the religious endowments which together ensured the financial independence of the ulama as an institution.

A considerable degree of political independence was also gained. At a national level, this was acquired adventitiously by the inability of the Qajar state to incorporate within its realms the *ᶜAtabát*, the holy 'thresholds' in Ottoman Iraq in which many of the Shiᶜi Imams were buried. From an Iranian viewpoint, these clergy-dominated cities – Karbalá, Najaf, Káẓimayn and Sámmará – effectively constituted an independent state free from Qajar control. At a local level, the independence of the higher clergy was acquired through their involvement in patrician politics and their deployment of their students and the local 'rowdies' (*lúṭís*) to act as their strong-arm supporters.

Comparatively free from state interference, the Shiᶜi ulama regulated their own institutions. Thus, at a formal level, increasing stress came to be placed on the distinction between those ulama who were qualified as *mujtahids* – that is, who had the right to make independent legal judgements (*ijtihád*) – and the rest. To become a *mujtahid* required the granting of a certificate of competence (*ijáẓa*) from an established *mujtahid*, but otherwise required no standardized procedure of appointment. The dominance of the *mujtahids* over the other ulama was effectively accomplished by the end of the eighteenth century, after a prolonged and bitter struggle with considerable recourse to physical intimidation and violence. Thereafter, the great *mujtahids* presented themselves as uniquely authoritative defenders of Islamic orthodoxy, readily gaining a place as members of the local and national notability of Qajar society. Whilst often competing between themselves for power and influence, the leading *mujtahids* came to resemble a self-perpetuating caste, linked by family ties and closely regulating the admission of new members. There was a tendency for a few *mujtahids* to be recognized as supreme exemplars, but no definite hierarchy came into being until the present century.

The rise of the *mujtahids* to dominance within the ranks of the ulama had considerable implications for religious dissent. Traditionally, Shiᶜism has not been confined to a narrow orthodoxy. Although dominated by legalistic concerns, Shiᶜi intellectual life has readily encompassed the implicitly dissenting traditions of speculative theology, philosophy and gnosis (*irfán*), albeit within certain limits of public expression. The dominance of the *mujtahids* – custodians of the holy law – redefined the role of dissent, leading to the persecution of the most organized traditions of intellectual dissent and putting pressure on individual exponents of speculative thought to observe strict outward conformity. This marginalization of the minority attracted by speculative thought provoked reaction, most notably amongst the adepts of Shaykhism, who powerfully challenged the intellectual control of the *mujtahids*, accusing them of narrow legalism and seeking to delegitimate their claim to unique authority.

EARLY SHAYKHISM

Shaykh Aḥmad al-Aḥsáʾí (1753–1826) was an Arab from a small village in the Ḥasá region near the Gulf coast of the Arabian Peninsula. Whilst his family had been Shiᶜis for generations, he appears to have been the first of them to have become a cleric. During the early 1790s he migrated to the *ᶜAtabát*. With a fast-growing reputation for piety and erudition, Shaykh Aḥmad, now in his forties, began to attract a personal following, not only in his homeland, but also in southern Iraq and in Iran, in both of which he travelled extensively. Remaining in Iran from 1806 until 1822, Shaykh Aḥmad, gained considerable support, not only from the ulama, but also from various members of the Qajar family, including Fatḥ ᶜAlí Sháh himself and the powerful governor of Kirmanshah, Muḥammad ᶜAlí Mírzá. In about 1822, he was accused of holding heretical views by Ḥájí

Mullá Muḥammad Taqí Baraghání, one of the leading ulama of Qazvin. After a vigorous campaign of denunciation, Baraghání's views were accepted by various ulama, including several influential figures at the ᶜ*Atabát*. Whilst Shaykh Aḥmad retained the sympathy of many leading ulama, the effect of this denunciation, as it gained wider support, was to mark off the particular followers of the Shaykh as being members of a separate school (*madhhab*) of Shiᶜism.

This tendency towards separation increased during the period of the Shaykh's successor, the Iranian-born Sayyid Káẓim Rashtí (died 1843/4). Clearly designated as the authorized expounder of the Shaykh's teachings, Sayyid Káẓim provided the focus around which a distinct Shaykhi sect might emerge. Following a largely peripatetic existence, Shaykh Aḥmad had made no attempt to form his followers into a separate congregation, and there seems to have been no clear distinction made between those who were his immediate disciples and the larger group of admirers and sympathizers. Again, even after the order of excommunication had been pronounced against him by Baraghání, his prestige and influence were such that this order had only limited effect. Sayyid Káẓim, by contrast, was initially a less prestigious figure amongst the ranks of the ulama and was more easily made the victim of a concerted campaign of denunciation, the distinction between the orthodox *Bálásarís* and the heterodox Shaykhis eventually coming to be generally accepted.[3] Remaining for the most part in Karbalá and exercising effective leadership. Sayyid Káẓim provided the amorphous group of the Shaykh's followers with a clear centre to which they might turn in response to the attacks directed against their former master. Whilst continuing to try to reintegrate the Shaykhi school within mainstream Shiᶜism, Sayyid Káẓim's forceful defence of the Shaykh's teachings, and the apologias written by his disciples, served only to emphasize the separate identity of the school.

Despite sustained opposition to Shaykhism on the part of certain ulama, the movement flourished under Sayyid Káẓim's leadership. A considerable number of adherents were gained (or their support was consolidated) throughout Iran, as well as in the southern part of Arab Iraq. Some small towns and villages seem to have become almost entirely Shaykhi. Significantly, several Qajar courtiers and princes also became his followers, including most of the family of the crown prince, ᶜAbbás Mírzá. Additionally, Sayyid Káẓim enjoyed the respect not only of a large number of 'orthodox' Shiᶜi ulama in Iran and the ᶜ*Atabát* who were unwilling to accept the pronouncements of Baraghání and his allies, but also of Shiᶜi ulama in Syria, Arabia and India, and even of Sunni dignitaries, such as the mufti of Baghdad, al-Alúsí, and ᶜAlí Riza Pasha, its governor. The Sayyid also gained considerable local prominence, both as one of the leading Shiᶜi ulama of the *ᶜAtabát* and as a community leader in Karbalá.

Shaykhi doctrine

Shaykh Aḥmad's role in the history of modern Shíᶜi thought has yet to be properly evaluated. He has been described as an *ᶜárif* (gnostic) amongst the ulama and an *ᶜálim* (cleric) amongst the gnostics,[4] and it is perhaps this combination of perspectives which constituted his distinctive contribution to modern Shiᶜism. Early Shaykhism, from this standpoint, may be seen as an attempted bridge between the main intellectual traditions of the contemporary Shiᶜi world: seeking to reconcile revelation with the use of reason, and theology with philosophy. As such, it was a precarious vision, which, deriving much of its driving power from the particular loyalty displayed towards its founders, perished with their deaths.

Although many of Shaykh Aḥmad's views seriously diverged from those of the theosophical thinkers of the Safavid period (whom he condemned repeatedly and severely), his main intellectual roots are clearly within that same general tradition. Similarly, part at least of his appeal is likely to have stemmed from his powerful reassertion of the concerns of Shiᶜi esotericism at a time when that tradition had no great master to promulgate its teachings.[5] Shaykh Aḥmad's own prestige, erudition and pious reputation made him more than merely a theosophical master, however, and whilst Shaykhism crystallized into a distinct and anathematized school under the leadership of Sayyid Káẓim, it nevertheless retained a broader appeal and importance. That this broader appeal was possible was doubtless due in part to the two leaders' facility in combining exoteric and esoteric viewpoints and statuses. Thus, both Shaykh Aḥmad and Sayyid Káẓim possessed the exoteric authority of 'orthodox' ulama, as well as the esoteric authority based on their own special claims. In this regard, both were leading *mujtahids*, each with a following of theological students, lesser ulama and laity. Sayyid Káẓim also acted as an important community leader. Again, whilst never entirely concealed, the full import of their esoteric teachings and claims were veiled in the obscure style of much of their writings, the Shaykhi leaders adopting the common esotericist strategy of writing and speaking in different ways for different levels of audience, reserving their more controversial teachings for the trusted audience of their closer disciples.

Central to Shaykh Aḥmad's teachings was the belief that it was essential for Shiᶜism to be purified from intellectual innovations by a return to infallible sources of guidance. Overtly, these sources were the Quran, the *ḥadíths* (Islamic traditions), and the Imams. At the same time, however, whilst many Quranic verses were clear in their meaning and directly in harmony with reason, others were not, and these were interpreted with the aid of reason and (the Shaykh's) esoteric knowledge, which was derived from intimate spiritual communion with the Imams. Herein lay the Shaykh's evident and implicit heterodoxy, for not only was Shaykh Aḥmad's imamology highly suspect, coming perilously close to the deification of the Imams – a charge which was certainly levelled against him – but his own esoteric relationship with the Imams formed the basis for an implicit claim to unique authority. Thus, according to the Shaykh, as God's essence was totally beyond the reach and comprehension of man, it was necessary for there to be intermediaries in order for man to gain access to any of the divine attributes and teachings. These intermediaries, themselves in their essence neither God nor men, were the prophets and Imams, who, as the causal and creative agents of the Primal Will, occupied a status almost of demiurges. Given that God was inaccessible, these holy, infallible and sinless beings were the manifestations of God's grace to mankind, and as such they constituted the sole refuge for all created things. The distinctively Shaykhi addition to this schema was the doctrine of the Fourth Support. After logically reducing the traditional Shiᶜi beliefs which constituted the foundations of true religion to three – beliefs in the unity of God (*tawḥíd*), in prophethood (*nubuwwa*) and in the imamate (*imáma*) – the Shaykhis added a Fourth Support (*ruknuʾr-rábiᶜ*) of their own, namely the doctrine that there must always exist amongst the Shiᶜis those capable of acting as the agents of grace between the Hidden Imam and his followers. It seems clear that, at least by their immediate disciples, Shaykh Aḥmad and after him Sayyid Káẓim were each regarded as in some way the 'bearer' of this Fourth Support, that is, as the perfect Shiᶜis who were the intermediaries of the Imam.

The nature of the Shaykhi leaders' special relationship with the Imams emerges from their own writings. Thus, Shaykh Aḥmad himself described a series of visionary experiences in which he met various Imams and also the Prophet, receiving from these personages certificates of competence (*ijázát*), as well as special verses by which he might consult the Imams directly when needing to elucidate some problem. He also claimed to have imbibed the saliva of the Imam Ḥasan and of the Prophet in these initiatory visions, an image redolent of the transmission of spiritual power (*baraka*). Thus whilst other ulama derived their knowledge from each other, Shaykh Aḥmad was able to claim to have followed a different path: 'I have derived what I know from the Imams of guidance, and error cannot find its way into my words, since all that I confirm in my books is from them and they are preserved from sin and ignorance and error'.[6] By recurrent visionary experience, he claimed, he was shown the answers to all questions, the inner meanings of things being unveiled to his eyes. Again, according to Sayyid Káẓim, the first twelve centuries of Islam had constituted the age during which its outward observances had been perfected; now, from the beginning of the thirteenth century (i.e. from AD 1785), these observances were to be subordinate to the elucidation of inner truth, Shaykh Aḥmad being the first promulgator (*muwarrij*) of this new age of inward realities.[7] Sayyid Káẓim, in turn, was the custodian of this innate knowledge, the appointed interpreter of the esoteric truths imparted by the Imams to Shaykh Aḥmad.

A particularly controversial element in these esoteric truths were the Shaykhi teachings on eschatology, and it was these which constituted the grounds for the initial pronouncement of excommunication against Shaykh Aḥmad. In sharp contrast to orthodox Shiʿi views, Shaykh Aḥmad taught that on the Day of Judgement, creation would return, not to God as its source but to the Primal Will; that the resurrection would take place, not in the corporeal body but in a 'subtle body' which came into being in the realm of *Húrqalyá*, the theosophical interworld between the material and heavenly realms; and that there were two hells and two paradises, one each in this world and the next, and that in one sense paradise was recognition of the *Qáʾim*, the Twelfth Imam, on the Day of Judgement. Besides these views the Shaykh also taught that Muhammad's 'night journey' to heaven was made only within the created realm and with the Prophet's subtle rather than material body.

Babi and Bahaʾi writers have also attributed millenarian views to the Shaykhi leaders, the Báb himself stating that Sayyid Káẓim repeatedly asked his disciples whether they did not want him to depart so that 'God may appear'.[8] This attribution is problematic, in that overt millenarian views are not given any prominence in the writings of the two leaders, the passages regarded as foretelling the coming of the Báb and Baháʾuʾlláh being amongst the more cryptic and allusive of their statements. However, given a milieu in which controversial ideas were veiled in allusive language, free use made of dissimulation (*taqiyya*), and esoteric truth only imparted to an inner circle of elite disciples, there is no reason to suppose that such views may not have been given prominence in their oral teachings. That a substantial number of Shaykhis later gave their allegiance to a millenarian movement certainly suggests that millenarian views may already have been held by at least some groups of Shaykhis.

THE EMERGENCE OF BABISM, 1844–5

Whatever the substance of Sayyid Káẓim's oral teachings, when he died (31 December 1843/1 January 1844) without appointing a successor, his disciples were thrown into confusion. Claims to successorship of some sort soon came to be advanced by several of the Sayyid's leading disciples, rival claims being made in Karbalá, Tabriz and Kirman. Of these claimants, the most successful was Ḥájí Muḥammad Karím Khán Kirmání (1809/10–1870/1), who soon established a widespread network of followers throughout the Shaykhi communities of Iran. Nevertheless, the former unity of Shaykhism was shattered as personal and doctrinal divisions separated the disciples.

Sayyid ʿAlí Muḥammad Shírází, the Báb

In the midst of this confused situation the new religion of Babism gradually emerged. Headed by Mullá Ḥusayn Bushrúʾí (1814–49), one of the most eminent of the late Sayyid's disciples and students, increasing numbers of Shaykhis chose to reject all of the clerical contenders for authority and instead to give their allegiance to a young and almost unknown merchant from southern Iran, Sayyid ʿAlí Muḥammad Shírází (1819–50). Lacking the formal authority and training of the ulama, ʿAlí Muḥammad initially claimed authority on the basis of his esoteric and messianic status as the *báb*, the 'gate' to the Hidden Imam, his followers thus coming to be known as *Bábís*.

Born into a family of prosperous Shirazi merchants, ʿAlí Muḥammad grew up under the guardianship of a maternal uncle who, after the early death of his father, provided him with the commercial training to join the family in the wholesale cloth trade. Fervently religious since childhood, ʿAlí Muḥammad soon wearied of commercial pursuits, however, finding solace in long hours of devotional practice and the private study of works of Shiʿi scholarship. Finally in 1839/40, at the age of 20, ʿAlí Muḥammad closed his commercial office and embarked on an extended pilgrimage to the shrine cities of Iraq, where he remained for about a year. Although never embarking on a formal religious training, the young merchant attended some of Sayyid Káẓim's classes during this time, attracting the attention of some of his fellow Shaykhis by his extreme piety. According to the Babi–Baha'i account he also came to the attention of Sayyid Káẓim, who treated him with marvellous respect. Returning to Shiraz in 1840 or 1841, ʿAlí Muḥammad then married and appeared to settle down, presumably much to the pleasure of his family, who were opposed to his pronounced religiosity. In 1843 and 1844, however, he experienced a number of visions, in the most dramatic of which he saw the severed head of the Imam Ḥusayn, drops of whose blood he drank and from the grace of which, as he was later to write, 'my breast was filled with convincing verses and mighty prayers' and, the spirit of God having 'permeated and taken possession of my soul', 'the mysteries of His revelation were unfolded before my eyes in all their glory.'[9]

After Sayyid Káẓim's death a number of the Shaykhis at Karbalá had entered into a period of religious retreat in search of divine guidance. Amongst these was Mullá Ḥusayn Bushrú'í, who on his re-emergence made his way to Shiraz (perhaps *en route* to Karím Khán in Kirman?), where he met the Báb and accepted his claims, the Báb's declaration of his mission being made during a secret meeting with Mullá Ḥusayn during the night of 22–23 May 1844. Although he initially doubted that an unlearned merchant could be Sayyid Káẓim's successor and the *báb* of the Imam, Bushrú'í soon became convinced of the Báb's innate knowledge and spiritual potency. A number of his fellow disciples who were with him also came to give their allegiance. Initially, the Báb enrolled a total of 18 Shaykhis as his first disciples, the *ḥurúfu'l-ḥayy* or 'Letters of the Living'. This inner circle of disciples in turn undertook the promulgation of the Báb's claims to the rest of the Shaykhi community, and beyond them to the Shiʿi world in general.

The Báb's early claims. The precise nature of the Báb's claims during the first few years of his mission are not entirely clear. Claiming at the least to be the 'bearer' of the esoteric knowledge of the Imams in succession to Shaykh Aḥmad and Sayyid Káẓim and to be the Imam's representative (*náʾib*) in the world, the *bábu'l-imám*, ʿAlí Muḥammad evidently implied that he also occupied some higher spiritual station. Thus his conception of '*báb*-hood' (*bábiyyat*) entailed a close identity with the Imam himself. He was, in the words of the Imam as recorded in the *Qayyúmu'l-Asmá* (the first book of the Báb's mission), 'my own self in the worlds of command and creation'.[10] Indeed, to follow, obey or visit the Báb was the same as following, obeying or visiting not only the Imam, but God himself seated upon his throne. Disbelief in the Báb, on the other hand, constituted rejection of the only path to the Imam and disbelief in Muhammad and the

Quran. Moreover, to the clerical reader, the Báb's own first book, the *Qayyúmuʾl-Asmá*, clearly purported to be the 'descent' (*nuzúl*) of 'divine revelation' (*waḥy*), a status traditionally not even accorded to the writings of the Imams.[11]

Whilst in 1848 the Báb was to announce publicly that he was the *Qáʾim*, the return of the Hidden Imam, and to make further higher claims, it seems probable that higher claims were already implicit in his earlier writings and were perceived by the Báb's leading disciples.[12] Such claims may even have been directly communicated to them in the Báb's oral teachings, an exoteric claim to be the *bábuʾl-imám* gaining currency amongst the generality of the Babis whilst the Babi elite were privy to an esoteric claim to some higher station.

The initial proclamation of the Báb's claims. Leaving Shiraz in the summer of 1844, the Letters of the Living dispersed throughout Iran to establish the new religion, meeting with a rapid and widespread success even beyond the Shaykhi community. Although not divulging the name of the Báb, the disciples taught that the *bábʾl-imám* had appeared and would shortly enter Karbalá to fulfil the messianic prophecies and lend support to the *Qáʾim*, whose advent was soon to occur. The most prominent of the disciples were also given specific proclamatory missions: Mullá Ḥusayn being directed to Tehran to apprise Muḥammad Sháh and his chief minister of the Báb's cause, whilst Mullá ᶜAlí Basṭámí was sent to the *ᶜAtabát* to announce the Báb's claims to the leading Shiᶜi cleric, Shaykh Muḥammad Ḥasan an-Najafí (*c.* 1788–1850). The Báb for his part prepared to make his way to Mecca for the *ḥajj*, there to announce his claims to the Sharif, the Custodian of the holy shrine of the Kaᶜba. In the event, Mullá Ḥusayn was unable to gain access to the Shah, Mullá ᶜAlí was arrested, condemned before a joint tribunal of Sunni and Shiᶜi ulama for disseminating heresy and unbelief, and sentenced to hard labour in Istanbul's naval dockyards, and the Báb failed to elicit any response in Mecca.

Large crowds, meanwhile, had gathered in Karbalá, many in response to the Babi call to await the Imam's reappearance. Many of these had purchased arms in accordance with the instructions of the *Qayyúmuʾl-Asmá* so as to aid the Imam in the final holy war against unbelief. Messianic expectation had come to centre on the beginning of the year AH 1261 (10 January 1845 onwards), that is just over a thousand years after the Imam's disappearance in AH 260. By the expected dates in January and March 1845, however, the Báb had still not returned from his pilgrimage journey, whilst the ulama's condemnation of the new movement was soon widely known. Millenarian excitement rapidly subsided and there was widespread disappointment on the part of the followers of the, as yet, unnamed Báb. By the summer of 1845, 'only a tiny band' of Babis were left at Karbalá, many having abandoned their faith, leaving only those diehards who had been able to interpret the Báb's change of plan as *badá*, the alteration of divine decree in response to changed circumstances, a doctrine more acceptable to Shaykhis than to those Balasaris or Sunnis who may have briefly been caught up in the millenarian fervour of 1261.

EXPANSION AND THE GROWTH OF OPPOSITION, 1845–8

With the apparent failure of the initial proclamation of the Báb's claims in Mecca and Karbalá, the centre of events again shifted to Iran. The Báb himself returned to Shiraz in July 1845. At his instructions, a Babi *mujtahid* in the city had already publicly added the name of ʿAlí Muḥammad to the Muslim call to prayer. This provoked such a public commotion that on his arrival, the Báb was placed under house arrest. There he remained until he escaped from the city in September 1846. Although restricted in his public activities, the Báb was now able to consolidate the movement which he had inspired and of which he was now the clearly identified leader. Conducting an extensive correspondence and receiving visits from his followers and from enquirers, he was able to win new adherents and co-ordinate the activities of his missionaries. With a few amanuenses in attendance, he was also able to secure a widespread dissemination of his increasingly voluminous revelation writings.

After the crisis of the Báb's non-appearance in Karbalá, those original Babis who had remained steadfast were joined by increasing numbers of new believers, many of them non-Shaykhis. Many of these converts were in the north, several Letters of the Living – including Mullá Ḥusayn – establishing themselves in the shrine centre of Mashhad, whilst others settled in Qazvin and Azerbaijan. Important Babi communities also developed in Shiraz, Isfahan and Tabriz, whilst at Zanján the conversion of a leading cleric, Mullá Muḥammad ʿAlí (entitled *Ḥujjat* (Proof)), led to the mass conversion of several thousand of his fellow townspeople. At Karbalá meanwhile, the Babi remnant had been reanimated by the arrival of Fáṭimih Bigum Baraghání (1814–52), the only woman amongst the Letters of the Living and the niece and daughter-in-law of the cleric who had so bitterly denounced Shaykh Aḥmad. Entitled *Qurratuʾl-ʿAyn* (Solace of the Eyes) by Sayyid Káẓim, and later given the title of *Ṭáhirih* (Pure) by the Báb, Fáṭimih Bigum Baraghání was not only deeply learned, but also eloquent, vehement and controversial. Radical in her interpretations of Babism, her assumption of leadership split the Babi community in Karbalá between the more conservative Babis and her own circle of devotees.

As the Babi movement expanded and increasingly assumed its own identity, it naturally attracted the attention of the religious and secular authorities in Iran. Some leading clerics and a few members of the civil elite were converted, but the majority of those in authority came to oppose the movement. This growth of opposition was gradual. Given the messianic claims of the Báb and the challenge which this posed to all established authority, this opposition was probably inevitable. Those who first felt threatened were the ulama, the Shaykhis in particular. They responded with bitter condemnation and an increasingly effective mobilization of opposition. The secular authorities, by contrast, were more cautious in their response; their effective opposition to the movement only followed the Babis' alienation from the Qajar regime and the growth of Babi militancy.

The break with Shaykhism

Babism had effectively originated as a faction within Shaykhism in the period of confusion following Sayyid Káẓim's death. By the time of the Báb's return to Shiraz, however, a more definite break between the Babis and the other Shaykhis (particularly the Karim-Khanis) was developing. The radical nature of the Báb's interpretation of Shaykhism was rapidly becoming apparent as his writings became more widely available and as several of the contenders for Shaykhi leadership were personally confronted by Babi missionaries seeking to gain their allegiance for their master. Whatever the antagonisms which may have existed between them, most of the would-be leaders were soon united in their opposition to Babism. In Iraq, Mullá Ḥasan Gawhar's participation in the condemnation of the unnamed Báb and his followers at the trial of Mullá ᶜAli marked the first major challenge to Babism from a Shaykhi leader. In Kirman, Karím Khán, by now the leading Shaykhi cleric, also became a determined opponent of Babism, having Babi missionaries expelled from the city and writing a number of widely distributed refutations of the movement, in the first of which, the *Iẓháquʾl-Báṭil* (*The Crushing of Falsehood*), completed in July 1845, he declared the Báb to be an infidel and dismissed the Báb's followers as Shaykhis who were but 'new in this cause' and little informed of its realities.[13] In this and subsequent works, Karím Khán presented a wide-ranging anti-Babi polemic which was influential amongst both Shaykhis and Balasaris. Opposition to the Báb was also expressed by the Tabrizi Shaykhis, several of whom, including Mullá Muḥammad Mamaqání, took part in the Báb's trial in 1848, which led to him receiving the bastinado. Mamaqání also wrote a book attacking Babism, and was one of the ulama who signed the Báb's death warrant.

The Babis, for their part, were not slow to return the fire, writing counterpolemics and condemning their Shaykhi opponents in no uncertain terms. Karím Khán in particular was regarded with disdain, the Báb referring to him as the 'Tree of Negation' and the 'Embodiment of Hellfire', whilst his disciples identified him with the evil eschatological figures of the Antichrist (*dajjál*) or the Sufyání. Indeed, some Babis went further, totally dissociating themselves from Shaykhism. Thus in Karbalá, the local Babi community was split between a 'conservative' faction, whose members still regarded themselves as part of the Shaykhi tradition, and a 'radical' faction, whose leader, Qurratuʾl-ʿAyn, regarded the Shaykhi tradition as having been abrogated by the Báb's revelation and even dismissed as unbelievers those local Babis who still clung to Shaykhism.

Increasingly the Shaykhi community became polarized between Babi and non-Babi elements, although in what proportions is unknown. Each side became fiercely antagonistic towards the other, the development of a distinctive Babi doctrine and the conversion of many non-Shaykhis to Babism reinforcing the growing separateness of the two groups. Uncomfortably aware of their common origin with Babism, as well as of the presumed identity which non-Shaykhis were inclined to impute to the two groups, the non-Babi Shaykhis witnessed the increasing heterodoxy of Babism and reacted, not only by forcefully condemning the Babis as unbelievers who had separated themselves from true Shaykhism, but also by emphasizing their own fidelity to Islamic orthodoxy. As MacEoin has argued, the emergence of Babism caused the Shaykhi leaders to redefine the nature of Shaykhism, toning down its more controversial teachings and expressing its identity with mainstream Shiʿism in an attempt at *rapprochement* with the Balasari majority.[14] This attempted *rapprochement* was particularly far-reaching in the case of the Tabrizi Shaykhis, whose beliefs appeared to become almost indistinguishable from those of conventional Shiʿis, but the attempt was also evident in the teachings of Karím Khán, who insisted that in all particulars the Shaykhis were agreed with the rest of the Shiʿis.

The clerical rejection of Babism

The increasing separation between Babism and Shaykhism was in turn reflective of the growing alienation between Babism and Shiʿi orthodoxy and facilitated Babism's rejection by the majority of the ulama. At a theoretical level, the Báb's claims constituted an inherent challenge to clerical authority even from the beginning of his mission. Theoretically, the ulama possessed their authority as the representatives of the absent Imam on a provisional basis, pending his return. Thus, even if only claiming to be the *bábuʾl-imám*, with direct access to the Imam, the Báb effectively called into question the continuing legitimacy of clerical authority. The ulama were called upon to recognize his claims and submit to his authority; only thus could they retain any legitimate authority of their own. When the absolute nature of this challenge became clear to them, most of the ulama evidently felt that they were really faced with only one of two choices, either to accept the Báb (openly or secretly), or to condemn him as an impostor.

Thus, whilst a number of ulama actually became Babis, supplying the movement with almost all of its leaders, and whilst there remained non-Babi ulama who regarded the Báb himself with a certain degree of sympathy, the majority of the ulama came to oppose Babism, labelling it as a dangerous heresy which threatened the foundations of orthodox Shiʿism. Under clerical inspiration, popular feeling was increasingly aroused against the Babis as a perceived anti-Islamic heresy, and in some localities physical assaults were aimed at Babi missionaries. However, whilst opposition to Babism soon became widespread – mirroring the rapid geographical expansion of Babism – no sustained and systematic campaign to counter its influence was at first initiated. Given the fragmented nature of authority amongst the Shiʿi ulama, it was almost inevitable that this should be so and that the situation should vary from city to city. As early as 1845, a *fatwá* (legal pronouncement) had been signed at Baghdad by the leading cleric of the Shiʿi world, condemning the unnamed Báb to death as an unbeliever, but this had had no binding effect on the ulama elsewhere. Again, *fatwás* were issued against the Báb personally at Shiraz, Isfahan, and later at Tabriz, but beyond reflecting the consolidation of anti-Babi sentiment, had no immediate effect.

Ultimately, of course, the Báb's execution in 1850 was a matter of state policy, for which clerical *fatwás* only provided legal justification, and by the time of the examination of the Báb at Tabriz in 1848 it seems likely that it was only the unwillingness of the state officials to order an execution that prevented such *fatwás* being put into effect. At Shiraz and Isfahan, however, whilst the Báb encountered the opposition of the majority of the ulama, he retained a measure of support from the Imam-Jumʿihs of the two cities. Whilst the Báb was plainly making highly unorthodox claims for himself, it was still possible at that stage to regard him and his followers as being just within the bounds of Shiʿism, if those bounds were defined with sufficient tolerance. Even for some of the ulama who did not themselves become Babis, it was initially possible to regard the Báb with a certain degree of sympathy, his general demeanour, and particularly his extreme piety, creating a favourable impression. Even the heterodoxy of his claims could be to some extent excused as the excesses of a deeply religious man whose enthusiasm had on occasion got the better of him. From such a standpoint, the increasingly evident unorthodoxy of Babism, merited not the Báb's execution as an unbeliever, but rather the admission that he was 'devoid of reason and judgement'. Such, certainly, was the eventual conclusion reached by the Imam-Jumʿih of Isfahan, and such, again, was the justification employed at Tabriz for not putting the Báb to death as an unbeliever at the time when the 1848 *fatwá* had been issued against him.[15]

Alienation from the Qajar regime

If the ulama were generally antagonistic towards the new religion, the attitude of the secular authorities was at first fairly neutral. Where actions against the Babis occurred they were localized, and occasioned by local political factors. Even as late as the trial of the Báb in July 1848, the major state officials involved seem to have adopted an attitude of bemused indifference towards the proceedings, whilst the task of inflicting the bastinado on the Báb – the first formal punishment which he had received – was left to the Shaykhuʾl-Islám or one of his entourage. This tolerance of Babism by the Qajar state was undoubtedly a major factor in facilitating the initial expansion and consolidation of the movement: when the Qajar regime did act against Babism, it was already well established and could only be extirpated at considerable cost.

During this interim period, the Babi attitude towards the regime was sympathetic, at least on a provisional basis. Whilst the Báb had asserted the Shiʿi principle that only the Imam or his representative might exercise legitimate authority, he clearly regarded the Shah as a potential ally. If Muḥammad Sháh (reigned 1834–48) would but proffer his assistance to the Báb, then he would be greatly blessed. Accordingly a number of unsuccessful attempts were made to enlist his aid. The early conversion of Sayyid Yaḥyá Darábí, one of the prominent ulama who frequented the court, was propitious here, but it was only with the Báb's sojourn in Isfahan (October 1846 to March 1847) that an audience with the Shah became a definite possibility, the Governor of Isfahan, Manúchihr Khán, receiving the Báb sympathetically and offering him his support. Such hopes were soon frustrated by Manúchihr Khán's death, however. Whilst the Báb was now invited to proceed to Tehran for an audience with the Shah, he proceeded under armed escort and at the last moment was taken instead to Mákú, a remote fortress on Iran's north-western border.

The Báb had effectively become a prisoner of state held in internal exile. His attitude towards the Qajar court became hostile. The Shah's chief minister, Ḥájí Mírzá Áqásí, was held particularly responsible for the Báb's plight. It was at his instigation that the Báb had been exiled, and again it was he who caused the Báb to be brought before the tribunal of ulama in Tabriz in July 1848. After the trial he was severely condemned in the Báb's *Khuṭbi-yi Qahriyyih* (*Sermon of Wrath*) and was denounced as 'Satan'. In the meantime, the Báb continued to write to the Shah, increasingly in condemnatory tones as the months of his imprisonment lengthened. In these letters, the Báb wrote that whilst he had waited that perchance the Shah might take heed of his guidance, 'the fateful hour' was now drawing near, and with it the Shah's last chance to make amends for the suffering which had been inflicted on the Báb. All who opposed the Báb were consigned to the lowest depths of hell-fire. The court was declared to have become the object of God's wrath. The 'day of chastisement' was approaching and Muḥammad Sháh himself was soon to die. If he remained an unbeliever, then he would lose not only this world but the world to come.

The growth of Babi militancy

The degree and nature of Babi militancy remains a matter of controversy.[16] At a theoretical level at least, the Báb clearly endorsed the traditional Islamic concept of holy war (*jihád*), according it the status of one of the pillars of Islam. Thus the *Qayyúmu'l-Asmá* called upon the Babis to prepare to 'conquer the countries and their people for the pure faith of God'. They should purchase arms and prepare for the 'day of slaughter' when god would slay the unbelievers, and the Imams and angelic hosts would aid them in battle and their martyrs would receive their due reward.[17] No such *jihád* was ever called, however, and according to the

Báb's own account he avoided going to Karbalá in 1845 – where many would-be followers had brought swords – specifically to avoid conflict and sedition.[18]

Whatever the Báb's ultimate intentions, the actual means of propagation which were adopted were non-militant missionary activity and the challenging of opponents to divine judgement (*mubáhala*). Such actions readily provoked opposition from powerful clerics and their followers, especially in response to the more vehement and uncompromising of the Babi missionaries. Physical assaults on the Babis became common. At the same time, at least some of the Babis very evidently still expected that the final *jihád* against the forces of unbelief would soon begin. Some began to prepare assiduously for that climactic moment, Ḥádí Farhádí, a member of a leading Babi merchant family in Qazvin, going so far as to begin the manufacture of swords in the basement of his home for that purpose. Whether more as a self-defensive response to the external situation, or as a conscious preparation for the approaching *jihád*, some Babis now began to carry weapons openly. The potential for violent confrontation increased.

The outspoken Qurratu'l-ʿAyn was a particular catalyst in this worsening situation. She had been expelled from Iraq by the Ottoman authorities after sparking off disturbances in Karbalá by her unorthodox and challenging behaviour. After making a proclamatory progress through western Iran in the spring and summer of 1847, she returned to her home city of Qazvin. Here she further antagonized her powerful uncle and father-in-law, Muḥammad Taqí Baraghání, by refusing to have any dealings with her husband, whom she now regarded as an unbeliever, and hence ritually impure. She created further controversy by openly proclaiming Babism. At her uncle's instigation leading Babis in the town were arrested and bastinadoed. Shortly thereafter, Baraghání was murdered. This murder, occurring towards the end of October 1847, marked a turning-point in the history of Babism in Iran. Although denying complicity, the Babis were readily accused of the murder and a large-scale persecution of the Qazvini Babis was instigated, several individuals being done to death. Qurratu'l-ʿAyn herself was spirited away to Tehran by her co-religionists. More generally, and no matter how unjustly, the incident served to label the Babis as a whole as being violent opponents of the ulama and hence to exacerbate dramatically clerical antagonism to the movement.

THE RADICALIZATION OF BABISM, 1848–53

Having established a widespread religious movement throughout much of Iran, the Babis had come into conflict with the guardians of religious orthodoxy. During the course of this conflict, some Babis had become militant and several violent incidents had occurred. Although the Báb had been imprisoned, the civil authorities had done little to prevent the expansion and consolidation of the movement. During the summer of 1848 this situation changed drastically. Central here was the Báb's open claim to Mahdihood, but this claim represented only part of a wider process of 'radicalization'. The structure of authority within the movement also changed significantly, whilst Babi doctrine underwent a transformation which – as we shall see in the next chapter – carried the movement far beyond the confines of Islamic orthodoxy. All of these changes are overshadowed, however, by the militant conflicts within which many of the Babis became involved.

The proclamation of the Báb's higher claims

From the beginning of his ministry, the Báb had implicitly claimed some higher spiritual station than merely that of being the *bábu'l-imám*. From the early months of 1848, whilst still in prison in Mákú, the Báb proceeded to advance a number of higher claims. Most importantly, he proclaimed himself to be the Imam Mahdi, the promised *Qá'im* (He who will arise), the inaugurator of the Resurrection, and the abrogator of the Islamic holy law. The Báb also promulgated a new code of holy law in his book, the *Bayán*, but this does not appear to have been widely circulated. The full implications of this claim were revolutionary. It was no mere declaration of privileged access to religious truth or authority that had been made. The claim to Mahdihood was a challenge to the entire existing religious, social and political order. In the presence of the Mahdi, no one had the right to independent authority.

The claim to Mahdihood was made public in the summer of 1848. In Tabriz, the Báb himself proclaimed his higher claim when he was brought to face a tribunal of ulama, presided over by the crown-prince, the future Náṣiri'd-Dín Sháh, in late July. For his pains he was publicly ridiculed and bastinadoed. Meanwhile, some of his leading disciples had gathered together a large group of rank-and-file Babis in order to communicate the Báb's higher claims to them and to consider the means by which the Báb might be released from prison. This gathering was held during June and July at Badasht, an isolated village near Sháhrúd. Accounts of the meeting vary, but it is clear that the effect on many of the participants was dramatic. For some the abrogation of Islamic law destroyed their faith. For others it became reason 'to gratify their selfish desires'.[19] Indeed, in the new circumstances, a deliberate antinomianism may have seemed to constitute a deliberate messianic act. Thus Qurratuʾl-ʿAyn's appearance with her face unveiled assumed a messianic significance. Again, in a sermon which is attributed to one of the leaders at Badasht, it is argued that not only are the laws of the Sharíʿa abrogated, but that all laws in general are only necessary until such a time as the true nature of the divine manifestation of the age is recognized.[20] It is not known how common such attitudes were, or how many 'selfish desires' were gratified, but the impression that something untoward had occurred was a strong one. Muslim suspicions of Babi behaviour gave credence to allegations of immorality and lawlessness. More conservative Babis were also outraged, and Mullá Ḥusayn, at least, threatened to 'scourge the participants at Badasht'.[21]

The dispersion of charismatic authority

A further aspect of the 'radicalization' of Babism was the emergence of what Peter Berger has termed a 'charismatic field'.[22] With the Báb's imprisonment in the remote north-west there were evidently practical difficulties in the co-ordination of a far-flung religious movement. In this context, the Báb's chief disciples increasingly came to exercise an independent charismatic authority. Whereas previously the leading disciples had exercised their authority as derived from the Báb, they now came close to claiming (or having claimed on their behalf) an authority based on their own separate possession of charisma. In part at least this charisma was related to the Babi concept of theophany (*ẓuhúr*), the Báb himself increasingly being seen not just as the Mahdi, but as a manifestation of the divine will or logos.

Already, prior to 1848, the question of the exact status of the Letters of the Living had caused dissension amongst the Babis. According to a particularly controversial belief, they were to be identified with the return of the inward reality of the sacred figures of Shiʿism: the 'fourteen immaculate ones' (the Prophet Muhammad, the twelve Imams and the Prophet's daughter, Fáṭima) together with the four original *abwáb*. By 1848 this belief appears to have become widely accepted, and higher claims were being advanced by, or on behalf of, some of the leading Letters of the Living. Qurratuʾl-ʿAyn was prominent amongst these, being said to have laid claim to divine status during the Badasht conference. The most important claims, however, were those advanced for Mullá Muḥammad ʿAlí Bárfurúshí, known after Badasht by the title *Quddús* (Holy). At the least, Quddús appears to have claimed to be the

Qāʾim, and certainly he was widely regarded as such. Again, later, in Bahaʾi belief – and presumably reflecting Babi ideas – he was regarded as the *nuqṭi-yi ukhrá* (the Last Point (of Revelation)) and as a divine messenger, the Báb being the *nuqṭi-yi úlá* (the Primal Point). Claims were also made concerning Mullá Ḥusayn, who was referred to as the *báb* (ᶜAlí Muḥammad supposedly having given him the title when he dispensed with it and made higher claims), as the Prince of Martyrs (the Imám Ḥusayn), and as the bearer of the Fourth Support.[23]

Whatever the precise spiritual stations accorded to these three disciples, it is clear that they now felt themselves able, at least in part, to fulfil the Báb's messianic role, whilst he was prevented from so doing by his captivity. Their actions at Badasht, at Mashhad and at the shrine of Shaykh Ṭabarsí came to be regarded as having fulfilled the prophetic traditions associated with the Mahdi. In some way all three disciples had come to share the Báb's authority. With him, they were the 'four banners' of truth referred to in tradition.[24] The Báb's authority as *Qāʾim* had effectively become a transferrable attribute which others might share, or as a role which they might perform.

As the Babis became increasingly radical and assertive and the Qajar authorities more hostile, tension between them understandably increased. Whatever the intentions of the Báb himself, one of the chief effects of the declaration of his higher claims was to further radicalize his followers. Whilst news of the Báb's claim to Mahdihood caused some to distance themselves from the movement, the general Babi reaction would seem to have been a great increase in fervour. As those who withdrew were likely to have been amongst the more 'conservative' Babis, this development provided support for those who held more radical interpretations as to the nature and purpose of their religion. Nor was this purely a religious radicalism. The claim to Mahdihood carried clear political implications, for in the presence of the Mahdi no secular government possessed any legitimacy except by his leave. The challenge to the ulama now also became overt, for they had assumed authority only in the absence of the Imam. Babism had now changed from being merely a sectarian development within Shiᶜism into an implicitly revolutionary movement which challenged the authority of both State and Church. Henceforth, Babism was to face the united opposition of both secular and religious authorities. In retrospect, its eventual extirpation may seem to have been only a matter of course. For the Babis, fervent in their expectation of the Resurrection, however, such opposition assumed millenarian significance. God's cause would surely triumph over the gathering forces of unbelief. The battle lines for the final conflict between good and evil were being drawn.

Armed conflict in Mazandaran

Initially, indeed, the Babis perceived their opponents in evident disarray, for the political situation was rapidly deteriorating. Racked by fiscal crisis and a major rebellion in the north-east, the government tottered towards collapse. On the eve of 4 September 1848, Muḥammad Sháh died and all was chaos. Even after the successful accession of the new Shah in October, disturbances continued and it was not until late in the spring of 1849 that the new regime was firmly in control. Men spoke openly of the final downfall of the Qajar dynasty and the break-up of the Iranian state.[25]

In the midst of this confused situation a group of Babis under Mullá Ḥusayn left Mashhad, on 21 July, and raised the messianic symbol of the Black Standard. Intending perhaps to journey to Chihríq to secure the Báb's release, the party proceeded westward out of Khurasan, proclaiming their faith in the towns and villages through which they passed. Preaching detachment to his followers, Mullá Ḥusayn bade them abandon their possessions and content themselves only with their 'steeds and swords'.[26] Approaching Bárfurúsh, they found themselves opposed for the first time by a mob of townspeople summoned together by a local cleric. Shots were fired at the Babis and several were killed. Mullá Ḥusayn then called upon his companions to counterattack, killing, according to one account, over 150 of their opponents. Attacked again, the Babis left the town and retired to the nearby shrine of Shaykh Ṭabarsí. After further attacks they constructed fortifications and prepared themselves for a siege.

The seven-month siege of Shaykh Ṭabarsí (October 1848 to May 1849) remains one of the most enigmatic episodes in Babi history. Contemporary Muslim historians were in no doubt that the Babis at Ṭabarsí, and later at Nayríz and Zanján, were intent upon insurrection, a view which has been accepted or amplified by various modern historians.[27] On balance, however, a straightforward insurrection does not appear to have been the Babis' intention. Certainly their actions were only secondarily 'political' in nature. Augmented by groups of Babis from other parts of Iran, the numbers of defendants at Ṭabarsí rose to perhaps 500–600 individuals. At their centre was a large group of highly motivated clerics and theological students. For men such as these, schooled in the subtleties of Shaykhi esotericism and steeped in the Shiʿi traditions of martyrdom and sacrifice, armed struggle appears to have assumed a complex symbolic role, besides the attainment of any more 'realistic' objectives. The ideal of the Imam Ḥusayn's struggle and martyrdom at Karbalá provided a paradigm for their actions. Fighting a defensive *jihád* against the forces of unbelief, the defenders gave testimony to God's truth, both by the dispatch of their opponents 'to hell' and by their own martyrdoms.

More practical objectives were not necessarily precluded, however. As a means of hastening the longed-for Babi theocracy, the defenders may well have seen their actions in 'completing the proof' as a form of spiritual pronunciamento, a call to their fellow countrymen to accept the Báb and to establish the new theocratic order. Their deeds demonstrated both the fulfilment of prophecy and the illegitimacy of the Qajar state. Initially, there seemed to be prospects for success. Whether or not as a result of the widespread disaffection with the Qajars which then obtained in Mazandaran, many local villagers came to their aid and even the local military chiefs did little to oppose them. At least one local dignitary joined them. Mazandaran as a whole did not rise to their aid, however. Nor were there any movements of support elsewhere. Although the Babis fought grimly to the last, their fervour and discipline striking terror into the hearts of the troops sent against them, defeat drew nearer. Eventually, weakened by starvation and decimated by the fighting and artillery and mortar bombardment, the Babi remnant responded to a false truce and were massacred or enslaved.

The events and upheavals of 1850

Ṭabarsí represented a major turning-point for the Babis. Whatever the exact political intentions of the combatants, the movement as a whole was now surely identified by the civil authorities as insurrectionary in nature. For their part, the Babis had lost many of their leaders and many of the most energetic of their rank and file. Half of the Letters of the Living had been killed at Ṭabarsí. With these losses, and forced into a semi-secret existence, effective co-ordination of the movement is likely to have become extremely difficult. The tendencies towards loss of cohesion, which later became so pronounced, may already have begun to make themselves felt.

With the extinction of the Babis at Ṭabarsí in May 1849, the government doubtless felt that the situation had been mastered. A period of quiescence certainly followed, but events in 1850 soon showed this to have been illusory. In January or February the Babis became involved in an existing dispute in the southern city of Yazd. Fighting between the governor and the townspeople had only recently subsided when the Babi missionary, Sayyid Yahyá Darábí, arrived. Himself a local dignitary, Darábí's proclamation of the Báb's higher claims provoked fresh disturbances in which a popular rebel leader intervened on Darábí's side. A number of people were killed, and Darábí then left the city to undertake an extended missionary journey through the towns and villages on the way to Nayríz in the province of Fars.

Meanwhile, in Tehran, the Babi group had been infiltrated by an informer who betrayed about fifty of its members to the authorities. Fearing a plot, the government had seven of the leading members of the group executed (19/20 February). These individuals, who included the Báb's uncle and guardian, were men of high social status: three merchants, two prominent ulama, a Sufi *murshid* (spiritual guide), and a government official.

In May further disturbances broke out. In the south Darábí had now reached the small town of Nayríz, where he already had a devoted following. As in Yazd, his missionary enterprise exacerbated existing conflicts. This time, however, the conversion of perhaps one-third of the townsfolk heralded a bloody struggle, from 27 May to 21 June 1850, in which Darábí and many of his followers were killed. Almost simultaneously (*c.* 13 May), a conflict had broken out in Zanján in the north. This was more serious. Zanján was a major centre on the road between Tabriz and Tehran, and the Babis maintained a lengthy resistance there which was ended only in January 1851. As at Ṭabarsí and Nayríz, the Babi zealots fought with a commitment and an aura of religious devotion which dismayed many of the common soldiers who fought against them. Unskilled in arms, the Babis acquitted themselves well against greatly superior forces possessed of superior weaponry. As at Ṭabarsí and Nayríz, they were finally overcome by attrition and a broken pledge of truce, and this was followed by a general massacre of the survivors.

The genesis and motivation of these conflicts is likely to remain unclear. Viewed separately, local factors appear to have been crucial. In each case, an exceptionally large local Babi community professed allegiance to a leading Babi cleric (Vaḥíd Darábí, Ḥujjat Zanjání) who was also a local notable. Local social and political tensions readily involved the Babis, and religious identification became a basis for social division. Given this emotional charge and the volatility of the local political situations, major conflicts were easily engendered. Both orthodox Muslims and Babis readily took up arms.

Whether or not local factors were primarily the cause, the government had ready reason to be alarmed. Seeking to end the movement once and for all, the Qajar authorities had the Báb brought again to Tabriz and executed (8/9 July). This did not end the fighting. In Zanján, the Babis continued their struggle until the winter (January 1851), whilst in Nayríz a second conflict between the Babis and their opponents occurred in 1853.

The collapse of Babism as an organized movement

By the beginning of 1851, Babism had already received such devastating blows that its complete extirpation as a religious movement would scarcely have been surprising. With the death of its founder, most of his leading disciples and many of the most devoted of the rank and file, Babism had lost not only its focal point, but much of its leadership cadre and dynamism. The movement now entered a period of persecuted underground existence, decline and fragmentation. Never completely united in doctrine or organization, the Babis now tended to break up into rival factions or to follow particular local leaders. The nominal leader of the movement in succession to the Báb was Mírzá Yaḥyá Núrí, entitled *Ṣubḥ-i Azal* (Morn of Eternity) (*c.* 1830–1912), a younger son of a Mazandarani land-owner and courtier. Youthful, inexperienced and preferring to live a life of near-seclusion, Ṣubḥ-i Azal appears to have become little more than an overall figurehead, whilst such local co-ordination and leadership as survived or emerged devolved upon those who were, or aspired to be, prominent members of the various Babi communities. Many of such local leaders soon laid claim to some sort of spiritual station, including that of the millenarian figure of *Man-yuẓhiruhu'lláh* (He whom God shall make manifest) foretold by the Báb. According to ʿAbduʾl-Bahá, no less than 25 individuals advanced such claims and the figure may have been higher.[28] Such claims were especially rife from 1850 until 1852, when several claimants were killed by the authorities. The claimants came from all parts of Iran and also from Baghdad, comprising an even larger 'charismatic field', indicative presumably of an intense longing for some sort of guidance and leadership. Mírzá Yaḥyá for his part appears to have accepted the chaos of competing claims, which he could do little to prevent, describing them as adding to the glory of the theophany.

Lacking central direction, those who remained Babis increasingly broke into rival factions divided by personal allegiance and doctrinal speculation. Whilst some appear to have given themselves over to gnostic ecstasy and antinomianism, others retained strongly political objectives, sharpened by the desire for revenge against those who had persecuted and killed the Báb and his saints. In Tehran, a conspiratorial circle emerged, led by a Khurasani cleric, Mullá Shaykh ᶜAlí Turshízí entitled ᶜ*Aẓím* (Great), and including Ḥájí Sulaymán Khán, the son of a Tabrizi notable, and perhaps as many as 70 others. Whether properly co-ordinated or not, in August 1852, individuals associated with this group made an unsuccessful attempt to assassinate the Shah, whilst at about the same time Ṣubḥ-i Azal sought to seize control of Núr. Briefly there was chaos – 'every bush was a Babee, or concealed one'[29] – but order was rapidly reimposed and a great persecution of Babis commenced, with some 30 to 40 prominent Babis slain – not all of them in any way associated with the conspiracy – and possibly hundreds of others also killed. Qurratuʾl-ᶜAyn was amongst those killed at this time. Ṣubḥ-i Azal himself went into hiding.

Whilst the Babis at Ṭabarsí had doubtless been able to regard their sufferings as 'messianic woes' presaging the final act in the divine drama of God's purpose for mankind, it is doubtful whether many of the remaining Babis after 1852 were able to sustain much optimism about the future. Their defeat had been crushing. Most of their remaining leaders had now been killed. The lack of effective overall leadership combined with the destruction or concealment of Babi manuscripts to compound existing confusions regarding doctrine. Without such leadership there was little way in which the Babis could successfully restructure their religion to survive an underground existence, nor were there any ideologues who might provide the ideological rationale which might have enabled them to come to terms with their sufferings. Disillusioned and dispirited, some Babis doubtless returned to orthodox Islam; many probably resorted to the traditional Shiᶜi practice of pious dissimulation (*taqiyya*). Henceforth, the threat of persecution required the Babis' abandonment of their activities or the exercise of extreme caution and secrecy. Regarded both as heretics and insurrectionaries, the remaining Babis faced not only real physical dangers, but also psychological isolation. Their beliefs were safest kept secret. One-time sympathizers were now likely to keep their distance. And the task of effectively countering the myth-making which linked Babism to every heretical doctrine and practice since the days of Mazdak was impossible. Isolated and fragmented, Babism now effectively disappeared from public view, the activities of the Babi remnant being largely unknown until the 1870s, when most transferred their allegiances to Baháʾuʾlláh as *Man-yuẓhiruhuʾlláh*. Had it not been for the transformation of Babism effected by Baháʾuʾlláh, it must be presumed that Babism would most probably have simply ceased to exist.

2

BABI DOCTRINE AND DOMINANT MOTIFS

As a religious movement, Babism may be characterized by four interrelated religious motifs: legalism, esotericism, 'polarity' and millenarianism. Holy war and martyrdom represent supplementary themes. In varying ways these motifs express both the movement's continuity and its disjunction with the Shiᶜi–Shaykhi tradition.

In the case of Babism these motifs are more or less rooted in the writings of the founder, Sayyid ᶜAlí Muḥammad. Motifs represent fundamental patterns of religious experience and are not just summaries of official doctrine, however. That the Báb's writings assumed such a fundamental role is itself a characteristic of the movement. The centrality of his writings reflects both the importance which the Babis attached to revelation, and, for the early period at least, the speed and efficiency with which these writings were transcribed and distributed amongst the faithful. A logistical distinction needs to be drawn here, however, and this closely parallels the theological and social transformation of Babism.

We may conveniently divide the history of the Babi movement between the periods preceding and following the open declaration of his higher claims in the summer of 1848. Although increasingly deviating from the standards of Islamic orthodoxy, early Babism (1844–8) remained fundamentally Islamic in tone and appeared primarily as an expression of sectarian religiosity. In this early period the Báb's writings were for the most part readily disseminated and, together with the transmission of his correspondence, provided a focal link for a relatively unified movement. The efficiency of this system began to decline in 1847 with the Báb's imprisonment in the fortress of Mákú. After 1848 the Babis posed a clear challenge to the entire religious and political order. The movement appeared effectively as a new religion and, to the state authorities at least, as a source of insurrection. At the same time, however, the difficulties in transmitting the Báb's writings augmented the increasing problem of co-ordinating the movement as a whole. The Báb remained the symbolic focus of the movement, but leadership and charismatic authority were dispersed. The Báb's writings no longer provided a clear focus for unity. Only a fraction of his prison writings appear to have been fully transmitted to the rank and file, and the possibilities for differing interpretations increased as the central core of leaders lost their lives. Whilst some Babis may well have continued to cling to the more Islamic concerns of early Babism, those others who accepted the Báb's new and more radical teachings were not able to make a uniform response. Unfortunately, the sheer pressure of events, together with the later destruction of Babi documents makes it difficult to reconstruct these various responses in detail.

The Báb's writings

From the first, the Báb's writings were voluminous. He lived in 'an atmosphere of revelation'.[1] Indeed, the enormous quantity of 'verses' (*áyát*) which he revealed both in Arabic and Persian, together with the tremendous speed with which he recorded them, were regarded as important proofs of his mission. The Quran itself, revealed over a 22-year period, consisted of only a little more than 6,000 verses. By contrast, according to the Báb's own account in the Persian *Bayán* (1847), he had by then revealed some 500,000 verses, 100,000 of which had been circulated.[2]

Of the Báb's writings, the pre-eminent works were the *Qayyúmu'l-Asmá*, the first and most widely circulated book of his mission, and the *Bayán-i Fársí* (*Persian Exposition*), his lengthy book of laws, composed during his imprisonment at Mákú. Of these, it was the *Qayyúmu'l-Asmá* which was effectively regarded as the Babis' own Quran for almost the entirety of the Báb's mission.[3] The *Bayán* appears to have been far less effectively distributed. The Báb's other writings included proclamatory letters to the Shah and his chief ministers, letters to the ulama of every city of Iran and the shrine cities of Iraq, treatises on Islamic law, commentaries on various Quranic verses and letters (including nine separate commentaries on the whole Quran), directions for spiritual exercises, a lengthy enumeration of variations on the names of God (the *Kitábu'l-Asmá* or *Book of Names*), and numbers of talismanic devices.

The writings of the chief disciples

With the dispersion of charismatic authority in later Babism, the teachings and writings of his leading disciples assumed increasing importance. The writings of these individuals were also voluminous. During the struggle at Ṭabarsí, for example, Quddús was engaged in writing perhaps up to 30,000 verses on the letter *ṣad* (ṣ) of the word *ṣamad* (eternal). Unlike the writings of the Báb, however, many of those of his disciples have been lost.

LEGALISM

As a religious motif, legalism may be characterized as the concern with structuring society according to the provisions of a holy law. In Islam, as in Judaism, this motif is central to 'official' definitions of religious life. The revelation of a divine law is regarded as having been an essential part of the prophetic role. Thus, although elaborated and formalized by later generations of ulama, Islamic law, the *sharíʿa*, derives its initial inspiration from the precepts of the Quran and from the example of Muhammad's own life and of his administration of the early Islamic state. Consequently, the *sharíʿa* is regarded as the well-trodden path of righteousness, the immutable divine standard to which human beings and human societies are called upon to conform.

For many devout Muslims, observance of the *sharíʿa* has become the central reality of an Islamic identity. By contrast, Islamic esotericists – such as the Shaykhis and most of the Babis – sought to identify a level of reality behind mere legal observance. Legalism still remained an important motif for them, however. The Shaykhi masters were qualified jurisconsults and acted as legal exemplars for their followers. Whilst heterodox in the doctrines they taught, they did not deviate from the orthopraxy of their day. Similarly, despite the novelty of his claims, the Báb initially commanded his followers to adhere strictly to Islamic law. Such laws were to be binding upon all 'until the resurrection'. Where he diverged from the orthopraxy of his day, it was only to make practices and prohibitions which Islamic law only encouraged or reproved into obligatory ones, and to promote various distinctive practices of a pietistic nature. The early Babis were thus enjoined to recite special and additional prayers, to abstain from smoking, and to perform the prostration at the grave of the Imam Ḥusayn in a particular manner indicative of extreme reverence. Again the Báb set out a demanding programme of prayer, devotional practice, fasting and study to be pursued by the spiritual seeker. Many Babis also observed a fast of three consecutive months (the Islamic fast being only for one month), and refrained from using the Abbasid colour of black in their clothes, or even black ink in the books they wrote, as the Abbasids had persecuted the Imams. Whilst not specifically un-Islamic, such practices were distinctive, marking off the Babis as a group set apart, not only by their allegiance to ᶜAlí Muḥammad as the Báb, but also by their particular veneration of the Imams, their pietistic legalism and their rigorous devotionalism.

This strict orthopraxy underwent a revolutionary transformation in later Babism. The Báb both abrogated the *sharíᶜa* and substituted his own code of laws in the *Bayán*. In that news of the abrogation appears to have been far more readily transmitted to the rank and file than were the detailed provisions of the *Bayán,* clear antinomian tendencies emerged. It is not possible to say how widespread these tendencies were, or how much confusion resulted. Extreme antinomianism was doubtless checked by even the partial transmission of the *Bayán*, as well as by the social realities of persecution. These same realities are also likely to have limited the public observance of the laws of the *Bayán*.

It is not necessary to provide here a detailed description of the requirements of Babi law.[4] Suffice it to say that in all major areas of law the regulations of the *Bayán* differed significantly from those of the Islamic *sharíᶜa*. Of the chief Islamic obligations of the individual believer towards God (*ᶜibádát*), the Báb detailed specific Babi forms of ritual prayer (*ṣalát*), fasting (*sawm*), pilgrimage (*ḥajj*) and holy war (*jihád*). Moreover, not only was the form of *ṣalát* changed, but this rite, so central to Islamic practice and identity, was given far less emphasis than the repetition (*dhikr*) of various scriptural verses and invocations and the general importance of individual prayerfulness. Again, the requirements of ritual purity, which are so important in Shiᶜism, were considerably de-emphasized and linked to ideas of physical cleanliness and spiritual purity. *Ḥajj* was to be made to the Báb's house in Shiraz rather than to Mecca.

As to the regulation of personal status and community affairs, perhaps the most important elements of Babi law concerned the attitude towards non-believers, the regulation of marriage, and various ordinances concerning economic life. Thus a sharp division was made between believers and unbelievers. With the exception of merchants and others engaged in useful professions, only believers were to be allowed to reside in Babi states. Non-Babi books were to be destroyed. Again, whilst non-Babis were to be treated with justice and not compelled to convert, the believers were to avoid contact with them and were strictly forbidden to intermarry with them. As to marriage, this was considered obligatory from the age of eleven – the Babi age of maturity. Again, polygamy was discouraged, concubinage was forbidden, and divorce was permitted only after a year of waiting. (All this contrasts with the Shiᶜi practice of the time in which child marriage, polygamy, concubinage, and instant divorce by the husband were common.)

With regard to economic affairs, Babi law offered a plain critique of contemporary Iranian practice: the confidentiality of mercantile correspondence was declared inviolate; the exact weight of the coinage was specified; the need for a stable monetary system was asserted; debts were required to be discharged; the good organization of the posts and communications in the lands of the Franks (Europeans) were commended, and the need for them to be so organized in Iran asserted; and – in radical contrast to Islamic law – the charging of interest was permitted. Additionally, travelling was discouraged except for purposes of trade. A specific Babi calendar was introduced, the Báb replacing the Islamic lunar year with a solar year of 19 months of 19 days, the year beginning on the traditional Iranian New Year's Day (*naw-rúz*) of the spring equinox. Detailed instructions were given for the manufacture of talismans. And the study of grammar (except to understand the *Bayán*), jurisprudence (*fiqh*), logic, philosophy and dead languages were specifically forbidden.

ESOTERICISM

The belief in hidden salvatory knowledge has often represented a counterpoint to Islamic legalism, especially amongst those influenced by Sufi or Shiᶜi ideas. Islamic law has thus been seen as an exoteric reality within which a level of esoteric meaning must be discerned in order to achieve spiritual progress or salvation. Although the more extreme expressions of this view have led to a disregard for Islamic law, its more moderate expressions have been able to be accommodated within Shiᶜi orthodoxy, gnosis coming to be viewed as an inner reality of faith.

Shaykhism represented a forceful reassertion of the tradition of Shiᶜi esotericism. The age of outward religious truth having been perfected, the Shaykhi masters maintained that a new age of esoteric truth was beginning of which they were the promulgators. This theme was continued by the Babis. As the bearer of exoteric truth, the Báb was initially regarded as the successor of the Shaykhi masters. He was the 'gate' to divine knowledge and the bearer of the Fourth Support. His historical role was different from that of his predecessors, however. Whilst they had revealed hidden knowledge, they had also concealed their real central teachings. With the near advent of the Imam, the time was approaching for the revelation of the inmost reality of the inner realities of truth. When the Báb made public his higher claims, in a sense Babi esotericism came to an end: the Lord of the Age had appeared and the Resurrection had begun. After the Báb had been executed, however, there was a rapid return to esotericism. The Babis had a desperate need to interpret the catastrophic events which had befallen them, and the possibilities of hidden truth bore a ready appeal.

Esotericism inevitably implies hierarchy, with at least a two-fold division between the believers and unbelievers. Thus whilst both the Shaykhis and the early Babis regarded themselves as Shiᶜi Muslims, the logic of their beliefs implied a considerable sense of spiritual elitism. They were the enlightened elite, and the rest of the Shiᶜis were at best an ignorant generality. The Babis went further. By rejecting the Báb, the Shiᶜi majority had simply ceased to be Muslims. They were consigned to hell.[5] Not surprisingly, such attitudes were generally concealed. The Shiᶜi doctrine of *taqiyya* (pious dissimulation to avoid danger) was readily employed by both Shaykhis and Babis. For Shiᶜi esotericists in particular, *taqiyya* provides both a means of protection for the holder of controversial beliefs and a means of guarding true belief from the ungodly and the uninitiated.

Of course, *taqiyya* contradicts the principle of making manifest the hidden realities of esoteric truth. For Babi radicals, such as Qurratuʾl-ᶜAyn, the desire to unveil the truth far outweighed considerations of caution. Thus, as most Shiᶜis were no longer true believers, they and their products were to be avoided as ritually impure. Food from their bazaars needed to be ritually purified before it could be used. Again, for Qurratuʾl-ᶜAyn, cohabitation with her unbelieving husband was no longer possible. Such action provoked both the enmity of non-Babis and controversy with Qurratuʾl-ᶜAyn's more cautious co-religionists. Whilst some sought to avoid all controversy, many adopted the strategy of only gradually unveiling the truth. The Báb himself appears to have favoured such an approach. For the first year of his mission his identity was not divulged to those who wished to convert. The precise nature of his claims was obscured and, at least according to his own later account, a definite progression of claims was made so as to avoid provoking a commotion amongst the people.[6] Again, Babi missionaries cultivated the art of gradually revealing their teachings to potential converts, concealing the essence of their message until the one they sought to convince was 'ripe'.

Babi esotericism may also have involved some sort of hierarchy of knowledge within the movement. At the least, there was a division between the Babi elite who were aware of the Báb's identity from the start and had been taught by him, and the mass of the Babis who were taught in turn by the elite and were dependent on them for their understanding of the new religion. Again, when the Báb made known his higher claims, it was in the first instance to the elite, and it was they in turn who transmitted these claims to the rank and file. The later attribution of theophanic status to members of the elite reinforces this impression of internal hierarchy.

A further and very fundamental form of Babi esotericism concerned the nature of prophetic speech. Such speech, recorded in the Books of God, possessed different levels of meaning. The generality of the people had made do with its outer literal meaning. For the Babis its inner meaning stood revealed. As in extreme Shiᶜi esotericism such meaning was not necessarily related to the obvious meaning of particular words and phrases. At the least, scriptural texts were to be understood in terms of symbol and metaphor. Thus messianic prophecies were not to be literally fulfilled. Such stars as would fall from heaven were the ulama, the leading luminaries of Islam. The world that would end was a former cycle of revelation. Again, each verse, each letter even, contained a complex store of meaning which might be unveiled by one possessed of divine knowledge. Hundreds of verses could be revealed to expound the 'manifold implications' of even a single letter of the Quran.

To support these hermeneutic unveilings, much use was made of the cabalistic manipulation of words, the 'science of letters' that was traditional to Shiᶜi esotericism and much encouraged by the Báb. By translating words into their numerical equivalents and then transforming these into new words, manifest hidden meanings could be unveiled. By such means certain numbers assumed great symbolic value. In particular, the ubiquitous nineteen (equivalent to *wáḥid* (unity), and *wujúd* (God's absolute being)) came to be employed in the very structure of religious life in such areas as communal organization and the derivation of a new calendar.

Other traditional 'occult sciences' were also employed, most notably the 'science of talismans'.[7] Placing great stress on the Shiᶜi practice of using talismanic devices, the Báb required his followers to own and carry special Babi talismans, describing in detail how they should be produced. These, and the similarly engraved stones which were to be carried or worn as ringstones or pendants, were to provide the bearer with the 'talismanic protection of God' (*ḥirz-i haqq*).

The use of these occult sciences served to link Babism with the common corpus of Islamic gnostic and esoteric ideas, as did the use of alchemical and astrological symbolism. The use of talismans (and the actual manner of their use) also linked Babism with the tradition of Islamic magic, albeit at a somewhat refined level. More explicitly magical elements also entered the religion on several occasions of popular contact with the Báb, the Báb being perceived as a holy man and miracle worker whose transmitted holiness endowed material objects – such as the waters of the public baths – with healing properties.[8] Overall, however, magical elements do not appear to have been central to the movement. The spiritual forces which the Babis recognised as operating in the world were predominantly divine rather than animistic in nature. The Báb and Quddús might perform miracles – over 2,000 according to one Babi cleric[9] – but these were expressions of divine grace rather than magical practice as such. The word of God was endowed with such potency that its representation provided talismanic protection, but at Ṭabarsí it was the paradigm of heroic martyrdom which seems to have provided the basis for Babi fervour, and not any concept of talismanic invulnerability. Again, whilst God was commonly assumed to have destroyed or later punished those who rose up against the Babis, the Babis themselves made no use of magical practices against their enemies – in contrast, say, to the leading Shiᶜi cleric who was believed to have killed a Russian general by magic during the first Russo-Persian war.[10] Indeed, compared with the popular Shiᶜism of the time, official Babi doctrine de-emphasized certain aspects of the miraculous, most notably by the allegorical meanings attached to the expected events of the Resurrection. Again, it was the Báb's opponents who provided one of the most magical accounts of Babism when they originated the myth (still current among some Iranian Shiᶜis) that the Babis possessed some miraculous substance by which they could cause people to convert to their religion, Náṣiri'd-Dín Sháh himself being reported to have tried out such a substance on some of his state prisoners.[11]

POLARITY

The regard for authoritative and charismatic leadership represents one of the most powerful of religious motifs. It is a theme which I have termed the 'polar' motif from its Sufi expression in the figure of the *quṭb*, the 'axis' or 'pole' at the centre of the hierarchy of saints.[12] In its strongest form this motif is centred on an individual who is regarded as a divine incarnation. More loosely it may be linked with any holy figure who is believed to possess extraordinary authority and to whom extreme deference and obedience is due.

In Islam, this motif is most strongly expressed in the beliefs in divine vice-gerency and sainthood, beliefs which are largely confined to Sufism and Shiᶜism. In Sufism, it is represented by the dyadic relationship between disciple and spiritual master and by the hierarchy of saints. In Shiᶜism, it is most fully represented in the figures of the Imams, the rightful and real rulers of the Islamic community, who are the direct channels to the source of revelation and the interpreters of its esoteric truths. In the absence of the Imams, the motif has found expression in the devotion accorded to certain leading clerics who have come to be regarded as spiritual and moral exemplars and in some way as being the worldly representatives of the Hidden Imam. The motif was strongly reasserted in Shaykhism, the Shaykhi masters being accorded an extraordinary authority on the basis both of their esoteric claim to a special relationship with the Imams, and of their exoteric role as leading clerical exemplars.

The Báb's authority and the validation of his claims

Whilst the Babis initially appeared to be continuing this Shaykhi concern, they clearly soon surpassed it, as is evidenced most clearly by the Báb's claims to authority and the manner of the validation of his claims. Thus, unlike the Shaykhi masters, the Báb had no exoteric role as a leading cleric. His authority rested entirely on his claims to be some sort of unique divine intermediary, whether in terms of his being the special representative of the Imam on earth, or (after 1848) the Imam Mahdi himself, or the actual 'Point' (*nuqṭa*) of revelation, that is in Shiᶜi terms a prophet or messenger from God. Again, the nature of the Báb's claim to authority is indicated by the means he employed to validate it: the revelation of verses, 'these verses which prove my being' and which 'flow from my power'.[13] This was the same validation which had been employed in the Quran: none could produce such verses except God. Those who doubted its divine origin were challenged to produce its like.

On numerous occasions, then, the Báb would 'prove' his claims by writing copious verses in Quranic style. The great speed of composition was itself part of his proof. Untutored in Arabic or the religious sciences, he claimed that he was able 'without thought or hesitation' to write a thousand verses in five hours without pause of the pen. Again, he could produce 'commentaries and learned treatises of so high a degree of wisdom and understanding of the Divine Unity that doctors of religion and philosophers confess their inability to comprehend those passages'.[14] Combined with his fine penmanship and melodious reading voice, these occasions of public proof exercised a hypnotic fascination over his audience. Even the sympathetic unbeliever might find in this spectacle evidence of superhuman power and themselves become enraptured by 'the magic of His voice and the sweeping force of His revelation'.[15] More deeply, the truth and potency of the Báb's revelation was shown by its transformative impact on the lives of men. That his disciples should feel themselves spiritually regenerated by the Báb was a further proof of his divinely-derived authority.

The proof by revelation also had wider implications. The sheer facticity of revelation was to be seen as God's supreme testimony to humankind. In the face of such facticity, human learning and traditional beliefs and expectations were irrelevant. Even the performance of miracles or the fulfilment of prophecies were inferior to the proof of revelation. Indeed, such external proofs were implicitly abandoned or minimalized. The Báb was himself the measure by which truth could be distinguished from falsehood, the criterion by which he himself could be judged. In the words traditionally ascribed to him after his initial declaration to Mullá Ḥusayn:

> It is for God to test His servants, and not for His servants to judge Him in accordance with their deficient standards. Were I to fail to resolve your perplexities, could the Reality that shines within Me be regarded as powerless, or My knowledge be accused as faulty? Nay . . .[16]

Criteria external to the Báb's own self or his writings might provide supportive evidence for his claims, but of themselves they were neither necessary nor sufficient means of validation. The one exception to this was the proof by *mubáhala*. Common Shiʿi practice, *mubáhala* (mutual cursing) consisted in two parties calling down God's curse and judgement upon whichever one was speaking falsely. For Sayyid Káẓim, it was the only valid means by which rival claims to the truth could be put to the test.[17] Similarly, the Báb and his disciples attached great importance to it and used it widely as a means of propagating their faith by challenging the ulama. Like the proof by revelation, it transcended appeal to reason or tradition by an assertion of the potency of absolute authority.

As a corollary of the manner of the Báb's validation of his claims, true discipleship to him would seem to have entailed a decisive and unquestioning act of faith – a direct response both to the challenge which the Báb had proffered and to the numinous quality of his own being. As the movement veered steadily away from orthodoxy and traditional religious expectations, those who remained attached to traditional conceptions of religious authority and validation may be assumed to have experienced increasing cognitive pressure to make such an act of unquestioning faith or to abandon the movement in confusion or despair.

The Báb's leading disciples

The regard for authoritative and charismatic leadership was not focused only on the Báb. From the start of the Babi movement certain of the Báb's leading disciples were accorded an exalted status, and this became an increasingly characteristic feature of the movement after 1848. Such status was derived from two sources: traditional clerical roles and the dispersion of charismatic authority.

Given the extreme respect that was accorded to higher members of the Shiᶜi ulama, it was not surprising that the conversion of leading clerics should be an important element in the expansion of Babism. In general such conversions led to the incorporation of new networks of followers into the Babi community. In two significant instances, however, the new Babis retained a personal and fervent relationship with their original clerical mentors: Mullá Muḥammad ᶜAlí Ḥujjat in Zanján and Sayyid Yaḥyá Vaḥíd Darábí in Nayríz. In these two instances entire local communities converted at the instigation of their existing and venerated religious exemplars.

Zanján and Nayríz were exceptional locations of Babi activity and authority. More characteristic of Babism as a whole was the developing charismatic authority of the leading disciples. In status and organizational role the Letters of the Living occupied a unique position. For some Babis this position was recognized in the doctrine of the *sábiqún* (the foremost), an identification of the Letters of the Living with the leading figures of Shiᶜi history.[18] Whilst all of the Letters were thus honoured, only Mullá Ḥusayn, Qurratuʾl-ᶜAyn and Quddús appear to have enjoyed any unusual degree of authority.

It was to these individuals that authority accrued in the aftermath of the Báb's imprisonment, and it was these individuals who were raised to almost theophanic status by their own followers.

The aftermath

The salience of the polar motif is further indicated by events which followed the execution of the Báb and these same leading disciples. As the movement collapsed, the great desire for a reassertion of charismatic leadership was expressed by the emergence of a plethora of claimants to divinely sanctioned authority. Again, it must be assumed that this desire contributed to the later rapid reunification and reanimation of the movement by Baháʾuʾlláh as a charismatic figure successfully and strongly embodying authoritative leadership.

MILLENARIANISM

In its particular Twelver Shiʿi form, millennial expectation centred on the expected return of the Twelfth Imam, Muḥammad al-Mahdí. He would come in the last days, battle against Antichrist (*Dajjál*) and the forces of evil, re-establish Shiʿism, 'fill the earth with justice', and usher in the reign of the saints and the events of the Resurrection (*qiyáma*) and the last judgement.

According to later Babi and Bahaʾi writers, the millennial promise formed a central part of the teachings of Shaykh Aḥmad and Sayyid Káẓim. Certainly some of their followers entertained adventist expectations and many Shaykhis responded eagerly to the explicit millenarianism of early Babism. This millenarianism also had a more widespread popular appeal and formed an important element in the initial expansion of the new movement. Even if the Báb was only regarded as the harbinger of the Imam, and not the Imam himself, this did not weaken the potential millenarian fervour which his claims might arouse. Whatever his role in the approaching Resurrection, the 'victory' and 'dominion' of God were now at hand. With the open declaration of his Mahdihood in 1848, the millenarian fervour of the Babis reached its peak. The reign of the saints was at hand. The lord was no longer nigh. He had come.

Despite the centrality of the millenarian motif in the Babi movement it is clear that it ultimately diverged quite radically from traditional Shiʿi millenarianism. This divergence became most apparent after 1848. Not only were the more miraculous 'signs of the end' given allegorical meaning but the Báb himself, by abrogating the Islamic *shariʿa*, revealing a new code of laws, and essentially inaugurating a new religion by his claim to be a divine messenger, increasingly failed to conform to the role which the Imam Mahdi would traditionally have been expected to fulfil. In early Babism, however, such divergences may not have been apparent. As harbinger of the Imam, the Báb challenged the existing framework of religious authority, but he did little to challenge the traditional expectations surrounding the approaching Resurrection. Indeed, in certain respects the Babis closely tied their appeal to those expectations. After all, the year of the Báb's declaration was exactly one thousand lunar years – a full millennium – after the disappearance of the last Imam in AH 260. Again, the Babis argued that ʿAlí Muḥammad possessed all the personal characteristics associated with the promised one: he was a sayyid of pure lineage; he was in his twenties, of medium height, a non-smoker, free from bodily deficiency; he had a gap between his front teeth and a mole on his forehead; and he claimed endowment with innate knowledge.[19]

It is less clear whether the early Babis shared the other traditional expectations concerning the Resurrection. Certainly those Shiᶜis who flocked to Karbalá in 1845 in response to the Báb's call to gather are likely to have shared the traditional expectations of miraculous events, but many of these readily turned away from the movement when the Báb failed to appear. For the core of the believers who were left – schooled as they were in the subtleties of Shaykhi esotericism – the allegorization of such events was doubtless more acceptable.

Rajᶜa

In one particular regard, however, Babi doctrine transcended the limitations of allegory. Shiᶜis expected that the Resurrection would be accompanied both by the appearance of various eschatological figures who would fight against the Mahdi and by the return of the Imam Ḥusayn, the Prophet Muhammad and the other Imams, who would participate in a victorious *jihád* against the forces of unbelief. The Babis believed that these various figures had all appeared. Central here was the Babi doctrine of 'return' (*rajᶜa*), a controversial concept which was capable of various interpretations. According to the more 'restrained' interpretation – such as is contained in the Bahaʾi schema and seemingly in the Báb's own account – each religious dispensation (*ẓuhúr*) is characterized by the appearance of very much the same *dramatis personae*. Around the central figure of the Divine Manifestation circle his chief disciples; opposing him gather the forces of negation headed by the *Dajjál* or Antichrist; and preceding him appear his forerunners, who prepare humanity for the new revelation at the times of its deepest spiritual darkness. Thus, the Báb, his Shaykhi predecessors, his followers and opponents were all re-enacting established 'roles' in the dispensational drama. In this sense Mullá Ḥusayn and the other Letters of the Living were the return of the holy ones of Shiᶜism, Karbalá was re-enacted at Ṭabarsí, the Qajars took on the identity of the hated Umayyads who had opposed the Imams, and Karím Khán Kirmání and Ḥají Mírzá Áqásí performed the roles of the one-eyed Antichrist and his companion, the hideous Sufyání. A far less symbolic interpretation was also possible, however, and it is clear that for some Babis at least the dispensational drama comprised not re-enactments of former 'roles', but re-embodiments of former personages. From an Islamic standpoint such notions came very close to the doctrine of metempsychosis, a heretical belief recurrent in extremist Shiᶜism.

Man-yuẓhiruhu'lláh

A final complexity in the consideration of Babi millenarianism is the doctrine of *Man-yuẓhiruhu'lláh*. Already transcending the traditional role of the Mahdi by claiming to be a new Divine Manifestation, and thus in essence the inaugurator of a new religion, the Báb extended and revived millenarian expectation by referring to a further messianic figure whom he termed *Man-yuẓhiruhu'lláh* (He whom God shall make manifest). Moreover, after *Man-yuẓhiruhu'lláh*, there would be yet other Divine Manifestations – an assertion of progressive continuity rather than of eschatological endings.

The figure of *Man-yuẓhiruhu'lláh* dominates the Báb's later writings, and time and again the Báb's followers were bidden not to reject *Man-yuẓhiruhu'llah*. Those who rejected him ceased to be believers. None could advance such a claim falsely. No one had the right to question him. It was better to read but one of his verses than to read the *Bayán* a thousand times. He was the origin of all names and attributes. He would arise suddenly on a day known only to God. All must rise on hearing his name. And in every meeting a vacant place should be left for him. Given such a further messianic emphasis it was doubtless to be expected that after the Báb's execution various claimants to this station appeared. Most Babis appear to have been far more prepared to regard the messianic fulfilment as occurring shortly, as the Baha'i propagandists asserted, than as occurring in the distant future, as the Azali Babis came to assert.

HOLY WAR AND MARTYRDOM

In Twelver Shi'ism, the traditions of holy war against the enemies of Islam and of heroic and sacrificial death in defence of Islam are closely interlinked. These traditions receive their worldly focus in the passion drama of the Imam Ḥusayn, grandson of the Prophet Muhammad. Rebelling against the rule of the usurping Umayyads, Ḥusayn and his followers were killed in the battle of Karbalá in AD 680. Annually commemorating these events in a highly emotional display of ritual grief, Twelver Shi'is have constantly reidentified themselves with the traditions of struggle against perceived injustice and of suffering and martyrdom in the path of that struggle. All those who would proclaim the truth of God's cause are expected to face the evil opposition of those who have rebelled against God.

These twin themes of martyrdom and *jihád* were both strongly expressed in Babism. Clearly in his initial role as harbinger of the Imam, the Báb conformed to traditional expectations about the importance of *jihád* in securing the victory of God's cause. Nor was such 'traditionalism' confined to the sanguinary declarations of the *Qayyúmu'l-Asmá*. Many of those who journeyed to Karbalá in response to his summons brought weapons with them in preparation for the forthcoming 'day of slaughter'. No *jihád* was actually called, however, and whilst the later conflicts at Ṭabarsí, Zanján and Nayríz took on the characteristics of defensive holy wars, much ambiguity remains as to their genesis and motivation. At the same time, the Báb's later teachings place much less emphasis on the traditional conception of *jihád*.

By contrast, the continuing importance of martyrdom as a religious ideal is unambiguous. Throughout the Báb's career the sufferings inflicted upon himself and his followers were interpreted as evidence of the hostility of the evil doers towards God's truth. Finally, sustained by faith, the Babis fought and died as witnesses for their truth. The paradigm of martyrdom was fully re-enacted. Ṭabarsí *was* Karbalá. Whether sword in hand upon the field of battle, or in the grisly scenes of torture, mutilation and execution which followed, the Babi martyrs gave their companions and successors new models of devotion, and of defiant resistance to the ungodly. Even to their opponents such testimony could be taken as a sign of truth. Certainly the sustained resistance by relatively small groups of Babis against large numbers of government troops was aided by such perceptions, and by the resultant low morale of many of the soldiers.

RATIONALISM AND SOCIAL REFORMISM

It is often supposed that Babism represented a proto-modernist movement within Iranian Shiʿism, embodying in various ways distinct impulses towards rationalism and social reform. Whilst such impulses may be discerned within Babism, their nature was deeply ambiguous and it is difficult to maintain that these were dominant elements of the religion. As to Babi 'rationalism', this may be seen as a continuation of the anti-literalist symbolism of Shaykhism. According to this view not only were certain of the miraculous elements of religion transposed from their expected occurrence in the world of matter to the interworld or to the realm of symbolic appearances, but the overall attitude towards social change was significantly transformed.[20] The orthodox fatalism, by which the occultation of the Imam was seen as a period of endless social decay, was replaced by a more 'humanistic' conception by which human spiritual progress was anticipated, at least during the 'arc of ascent'. These anti-literalist and 'progressive' conceptions were far overshadowed, however, by the intense pietism of Babi devotionalism and the anti-intellectualist attitudes displayed in the laws governing the destruction of non-Babi books and the prohibition of various forms of study.

As to Babi social reformism, the reality seems much coloured by various myths which quickly grew up around the movement. According to one such myth, derived both from the traditional Muslim account of what heretical movements were supposed to practise and (conservative) European views of any supposed radicalism in the light of the European experience of the revolutions of 1848, the Babis were socialistic revolutionaries intent upon the overthrow of state and religion – Iranian Blanquists, as it were, in religious guise. Apart from the arguments about the Babis' political intentions, the main elements in this view are the Babis' supposed advocacy and practice of the communality of property and of women. According to the second main myth, this time springing mostly from Western liberals from the late nineteenth century onwards, the Babis were, by contrast, to be seen as heroic agents of progress, dedicated to tolerance and the emancipation of women.

Regarding the communality of property, there is no evidence that this ever became part of formal Babi practice and doctrine other than, as Curzon has remarked, in the New Testament sense of 'the sharing of goods in common by members of the faith, and the exercise of alms-giving, and an ample charity'.[21] Indeed, in so far as the Báb's own teachings relate to economic matters, the central element is undoubtedly the expressed need for the creation of a more favourable environment for trade rather than any egalitarianism. According to a controversial account in the *Nuqṭatu'l-Káf* (*The Point of the K*, an early Babi history), however, Quddús advocated something of the kind during the conference of Badasht, and, more definitely, the defenders at Shaykh Ṭabarsí shared their goods in common, but then only in the context of a self-perceived heroic and self-renunciatory struggle against the forces of evil.[22]

As to the belief, expressed amongst others by the British envoy in Iran, Justin Sheil, that there was 'no form of marriage' amongst the Babis, for 'a man and a woman live together as long as they please and no longer, and if another man desires to have possession of that woman, it rests with her, not with the man who has been her husband', there being no limit to the number of wives or husbands an individual might have, this must be dismissed as nonsense, reflecting Muslim fears and suspicions rather than

Babi belief or practice.[23] Thus, at a formal level, the Báb advocated marriage, either monogamously or in a limited form of polygamy; concubinage and adultery were forbidden; and divorce (as in Islam by the husband of the wife) was permitted only after the elapse of a year of waiting. Even at the level of common practice, the most that can be affirmed is that Qurratuʾl-ʿAyn defied and scandalized social convention with the freedom with which she spoke and travelled, and that on occasions she allowed herself to be seen unveiled. There is also the allegation that Qurratuʾl-ʿAyn – separated but not divorced from her husband – contracted some relationship with Quddús at Badasht, but there is no firm evidence to validate this statement.

Again with regard to the Babis' supposed emancipation of women, this must be viewed in very relative terms, for whilst there is no doubt that the Báb sought to elevate the (deplorably depressed) condition of Persian women – notably through the abolition of concubinage and the prohibition on instant divorce (and the consequent danger of destitution) – and regarded women sufficiently highly as to appoint a woman as one of his chief disciples, emancipatory moves beyond this were extremely limited: the necessity of veiling was removed, but this appears not to have been put into effect by his followers; strict seclusion of women was abolished and women were allowed to speak with men, but only to an extremely limited degree; and women were confined to attending the mosque separately at night. Likewise, in the case of Qurratuʾl-ʿAyn, whilst her fierce assertion of her own independence and religious standing must be regarded as an implicit declaration of her own emancipation as a woman, it is difficult to see her as the martyr for women's rights which she has sometimes been portrayed as in the West. Rather, she is more easily seen as a religious zealot whose zealotry was such as to impel her beyond normally sanctioned female social roles.

As to the supposed tolerance of the Babis, whilst the Báb himself openly read the Bible during his imprisonment (an act startlingly at variance with contemporary attitudes), and instructed in the *Bayán* that non-Babis should be treated with justice, it is difficult to regard the intended destruction of non-Babi books and the expulsion of unbelievers from Babi kingdoms as indicative of any modern spirit of tolerance. It is only with the emergence of the Bahaʾi Faith that there was a concern with tolerance, or indeed with social reform in general.

3
BABISM AS A SOCIO-RELIGIOUS MOVEMENT IN IRAN

Given the rapid expansion of the Babi movement and the violent conflicts which preceded its collapse, a number of writers have interpreted the movement as an expression of political or class conflict. Alternatively, it has been seen as a response to the Western impact on Iran. These views have more than mere historical import, because in stereotypical form they contribute to the contemporary image of Iranian Bahaʾism, the allegation that the Bahaʾi Faith 'is not a religion' being a commonly used justification for the persecution of Bahaʾis. For both historical and contemporary reasons, then, it is necessary to comment on Babism as a socio-religious movement in Iran.

GROWTH AND SOCIAL COMPOSITION

In the first instance it will be as well to emphasize the limited nature of our knowledge of the demography and social composition of the Babi movement. It is possible that at the peak of its expansion, Babism had as many as 100,000 adherents. If this is anywhere near correct, and if the total Iranian population at the time was in the region of six million (opinions differ considerably), of whom at least one-third were nomads, then the Babis may have comprised some 2.5 per cent of the settled population, a significant minority when well organized.[1]

The exact social composition of the Babi community is as uncertain as the figure for its total membership. Some of the main features seem clear enough, however. At a general level, although Babism was widely based in Iranian society, the pattern of expansion to different social groups was subject to various constraints and possibilities.

Ideologically, the messianic claims of Babism broadened the movement's appeal beyond the narrow confines of Shaykhi esotericism, creating the base for a widespread popular movement. Beyond this,

Babism remained within a Shiʿi conceptual universe. Converts to Babism were drawn almost entirely from amongst the Twelver Shiʿis, although there were some Kurdish Sunnis who were (transiently?) prepared to regard the Báb as a holy man and miracle worker, and contacts were established with groups of ʿAlíyuʾlláhís and Jews. The sizeable minorities of Zoroastrians and Christians, and most of the Sunni Muslims, were not contacted. There were also linguistic and geographic barriers. Although there were a few Arab Babis, the overwhelming majority were either Persians or Azeri Turks, the two groups who together comprised most of the settled Iranian Shiʿi population. Most of the tribal minorities – distinctive in language, religion and nomadic lifestyle – were not contacted. Nor were Babi missionaries generally active in such areas as the western mountains, the southern coast or the south-east, which were all relatively remote or inaccessible.

Babi missionaries initially utilized the pre-existing network of Shaykhi communities, thereby rapidly expanding throughout Iran and in some instances gaining the allegiance of entire local communities. At first generally cautious in their missionary endeavour, the Báb's disciples gained converts outside the Shaykhi fold as a result of personal contacts. As Babi preaching became more open larger numbers of non-Shaykhis converted, often in emulation of some local religious leader. Public preaching also generated forceful opposition, and where the local religious and civic leaders offered sustained and united opposition, the Babi missionaries were limited in their success, often being forced to flee the locality. On the other hand, where the local elite was divided in its response, rapid expansion might ensue, often along lines of existing neighbourhood divisions and patronage relationships. As the Babi missionaries travelled extensively, contacts were made in all major towns of the Iranian heartland. By contrast, though extensive contacts were made in some rural areas, expansion in such areas was far more uneven.

As between different regions of Iran, there is no support for the assertion that there was 'an element in the movement's origins of the protest of the south against the north'.[2] On the contrary, Babism appears to have been more successful in the north. Different areas and towns may well have varied in the radicalism of their Babi groups, however.

The Babis were drawn almost entirely from amongst the settled population of the Shiʿi heartland. This population was socially diverse and the incidence of conversion to Babism appears to have varied considerably between different social groups and classes. Of these, the ulama were quite clearly the dominant group within the movement, providing most of its leaders and a significant proportion of its most active membership. At Shaykh Ṭabarsí, for example, 37 per cent of those identified as participants were ulama.[3] As between high- and low-ranking ulama, significant numbers of each were converted. The Letters of the Living were all lesser ulama, however, and in general the more radical Babis were drawn from this grouping, especially from amongst the seminary students (*tulláb*). By contrast the higher-ranking ulama were generally amongst the more conservative and cautious Babis.

Of the non-ulama, such evidence as there is suggests that the overall incidence of conversion was probably greatest amongst the merchants and craftsmen of the bazaar. This was facilitated by Babi missionary endeavour being at first directed chiefly to the larger towns, and probably also by the fact that the pre-existing relationships between the clerics and the *bazárís* were often particularly strong: the bazaar was a natural place for clerical missionaries to look for converts. Thus, in the main commercial and manufacturing towns, *bazárís* soon became a major element in the Babi communities. Although skilled artisans and shopkeepers may well have comprised the majority, a significant number of merchant families also converted. Literate and possessed of both financial resources and a national network of communication, the Babi merchants provided a major linkage in the further dissemination of the new religion. Whether or not there were significant numbers of converts from amongst the unskilled urban workforce is unknown. It may well be that what distinguished the volatile situations in Zanján, Yazd and Nayríz was precisely the localized conversion of members of this class, but in Iran as a whole such converts attained no prominence within the movement. Similarly, although Iran was then predominantly a peasant society, peasants were not a prominent element in the Babi membership except in a number of localized instances where group conversions followed the conversion of local religious leaders, or in one case of a local landlord. Again, although there were some of the landed gentry who became Babis, they were few in number, as were converts from among Qajar officialdom.

With regard to differences between the sexes in the incidence of conversion, there has as yet been little research. Impressionistic evidence – including conversations with Iranian Bahaʾis regarding their Babi forebears – suggests that Babism may well have been a predominantly male preserve, at least in its initial diffusion. With the exception of those women contacted by Qurratuʾl-ʿAyn and her associates (including Mullá Ḥusayn's sister), most Babi women seem liable to have learnt of Babism from their menfolk. There were cases where converts concealed their religion from their immediate families, but in general it seems likely that the most active and committed Babis sought to secure their spouses' conversions. Although Babi women were for the most part little involved in the organization of the religion, they were numbered amongst the martyrs, and, at Zanján at least, amongst the combatants.

THE POLITICAL ASPECTS OF RELIGIOUS DISSENT

The Báb's claim to Mahdihood was an explicit challenge to the entire existing religious, social and political order. His followers' attempt to establish a theocracy was inevitably a political as well as a religious endeavour. In the course of rejection and defeat the Babis came to challenge openly the legitimacy of the Qajar regime, leading disciples later seeking to revenge themselves upon its head. Understandably, then, Babism has come to be seen as an insurrectionary movement. In so far as they can be discerned, the motivation of the Babi combatants and the complex developing relationship between the Babis and the Qajar regime belie a straightforwardly 'political' account, however. If the Babis had simply wished to stage a coup or mount an insurrection there was no need for them to have developed an elaborate religious ideology. Nineteenth-century Iranians were quite capable of mounting insurrections without the benefit of religious ideologies and indeed often did so to considerable effect. The sufferings engendered by the Qajars' brutal conquest of Khurasan may well have prompted the particular militancy of the Khurasani Babis, but for those Khurasanis who wanted to fight against Qajar oppression, Salár's rebellion surely provided a better means than Babism. Nor, indeed, were the Babis representative of social groups who were so remote from the political processes of the time as to constitute 'primitive rebels'. Even in practical terms, if the Babi movement was as extensive and as well organized as is usually supposed, then a few localized and spasmodic 'upheavals' hardly constitute effective insurrectionary action.

At a national level, at least, a 'religious' account seems far more plausible. Though conscious of the political implications of their claims in a society in which religious and political action interweaved, the Babis may still be seen primarily as religious zealots. Only in the context of interaction with the political environment did Babism assume a revolutionary stance. Intent upon religio-political change, the Babi leaders sought first to conduct a national campaign of missionary endeavour and to gain the allegiance of the Qajar regime. Failing in this later regard and encountering opposition from the Shiʿi ulama, many Babis became increasingly assertive in their missionary endeavour, the march with the Black Standard from Khurasan being the culmination of this tendency towards militant proclamation. In the midst of a deteriorating political situation such actions readily provoked a militant response, which in turn led the Babi zealots to witness for the truth of their faith in martyrdom and with the sword. Once acted out, such a confrontation defined the rival political roles of the Qajars and the Babis, but in its aftermath no unified Babi response developed. Increasingly, 'radicals' and 'conservatives' amongst the Babis diverged in their paths of action, further confrontations occurring in the context of adventitious local circumstances.

Religio-political interaction also characterized the development of the various local Babi communities, accentuating the movement's tendencies towards diversity. Wherever the Babis grew in numbers and importance they were increasingly and inevitably drawn into the intricate web of communal politics. Each Iranian town was invariably divided into a number of rival districts, each with its own patrician patrons and local associations. Sometimes engaging in bitter intercommunal fighting, these districts were often distinguished by allegiance to rival religious factions. Large-scale conversions to Babism naturally reflected these divisions. The old Niᶜmatí quarter of Bárfurúsh became successively the Shaykhi and then the Babi quarter. Similarly, support for the Báb in Shiraz reflected factional divisions, whilst Babi conversions in Zanján and Nayríz were concentrated within particular neighbourhoods. Patrician rivalries were also involved. Rivalries between the leading ulama in Qazvin may have been involved in Baraghání's original antagonism towards Shaykh Aḥmad. Thereafter, support for Shaykhism or Babism in Qazvin was also a symbolic gesture of assertiveness against Baraghání. Again, in Zanján, existing patrician rivalries involving the Babi leader were merely accentuated by his conversion and undoubtedly contributed to the subsequent escalation of hostilities. Finally, as leading patricians – particularly the clergy – generally had groups of strong-arm supporters, the possibilities for the escalation of violence were always present. Indeed, in Yazd, it was the leader of the local 'rowdies' (*lúṭís*), already in conflict with the local governor, who came to champion Darábí in his preaching of Babism.

SOCIAL DISCONTENT AND CLASS CONFLICT

Mid-nineteenth-century Iran was both socially divided and crisis-ridden. Although a major contextual element in the emergence of Babism, the exact nature of the relationship between these various social tensions and the new movement is far from clear, however.

Social class

As to the analysis of Babism in class terms, the most clear-cut portrayal is that provided by Mikhail Ivanov.[4] According to this interpretation the movement represented a two-fold struggle against feudalism and enslavement to foreign capital. Thus whilst the Báb promoted a bourgeois reformism reflective of his own class position, his leading disciples developed a radical popular movement with democratic tendencies, which dominated the insurrectionary period from 1848 to 1852. When defeat caused the movement to lose its popular mass character, some Babi leaders went over to terrorism.

The argument that Babism represented some form of bourgeois reformism is a difficult one to sustain. The Báb himself was a merchant, as were a number of his followers, but there is no evidence that economic concerns were prominent in the initial expansion of the movement. Although commercial and *bazárí* social networks became an important element in the movement's further diffusion, the primary 'carriers' of the religion were members of the Shaykhi ulama (of various class backgrounds). Again, although the Báb's book of laws included a few regulations favouring merchant interests, that book was not a major element in the religion's appeal, nor was it more than peripherally concerned with social reform.

Similarly, it is difficult to attribute Babism with any policy of resistance or reaction to Western encroachments, such as might be expected from an ideology of bourgeois nationalism. Certainly the *Bayán* contains elements that were later to be given such an interpretation by the Azali free-thinker, Mírzá Áqá Khán Kirmání,[5] but this does not seem to have been the interpretation given them by the early Babis. Although centring on the world of Iranian Shiʿism, the Babis plainly saw their mission as being pan-Islamic or even universal in scope. Islamic themes far outweighed those aspects of Persian culture – such as the new year (*naw rúz*) celebration – which received acknowledgement in the Báb's writings. Persian was made a language of revelation, but it augmented Arabic rather than replaced it. Again, in obvious contrast to the cultural xenophobia of the Shaykhi leader, Karím Khán,[6] the Báb supported the emulation of certain aspects of European life and manners, albeit that these were peripheral to the system he propounded. The Báb was aware of the impact and presence of the West, but the religion which he founded cannot usefully be thought of as either a reaction to, or an accommodation with, the West.

Ivanov's interpretation of the popular radicalism of later Babism represents a stronger argument. However, it remains debatable as to whether even popular Babism was significantly radical in terms of its socio-economic implications. The communality of property which was practised at Ṭabarsí and Zanján may have reflected the ideas of some of those at Badasht, but occurred in the very specific context of extreme privation and siege. The practice does not appear to have become common elsewhere and, whatever appeal it may have had to the poorer Zanjáni Babis, it readily alienated their more affluent co-religionists. In general, far from being advocates of social revolution, the Babi leaders may better be seen as proponents of traditional Islamic ideals of charity, the struggle against injustice, and the equitable treatment of all true believers. Again, neither in its official nor in its 'popular' forms was Babism democratic, being hierarchical, rather, and implicitly authoritarian.

More generally, it is difficult to interpret Babism in specific class terms at all, except in relationship to the very particular 'class' conflict that had emerged amongst the ulama. As Shaykhism had done before it, Babism explicitly challenged the dominance of the *mujtahids*. Although there is no conclusive evidence, it is more than possible that those ulama who opposed the *mujtahids'* dominance were at least amongst the most aquiescent in response to Babi missionary expansion, if not actually amongst the converts. Significantly, the two leading ulama who led the Babis at Zanján and Nayríz were respectively an Akhbárí traditionalist and the son of a leading esotericist, both with reason to oppose the newly developing orthodoxy. More conjecturally, there may have been an element of popular economic resentment against the increasingly rich and powerful higher clergy, and it is of note that at Badasht, it was specifically the non-payment of the substantial religious taxes which Quddús was alleged to have advocated.[7]

Class and related factors were important in the development of Babism, but their influence was largely indirect – facilitating rather than causative. Like many other religious movements in traditional societies, non-class social divisions (religion, ethnicity, communality, and patronage relationships) defined the social networks by which expansion of the movement occurred. Then again, whilst Babism succeeded in gaining converts from a wide range of social groups and classes (both elite and popular), the incidence of conversion varied widely, supporting the idea of an 'elective affinity' between particular social groups and the religion's ethos and ideology. Certainly the predominance in Babism of clerics, merchants and craftsmen supports Weber's assertions as to the social location of religions with rationalistic systems of ethics.[8] Again, as Babism became radicalized, the divisions between 'radicals' and 'conservatives' opened on predictable class lines, the more affluent amongst the laity and the more established amongst the clerics generally being the more conservative Babis.

Social discontent

It is generally supposed by social scientists and many historians that religious movements which promote strong millenarian expectations are in some way the product of extreme social discontent.[9] It is assumed that the urgent anticipation of a total and supernaturally derived transformation of this present world reflects the hopes of those for whom the experience or promise of that world has been one of alienation and suffering. Certainly, in the case of the Babi movement – with its strong appeal to millenarian expectation – an underlying context of social discontent can be readily identified. For perhaps most adult Iranians, the experience of life by the 1840s provided ample cause for millennial hope. Even if the all too commonplace miseries of dearth, earthquake and feudal oppression are left aside, there had been many potentially portentous 'signs of the end': the introduction and recurrence of epidemics of cholera from 1821 onwards (including two major outbreaks in the 1840s which killed thousands of Iranians);[10] the humiliating defeats of the Iranian 'armies of Islam' at the hands of the infidel Russians (1813, 1828) and the English (1839); the intervention of those same powers in Iranian political life, and the knowledge of the general threat which European imperialism posed to all the 'lands of Islam'; the twin sackings of the Shiᶜi holy city of Karbalá by the Wahhabis (1802) and the Turks (1843); and the devastating economic impact of both the war indemnity to Russia and Iran's incorporation into the European world economy.

Whether or not as a direct correlate of this catalogue of woe, generalized millenarian expectation appears to have become quite common in mid-nineteenth-century Iran.[11] Emphasizing the Báb's prophetic claims and his 'appearance' in the millennial year AH 1260 (AD 1844), the Babi missionaries were well able to channel such expectation into their own movement. It is tempting to make more specific correlations, but these are ambiguous in their application. Thus the particular success of Babism in the province of Khurasan[12] may well reflect the Khurasanis' experience of the Qajars' particularly brutal subjugation of their lands, but neither within Khurasan, nor within Iran as a whole, is there any simple correlation between the experience of Qajar subjugation and the response to Babism and militancy within it. Again, whilst the craft producers bore much of the brunt of the European economic impact (the collapse of traditional industries, financial crises), and were amongst those social groups most responsive to Babism, closer examination does not reveal any apparent correlation between conversion and the particular sectors of craft production, such as textiles, which were most adversely affected.

Finally it should be emphasized that, in contrast to many instances of millenarian activism, the Babi religion did not emerge in a context in which traditional religious values and institutions were under external threat. By 1850 Europe posed no ideological challenge to Iran. The few resident Europeans were objects of curiosity or contempt; they were not yet perceived as the bearers of revolutionary values. In so far as Babism embodied specific religious discontents, it was within the framework of traditional values, institutions and expectations. Pious hope for a better world freed from oppression fostered the appeal of the movement, but so did the traditional appeals of the exemplification of piety and holiness and the possession of that hidden knowledge and grace bestowed by the Imams. For all its radical departures from tradition, Babism remained part of the traditional world of Iranian Shiʿism and was extirpated as a heresy accordingly. Yet within twenty to thirty years of that final persecution that world had been transformed. Iran had become a mere pawn in the 'Great Game' of Anglo-Russian rivalry. The European economic impact had become pervasive and European ideas were being actively promoted to challenge all manner of traditional thinking. The Babis for their part had re-emerged as followers of a new religion which, by the end of the century, was to have gained adherents not only in India and Egypt, but even in America and Europe itself. The 'signs of holiness' had been transferred, and Babism, militant and millenarian, had been transformed into the Bahaʾi Faith, irenic, universalistic and increasingly assertive of its independence and separation from Shiʿism.

PART II: THE BAHAʾI FAITH IN THE EAST, *c.* 1866–1921

4

THE BABI RECOVERY AND THE EMERGENCE OF THE BAHAʾI FAITH

By the early 1850s, Babism had all but collapsed as a religious movement. The Iranian government, clearly, regarded its 'roots' as having been 'torn up',[1] and it would scarcely have been surprising if Babism had simply ceased to exist. That it did not is to be largely attributed to the transformation effected by Mírzá Ḥusayn ʿAlí Núr (1817–92), an older half-brother of Mírzá Yaḥyá Ṣubḥ-i Azal (1830/1–1912). Known to his followers by the title *Baháʾuʾlláh* (Glory of God), Ḥusayn ʿAlí first came to dominate the Babi movement and then, in 1866, laid claim to be the promised *Man-yuẓhiruhuʾlláh*. Most Babis thereafter become his adherents under the name of *Baháʾís*, the small minority who continued to accept Ṣubḥ-i Azal as their leader coming to be known as *Azalís*. The assessment of the careers of these two men prior to this date and of the deepening rift which developed between them is no easy matter in that the major sources for the period were written by their antagonistic and partisan followers after this division into two separate groups.

BAHÁʾUʾLLÁH AND THE REVIVAL OF BABISM, 1853–66

Baháʾuʾlláh and Ṣubḥ-i Azal[2] came from a family of land-owning notables in the district of Núr in the province of Mazandaran. In addition to land-owning, their father, Mírzá ʿAbbás Núrí (died 1839), had become politically influential and wealthy during the reign of Fatḥ ᶜAlí Sháh (reigned 1797–1834) and was appointed to various administrative posts. Most of this wealth and power was lost through the efforts of Ḥájí Mírzá Áqásí after he became chief minister in 1835, Mírzá ᶜAbbás having been a partisan of the ousted chief minister, Qáʾim-Maqám. Whilst distantly related to an eminent Nuri cleric, the family were clearly part of the civil elite and, as was typical of their class position, received no specialized religious education.

Early converts to Babism, Baháʾuʾlláh and Ṣubḥ-i Azal, along with several other members of their wider family, were amongst the most socially distinguished adherents of the new movement, and both brothers acquired a prominence within the movement which was probably unequalled by any other non-clerical disciple. Accepting the Báb's teachings in the summer of 1844, Baháʾuʾlláh, then in his late twenties, quickly proved himself to be one of the most energetic and resourceful of the Báb's followers. Thirteen years older than Ṣubḥ-i Azal and already a man of established prestige and wealth, he was able to provide considerable assistance to the movement and seems to have possessed a certain authority. He was not, however, amongst the main rank of leaders, all of whom were ulama.

Baháʾuʾlláh's social position initially afforded him some protection from the rising tide of opposition to Babism, but later led to the suspicion that he was a prime instigator of the Babi disturbances. Thus, some time after the Báb's execution, the chief minister, Amír Kabír, informed Baháʾuʾlláh that he believed that without his (Baháʾuʾlláh's) support and guidance the Babis at Ṭabarsí could not have withstood the government troops sent against them. He also offered him the post of minister of the court (*amír-i díván*) so that the abilities of 'so resourceful a person' might be employed in the service of the state and thus neutralized.[3] In the event, Baháʾuʾlláh retired to Karbalá in the summer of 1851, returning to Tehran less than a year later at the invitation of the newly installed chief minister, his distant relative, Mírzá Áqá Khán-i Núrí. Staying with that minister's brother at the time of the attempt on the life of the Shah, he was eventually placed under arrest and consigned under dreadful conditions to the subterranean *Síyáh Chál* (Black Pit), where other Babis suspected of complicity in the assassination attempt were imprisoned. Despite the absence of any evidence linking Baháʾuʾlláh to the conspirators he was condemned to life imprisonment, but after four months this sentence was commuted to one of exile, due in part at least to pressure from his family and from the Russian ambassador, whose legation secretary was Baháʾuʾlláh's brother-in-law. Refusing the offer of asylum in Russia, he and his family undertook the arduous winter journey to the Ottoman provincial capital of Baghdad, arriving there in April 1853.

The growing polarization within the Babi community in Iraq

The period from Bahá'u'lláh's arrival in Baghdad in 1853 to the open proclamation of his claims to the Babi community in 1866 is one of considerable complexity and obscurity. The main trend of events is clear, however. By 1853, the Babi movement had been driven into a secret existence by the severity of external repression; Ṣubḥ-i Azal's overall authority within the movement, whilst still recognized by many Babis, had been effectively challenged by the emergence of a number of counterclaimants to various levels of spiritual authority; and Babi doctrine was still unsystematized and subject to a variety of conflicting and speculative interpretations. In contrast, by 1866, many Babis were coming to accept the overall authority of Bahá'u'lláh, under whose leadership a new and less esoteric presentation of Babi beliefs was developing, and a growing self-confidence was beginning to stir within the Babi community as a whole which presaged the re-emergence of Babism as an active force in Iranian religious life, albeit in a greatly altered form.

The most significant development between 1853 and 1866 – the eclipse of Ṣubḥ-i Azal by Bahá'u'lláh – is also the most difficult to reconstruct given the sharply varying accounts provided by later Baha'i and Azali writers. Before proceeding, then, it will be as well to state what is agreed between the two traditions, namely that Ṣubḥ-i Azal had received some definite form of appointment by the Báb to act as leader of the community, and that Ṣubḥ-i Azal and Bahá'u'lláh were of very different temperaments and abilities, the former, during this period, being withdrawn and retiring, and the latter forceful and outgoing. In morally evaluative terms, what to the Baha'is was Ṣubḥ-i Azal's cowardice was to the Azalis his caution, and what to the Azalis was Bahá'u'lláh's ambition was to the Baha'is his care and concern for a fragmented and demoralized community. Behind these labels there were clearly significant and recognizable differences in leadership style and appeal, and it will be more useful, in the present instance, given the difficulties in reconstructing the historical narrative, to examine each leader in these more general terms.

Ṣubḥ-i Azal's leadership. It would appear that Ṣubḥ-i Azal's main appeal as a Babi leader, at least initially, was in his being the Báb's nominee. Whilst the precise nature of that nomination remains obscure, there seems no doubt that he was soon generally recognized as being in some sense the Báb's successor, after the latter's execution in 1850. Understandably, given the confusion of the early 1850s, some went further and regarded Ṣubḥ-i Azal as being *Man-yuẓhiruhu'lláh* himself, but this does not seem to have been a claim which he advanced on his own behalf. Ṣubḥ-i Azal does not appear to have been a very effective leader, the numerous counterclaimants to divinely inspired authority constituting a clear challenge to his leadership, which his subsequent preference for seclusion can have done little to rebuff. Having gone into hiding in the aftermath of the attempt on the life of the Shah, he had made his way secretly to Baghdad, where he made contact with his brother, but maintained a general seclusion from the Babis, communicating directly with only a trusted few. Indeed, according to Baha'i accounts, he even threatened at one stage to excommunicate any Babi who should reveal his identity or location.[4] Such seclusion cannot be regarded as a particularly forceful response to the growing demoralization and disintegration of the community in the early 1850s. This in itself may have caused dissatisfaction with his leadership. Unlike the pacific policies later adopted by Bahá'u'lláh, however, Ṣubḥ-i Azal continued the tradition of Babi militancy, seemingly encouraging his followers in Iraq to attack the hated Shi'is and dispatching one more would-be assassin against Náṣiri'd-Dín Sháh, again unsuccessfully. He also caused to have murdered the Babi claimant to special authority who was perhaps the most serious threat to his own position, the eminent Mírzá Asadu'lláh of Khúy, entitled *Dayyán*.[5] More generally, when contrasted with Bahá'u'lláh's later claims and teachings, Ṣubḥ-i Azal may well be seen as a 'conservative' leader, whose continuing appeal (albeit only to a minority) may in part have been to those Babis who objected to the innovatory nature of Bahá'u'lláh's leadership, perhaps in particular to his attempted *rapprochement* with the Iranian authorities.

Bahá'u'lláh's growing prominence as a Babi leader. In contrast to Ṣubḥ-i Azal's seclusion, Bahá'u'lláh was readily accessible and would soon appear to have begun to attract a following amongst the Babi community. Whether or not for this reason, some tension apparently developed between the two brothers during the first year of their sojourn in Baghdad, and in April 1854 Bahá'u'lláh left without warning and withdrew to the mountains of Kurdistan to live the life of a solitary dervish. Later, coming into contact with some of the Sufi leaders of Sulaymániyya and gaining a reputation as a respected spiritual teacher and mystic, Bahá'u'lláh adapted readily to the life of a dervish, enjoying, by his own account, an inner tranquillity which was only brought to an end when his family finally discovered his whereabouts and begged him to return to Baghdad. This he did in March 1856, two years after his withdrawal.

Back in Baghdad, Bahá'u'lláh now rapidly became the leading figure in the Babi community in Iraq, exerting also a growing influence throughout Iran. Increasingly, it was Bahá'u'lláh rather than Ṣubḥ-i Azal whom Babi pilgrims from Iran sought to see. This growing prominence was clearly perceived by those outside the community. Thus Capt. Arnold Burrowes Kemball, the British consul-general in Baghdad, referred to Mírzá Ḥusayn ʿAlí (Bahá'u'lláh) as the 'Chief' of the local Babis (June 1858), later stating that whilst his brother Mírzá Yaḥyá (Ṣubḥ-i Azal), 'who lies perdu and the secret of whose whereabouts is mysteriously preserved', was 'recognised by the Babis as the second incarnation of the looked for Imaum' (i.e. after the Báb), Mírzá Ḥusayn ʿAli enjoyed 'a consideration which partakes of absolute devotion and reverence on the part of his followers', being recognized as 'the Director and Guide of the Babees' of Iran 'with whom he maintains a constant correspondence' (September 1859).[6] Similarly, in 1862, when the Iranian Foreign Minister, Mírzá Saʿíd Khán, had come to fear a Babi revival and was seeking the expulsion of the Babis from Baghdad, it was solely to Mírzá Ḥusayn ʿAlí and 'his followers and familiars' to whom he referred; no mention was made of Mírzá Yaḥyá,[7]

Bahá'u'lláh's growing appeal to the Babi community was doubtless considerably aided by his competence as a leader, particularly his effective construction of a network of communication linking together the fragmented Babi communities in Iran and those in Iraq. Located in an area of major Shiʿi pilgrimage and yet not living under Iranian jurisdiction, Bahá'u'lláh was well situated to construct such a network. If necessary under the guise of Shiʿi pilgrims, Iranian Babis could travel to visit Bahá'u'lláh, taking with them letters and questions from their co-religionists and returning with the replies. Such Babi travellers, together with couriers specially dispatched by Bahá'u'lláh, could visit other localities *en route* and thus bring together the various local groups. Possessed again of a single and effective centre to which the whole community could turn, the Babis appear to have rallied and to have gradually reconstituted themselves as a cohesive religious movement.

The nature of Bahá'u'lláh's appeal as a Babi leader at this time went deeper than merely his location at the centre of a network of communication, however. The two most fundamental factors involved were almost certainly his accessibility and the dissemination of his writings. These factors were paramount in an account given by Ḥájí Mírzá Ḥaydar ʿAlí – a learned Babi, who later became an outstanding Bahaʾi teacher – of what had originally caused him to abandon his trust in Ṣubḥ-i Azal and turn to Baháʾuʾlláh. Thus Ḥaydar ʿAlí referred to his early dislike for Ṣubḥ-i Azal's leadership, seeing no difference between the 'hidden Azal' and the Shiʿi Hidden Imam, and considering that his writings were 'just nonsense'. Baháʾuʾlláh's writings, by contrast, he considered 'the greatest miracle ever performed'.[8] A similar sentiment appears in the Bahaʾi account of Baháʾuʾlláh's writing of the *Lawḥ-i Kulluʾṭ-ṭaʿám* (Tablet of All Food) in 1853 or 1854, a commentary on a particular Quranic verse written in response to a Babi questioner who had found Ṣubḥ-i Azal's response highly inadequate.[9]

At the same time as Baháʾuʾlláh was becoming increasingly prominent as a leader throughout the Babi community, he was plainly attracting his own local circle of devotees who were fiercely loyal to him and dedicated to the revival of Babism as he interpreted it – what might be termed 'neo-Babism'. As a result of Baháʾuʾlláh's extensive correspondence with the Babis in Iran and their visits to Baghdad, devotees were also gained in Iran, and, following Baháʾuʾlláh's emphasis on teaching and promulgating Babism, a number of new adherents, loyal to Baháʾuʾlláh, were also gained. Thus inside the larger Babi community there gradually developed an indistinct grouping of partisans of Baháʾuʾlláh, who, by such very partisanship, tended to devalue the overall leadership and status of Ṣubḥ-i Azal to that of merely a nominal headship.

Baháʾuʾlláh's early writings

The appeal of Baháʾuʾlláh's writings, both to the Babi community in general and to his own circle of devotees in particular, would seem to have been complex, the writings themselves displaying a considerable variety in both style and content. The actual volume of writings was now very great and for at least some of his disciples Baháʾuʾlláh's linguistic fluency and rapidity of composition constituted proof of greatness, and perhaps even of revelation. In the period after his return from Kurdistan Baháʾuʾlláh is reported to have been so prolific in his utterances that in a single hour he would 'reveal' a thousand verses, and in the course of 24 hours reveal the equivalent of the whole Quran (over 6,000 verses), itself revealed over the course of 23 years. That such fluency was regarded as evidence of spiritual potency reflects a continuation of the Babi fascination with language for its own sake. That Bahá'u'lláh revealed a vast number of verses and then ordered that hundreds of thousands of them be obliterated – there being none 'worthy to hear these melodies' – was, perhaps, in itself an indication to his followers of the divine origin of those verses.[10] Again, the fact that Bahá'u'lláh would, on occasion, chant in the '*badíᶜ* (unique) language', which was 'used by the denizens of one of the worlds of God', and which 'had a wonderful effect upon the listener', indicated contact with the heavenly worlds.[11] The importance attached to language was also shown by Bahá'u'lláh's various commentaries on the esoteric significance of individual words, or even letters of the Quran.

The matter of differing style pertains both to the writings of this early period and those composed later. In general, most of Bahá'u'lláh's writings can be roughly allocated to one of two stylistic categories, each with its own distinctive appeal. Firstly there are Bahá'u'lláh's 'rapturous' writings, characterized by the use of poetic and allusive language and often regarded by Baha'is as untranslatable. Such writings deal with Bahá'u'lláh's own religious experiences, such as his encounters with the 'Maid of Heaven' or with personified divine names, the nature of his own spiritual station, his sufferings and readiness for martyrdom, and with the glories and nature of the various spiritual worlds. Certain incantatory prayers, such as the so-called 'Long Healing Prayer', also fall into this category.[12] Whilst Baha'is may well find 'infinite meanings' in the symbolic language used, the appeal of these 'rapturous' writings would seem to lie particularly in the emotional or spiritual state which they produce in the devotee. Often making strong use of rhyme and rhythm and of a repeated chorus line, these writings, when chanted in Persian or Arabic can have an almost hypnotic effect. Regarded by Baha'is as being of unsurpassed beauty, their chanting 'creates an atmosphere of ecstasy', evoking feelings of 'awe and exitement within the soul'.[13]

In contrast to these 'rapturous' writings, the majority of Bahá'u'lláh's writings, in both Persian and Arabic, were written in a style which is far more readily comprehensible. Whilst they may contain abstruse or 'mystical' passages, or make use of symbolic language, or, in the case of some of his Persian writings, may contain substantial sections in Arabic and a heavily Arabicized vocabulary, most of Bahá'u'lláh's major works were (and are) accessible to those who had not received the extensive literary training of the ulama, or who were not overly familiar with the specialized terminology employed by Sufis. In the context of Babism in the 1850s and 1860s, the lucidity of books like the *Kitáb-i Íqán* (*Book of Certitude*) was revolutionary. To an unprecedented degree in terms of their own literary tradition the Babis now had access to books which not only evoked feelings of wonderment or spiritual ecstasy, but which communicated coherent statements of belief.

In terms of subject matter, prior to 1866 and the open claim made to the station of *Man-yuẓhiruhuʾlláh*, Baháʾuʾlláh's writings were predominantly concerned with mystical, ethical and doctrinal subjects which, whilst written within the general Babi framework, display a different pattern of emphases, which may well have been regarded as innovatory. Many of these early writings were essentially 'mystical' in nature, especially prior to Baháʾuʾlláh's return from Kurdistan. These mystical writings frequently display the peculiarities of 'rapturous' style already described. Some of these works, such as the *Qaṣída al-Warqáʾiyya* (*The Ode of the Dove*) and the *Haft Vádí* (*Seven Valleys*) were consciously modelled on classical Sufi writings, addressed Sufi themes, and in general displayed a considerable familiarity with Sufi writers and ideas. In terms of a distinctive position *vis-à-vis* these Sufi concepts, Baháʾuʾlláh clearly rejected the doctrine of existential monism (*waḥdatuʾl-wujúd*) together with any suggestion that the spiritually developed individual might attain annihilation (*fanáʾ*) in God. Rather, in keeping with the Shaykhi-Babi tradition he maintained that God was utterly transcendent and totally unapproachable.[14] Again, in the *Haft Vádí*, he emphasized that in his path towards the 'truth' (*haqíqat*) which is his goal, the seeker must not deviate in the slightest from the requirements of divine law (*sharíʿat*), thus dismissing the view held by some Sufis that attainment of the truth represented in some way a means of transcending the law.

There is a clear overlap between Baháʾuʾlláh's writings on the mystical path and those concerned with ethics. This overlap is particularly evident in the *Kitáb-i Íqán* in which Baháʾuʾlláh outlined the attributes required of the 'true seeker' as including not only such 'mystical' qualities as detachment and rapture, but also more 'mundane' 'ethical' qualities such as kindness (including kindness to animals) and avoidance of backbiting. This emphasis on the practical morality involved in the spiritual quest is very marked in many of Baháʾuʾlláh's writings throughout his career and may be said to constitute a distinctive attitude which contrasted quite clearly with the more metaphysical emphases found in both the Sufi and Babi traditions.

The *Kitáb-i Íqán* was also Baháʾuʾlláh's main doctrinal work at this time and, together with the *Kalimát-i Maknúnih* (*Hidden Words*) – a collection of poetic statements of religious and ethical injunctions – it became immensely popular within the Babi community and was extensively transcribed. Written in 1862 in response to questions by an as yet unconverted uncle of the Báb, the *Íqán* provides a clear account of religious history from a Babi perspective, outlining the Shaykhi–Babi conception of the unknowability of God's essence and the consequent necessity for a succession of manifestations of God; attributing the human rejection of this succession of God's messengers to the expectation that prophetic signs would be fulfilled literally, to the lack of spiritual perception on the part of successive clergies, and to the blind obedience shown by the rank and file to these religious leaders; discoursing at length on the symbolic fulfilment of prophecy, both with regard to the return of Christ (using Matthew 24: 29–31 as the text) and to the specific proofs of the Báb's mission; and stressing the spiritual qualities and need for intellectual independence of those who would wish to become true seekers.

The beginnings of revival and a further exile

With the growing cohesion of the Babi community, the Babis gathered in Iraq became increasingly assertive, individual Babis engaging in the militant defence of the faith against those who abused its leaders. As the evident leader of a large number of fanatically devoted followers, Baháʾuʾlláh was increasingly held in respect by many of the local Iranian and Ottoman dignitaries, several of whom became his fervent admirers. For at least some of these dignitaries it was Baháʾuʾlláh's supposed political potential which was especially attractive. The Babi movement was apparently reviving and the Qajar dynasty continued to be unpopular. Baháʾuʾlláh was evidently a figure well worth cultivating, not only by Iranian dissidents such as Malkum Khán, but also by the local British agent, who at one point is said to have offered Baháʾuʾlláh British citizenship.[15] According to Bahaʾi accounts such political overtures were firmly rejected by Baháʾuʾlláh, who was already seeking to pursue his policy of depoliticizing Babism and supressing its militant tendencies.

At the same time, as the Babi community in Iraq became more assertive and Baháʾuʾlláh's reputation and prestige increased, the fear and enmity of Shiʿi ulama and Qajar officials was rekindled. As the Iranian Foreign Minister was soon to write:

> I see beneath the ashes the glow of fire,
> And it wants but little to burst into a blaze[16]

Opposition to Baháʾuʾlláh mounted in intensity after 1860, largely as a result of the machinations of the newly appointed Persian consul and a visiting Shiʿi cleric. A succession of alarmist reports sent to the Iranian government eventually bore fruit, and after repeated petitioning to the Ottoman authorities an order was made to remove Bahá'u'lláh from Baghdad. Having by this time gained Ottoman citizenship, Bahá'u'lláh, his family and chosen attendants were not, as had been the Persians' hope, returned to Iran, but were invited to go to Istanbul.

Departing from his Baghdad home in April 1863, Bahá'u'lláh stayed for twelve days in the Najíbiyya garden on the outskirts of the city. During these days local dignitaries including the governor and the mufti, as well as many of the common people, visited him to pay their respects. Attended by a large and emotional crowd, he finally left the garden, people pressing forward to kiss his stirrups and even trying to throw themselves under his horse's hooves in a manner reminiscent of the devotion afforded leading Sufi shaykhs. For Baha'is these twelve days, in what they have come to call the Garden of Riḍván (Paradise), constitute a moment of supreme significance, Bahá'u'lláh there making the declaration to his intimate disciples and family that he was himself *Man-yuẓhiruhu'lláh*.[17]

Accompanied by his family and over twenty disciples who acted as his attendants, Bahá'u'lláh then undertook a four-month journey to the Ottoman capital, receiving every mark of respect from the government officials and notables of the districts through which he passed. Although he arrived in Istanbul as an honoured guest, the resentment occasioned by his reluctance to have any dealings with government ministers, combined with further representations from the Persian ambassador, led to an order of what was, in effect, exile – to Edirne in Rumelia. Arriving in Edirne in December 1863, the exiles remained in Rumelia until a further order of exile was issued, causing them to be moved again in the summer of 1868. By 1868, however, there was no longer a relatively unified Babi community, but rather two mutually opposed groups: Azali Babis and Baha'is.

THE EMERGENCE OF THE BAHA'I FAITH, 1866–1921

The definite separation between Azalis and Baha'is, 1866–8

Such had been the extent of Ṣubḥ-i Azal's concealment in Baghdad that when he joined Bahá'u'lláh's caravan at Mosul, most of the Babis had apparently not known who he was.[18] In Edirne, although living under an assumed name, he revealed his identity to the Babi colony and, according to Baha'i accounts, began to conspire against Bahá'u'lláh's increasing pre-eminence amongst the Babis. We are again confronted by mutually contradictory partisan sources which do not readily lend themselves to independent evaluation. Clearly, though, the internal situation in the Babi colony was deteriorating rapidly, and in the spring of 1866, at Bahá'u'lláh's instigation, a definite division was made in the colony, the majority siding with him and only a few individuals supporting Ṣubḥ-i Azal. After this 'Most Great Separation' Bahá'u'lláh made known his claim to be *Man-yuẓhiruhu'lláh*, at first to Ṣubḥ-i Azal and the other Babis in Edirne, and then in a series of letters and with the aid of specific emissaries to the Iranian Babi communities.

A large number of Babis in Iran were already sympathetic to Bahá'u'lláh's leadership, some being his outright devotees, and,

> since the Báb has always given the glad-tidings of the coming of 'Him Whom God shall make manifest', has not laid down any conditions or specified any time for His advent, has enjoined upon all to accept and acknowledge Him as soon as He reveals Himself, has prohibited investigation, caution or delay in accepting His message, has condemned to hell-fire those who do not recognize Him, has strictly forbidden the seeking of proofs from Him, and has regarded Himself as the servant and forerunner of 'Him Whom God shall make manifest',[19]

it was not overly surprising that after a year or two the claims of an already popular leader were accepted by the vast majority of the Babis. Nevertheless, the response to Bahá'u'lláh's claims was not always immediate: the Qazvin community, for example, was convulsed by the announcement, whilst in Dughábád, Bahá'u'lláh's emissary received a beating before he gained the support of the leading Babis.[20]

With the support of the majority of the Babi community, Bahá'u'lláh now fully emerged as the leader of an independent and essentially new religion, increasingly as distinct from Babism as it was from Islam. Henceforth the 'people of Bahá' (*ahl-i Bahá*), the Baha'is, asserted their separation from their Babi heritage, whilst those who rejected Bahá'u'lláh's claims asserted their adherence to the original tenets of Babism, either as the definite partisans of Ṣubḥ-i Azal – those whom we may thus term Azali Babis – or as essentially unattached *ahl-i Bayán* (people of the Bayán). This third group seems to have soon lost all importance in the development of the religion.

This definitive separation between the Baha'i majority and the Azali minority was before long given physical expression by the intervention of the Ottoman authorities in the lives of the Baha'is and Babis at Edirne. For the most part the Babi–Baha'i colony of Edirne seems to have enjoyed considerable sympathy from the local population and the successive governors, but to the authorities in Istanbul the colony seemed to pose a threat. Its numbers were growing. There were frequent visitors from Iran

1. Group of Baha'is in Edirne (ʿAbdu'l-Bahá is sitting third from left. Bahá'u'lláh's amanuensis, Khádimu'lláh, is standing immediately behind him)

and elsewhere. Reports were received of attempts to make proselytes from amongst the Muslim population. There were even allegations that Bahá'u'lláh was conspiring with Bulgarian revolutionaries to conquer Istanbul. Despite the submissions of Mehmet Hourshid Pasha, the governor of Edirne, that he had found no cause for complaint against the 'Babis' and that Bahá'u'lláh had good reason to complain about the Azalis (whom Baha'is accuse of fomenting much of the trouble), the investigating commission recommended the further exile of the colony, the fact that both Bahá'u'lláh and Ṣubḥ-i Azal were making religious claims being regarded as a potential source of disorder.[21] In August 1868, despite European consular intervention and in conditions of great uncertainty, the Babis and Baha'is were arrested, it eventually being determined that about seventy of the exiles (mostly Baha'is) would be sent to ʿAkká in Ottoman Syria, whilst the remaining few (mostly Azalis) should be sent to Famagusta in Cyprus. A few members of each faction were sent with the other group, presumably to act as potential spies. At about the same time, Bahá'u'lláh's property in Baghdad (valued at nearly £50,000) was confiscated, and thirty to forty leading Babis and Baha'is in Baghdad were exiled to Mosul. Deprived of Ottoman protection, several believers living in Iraq were murdered by Shiʿis, whilst in Egypt a number of newly settled

Baha'i merchants were imprisoned or mulcted of considerable sums of money at the instigation of the Persian consul.

Bahá'u'lláh's exile in Syria, 1868–92

The period of Bahá'u'lláh's exile in Syria (1868–92) saw the consolidation and expansion of the new religion which bore his name. Such consolidation was at first made difficult by the circumstances of Bahá'u'lláh's initial imprisonment in the fortress of St Jean d'Acre (ᶜAkká) from August 1868 until November 1870, these being extremely severe. Thereafter conditions eased somewhat and from 1877 Bahá'u'lláh was permitted to live outside the city, living the final years of his life at the mansion of Bahjí. During these years Bahá'u'lláh himself increasingly tended to live a life of semi-seclusion, granting audiences only to his followers and occasional visitors. Leaving much of the organization of the affairs of the 'Cause of God' (*amru'lláh*) in the capable hands of his eldest son, ᶜAbbás Effendi, (1844–1921), he devoted his time to his considerable correspondence with his followers in Iran, to the composition of his more general Tablets (*alwáḥ*), and to the enjoyment of nature and the countryside. Upon his father's death in 1892, ᶜAbbás (later better known as ᶜAbdu'l-Bahá) became leader of the Baha'i community as 'Centre' of his father's Covenant.

With the attainment of stability and relative security at the centre of the movement a process of consolidation and expansion was set in train. An important element in this process was the establishment of a reliable system of communications. The headquarters of the Baha'i movement were now established in Ottoman Syria whilst the majority of the Baha'is remained in Iran, anywhere from 700 to 1,500 miles away. The existing means of communication between the two areas were poor. Contact was maintained largely through correspondence and the continuing use of the earlier system of employing full-time Baha'i couriers to take letters back and forth. This was a procedure not without its dangers, letters having to be effectively smuggled across the Iranian border. In addition, letters were carried by those Baha'is who undertook the extensive and often hazardous journey to Syria for themselves in order to visit Bahá'u'lláh. Despite the difficulties, such visitors increased in numbers over the years, often using the established Baha'i communities in Iraq, Turkey, Syria and Egypt as staging-posts. At some point the latter stages of these journeys began to be regulated by the appointment of definite Baha'i agents at such centres as Beirut and Alexandria. These individuals were charged with easing the travellers' journeys and ensuring that definite permission had been received from Baháʾuʾlláh or ʿAbbás Effendi to allow them to approach ʿAkká.

These visits to ʿAkká or Bahjí were now clearly in the nature of pilgrimages, the high points of which were the granting of audiences with Baháʾuʾlláh. Even a non-Bahaʾi like E.G. Browne might be powerfully impressed by such a visitation, later describing how, after he had been conducted into what he felt was the 'wondrous' and awesome presence of Baháʾuʾlláh, 'I bowed myself before one who is the object of a devotion and love which kings might envy and emperors sigh for in vain', commenting:

> The face of him on whom I gazed I can never forget, though I cannot describe it. Those piercing eyes seemed to read one's very soul; power and authority sat on that ample brow; while the deep lines on the forehead and face implied an age which the jet-black hair and beard flowing down in indistinguishable luxuriance almost to the waist seemed to belie.[22]

The experience for Persian Bahaʾis was often completely overwhelming: thus Ḥaydar ʿAlí refers to the near impossibility of anyone actually looking into his eyes or uttering one complete sentence in his presence, commenting that Baháʾuʾlláh's 'every step and movement was like a miracle to me.'[23]

The succession of ʿAbduʾl-Bahá, 1892–1921

In his *Kitáb-i ʿAhdí* (*Book of My Covenant*), Baháʾuʾlláh unambiguously appointed his eldest son, ʿAbbás Effendi – ʿAbduʾl-Bahá, the *Ghuṣn-i Aʿẓam* (Most Great Branch) – to be the centre of authority after his passing, and after him in turn, his second son, Mírzá Muḥammad ʿAlí, the *Ghuṣn-i Akbar* (Greater Branch).[24] Although the exact circumstances of the events following Baháʾuʾlláh's death in May 1892 are far from clear, it is evident that within a remarkably short space of time, Muḥammad ʿAlí, supported by his brother-in-law Mírzá Majdiʾd-Dín, had succeeded in alienating the majority of Baháʾuʾlláh's family from their initial allegiance to ʿAbduʾl-Bahá. Of Baháʾuʾlláh's surviving family, including wives, children, nephews and nieces and their spouses – perhaps forty people in all – only ʿAbduʾl-Bahá's full sister, his daughters, his uncle and his family remained in support. Charging ʿAbduʾl-Bahá with exceeding the authority bestowed upon him by his father and with laying claim to the rank and prerogatives of a Manifestation of God, Muḥammad ʿAlí and his followers mounted an extensive campaign to challenge ʿAbduʾl-Bahá's authority throughout the Baha'i world, the resulting dissension dividing the Baha'is into two groups. One group regarded ʿAbdu'l-Bahá as the Centre of his father's Covenant and themselves as 'steadfast and firm' (*thábit*) Baha'is, contrasting themselves with the followers of Muḥammad ʿAlí, whom they termed *Náqiḍín* (violators of the Covenant, Covenant-breakers). The second group supported Muḥammad ʿAlí and referred to themselves as *muwaḥḥidún* (unitarians) and the followers of ʿAbbás as *mushrikún* (polytheists). Whilst the second group succeeded in consolidating their position in Syria and winning a number of supporters elsewhere – notably the prominent Iranian Baha'i teacher Áqá Jamál Burújirdí and the pioneer Baha'i teacher in the West, Ibrahim Kheiralla – the majority of Baha'is, both in the East and the West rallied to ʿAbdu'l-Bahá. Nevertheless, in occupation of Bahá'u'lláh's former residence at Bahjí and with the support of various local Ottoman officials, the followers of Muḥammad ʿAlí were initially in a very strong position and were able to create considerable local difficulties for ʿAbdu'l-Bahá, at least until the Young Turks' revolution of July 1908 brought freedom to all political and religious prisoners, ʿAbdu'l-Bahá amongst them. Thereafter the influence of the followers of Muḥammad ʿAlí waned rapidly, although they still remained a thorn in the side of both ʿAbdu'l-Bahá and his grandson, Shoghi Effendi, who later succeeded him. Remaining largely in the ʿAkká area, the followers of Muḥammad ʿAlí formed the nucleus of what Cohen has termed a 'residual religious community', a congeries of what was to become six extended families united only in their opposition to ʿAbdu'l-Bahá or his successor, isolated from each other, totally excluded from the wider Baha'i world, and ambivalently related to the environing Arab Muslim society.[25] ʿAbdu'l-Bahá, meanwhile, after his freedom from Ottoman captivity had been attained, all but abandoned ʿAkká as his centre of operations. In 1909 he moved his home to Haifa, across the bay from ʿAkká. He then proceeded on his extensive world travels, firstly in 1910 to Egypt, and then visiting his followers in the West from 1911 until his return to Palestine and Haifa in 1913. Henceforth, for all intents and purposes, Haifa has remained the world centre of the Baha'i Faith.

5

DOMINANT MOTIFS IN THE BAHAʾI FAITH IN THE EAST

In deriving the dominant motifs of the Bahaʾi Faith in the 1866–1921 period, particular attention needs to be given to the corpus of Bahaʾi scripture and to one or two secondary writings which between them provided the main sources for orthodox Bahaʾi belief during the period of Baháʾuʾlláh's leadership after the open declaration of his mission (1866–92), and at least for the Bahaʾis of the East, during the period of the leadership of ʿAbduʾl-Bahá (1892–1921). That the Bahaʾi Faith was (and is) a scriptural religion par excellence, in which great importance was attached to the writings of the founder and his successor, provides only partial justification for this stress on 'officially transmitted' doctrine as a key element in describing the motifs which dominated the religious concerns of the early Bahaʾis of the East. Of great importance, too, is the evidence that from an early date Baháʾuʾlláh's writings were widely available to his followers, that even before the first printed and lithographed editions of Bahaʾi works began to be produced in the 1890s at Bombay and Cairo a number of individuals were intensively involved in transcribing and circulating the more important writings,[1] that unlike Babi writings the actual style of most Bahaʾi writings was fairly accessible to moderately well-educated Iranians, that there existed a network of communication by which doctrine could be effectively transmitted to the rank and file by individuals well able to understand its rational meanings, and that great stress was laid on doctrinal unity.

It should be noted that whilst clear doctrinal continuities exist between Babi and Bahaʾi thought, the texts and concepts of Babism had been poorly communicated during its latter, hectic days. Most Bahaʾis had neither detailed knowledge of Babism, nor access to the major Babi texts, Baháʾuʾlláh himself claiming not to have had access to the *Bayán*.[2] At the same time, Baháʾuʾlláh's early writings, that is those composed prior to the open declaration of his mission, were readily available and were readily accorded the same status as his later writings.

THE POLAR/THEOPHANIC MOTIF

Central to both Baha'i doctrine and religious focus was the theophanic motif. Doctrinally, as in the Shaykhi-Babi tradition, Bahá'u'lláh asserted the absolute unknowability and unapproachability of the divine essence. Only through the intermediary of the *maẓhar-i iláhí*, the Manifestation of God, who manifested God's attributes to mankind, could the believer approach the object of his religious quest. Of these Manifestations, who included, amongst others, Abraham, Zoroaster, Moses, Christ, Muhammad and the Báb, Bahá'u'lláh was the latest, the point of religious focus for all humanity in this new age. Later messengers from God would appear but not until a thousand years had elapsed. Whilst by the doctrine of progressive revelation the particular teachings and laws promulgated by Bahá'u'lláh were deemed to be those most appropriate for the present age, for the most dedicated Baha'is it was the person of Bahá'u'lláh rather than such teachings or laws which constituted the centre of their religious faith and devotion.

To a considerable degree this devotion was simply transferred to the person of ʿAbdu'l-Bahá after his father's death, even though doctrinally he was not regarded as a Manifestation of God but rather as the Centre of his father's Covenant and the 'mystery of God' (*sirru'lláh*). The remarkable unity and centralized control of doctrine and organization which characterized the Baha'i Faith, and which so clearly differentiated it from Babism, doubtless depended on the efficient communications which linked the Baha'i community to its distant centre and on the clear and unambiguous instructions and doctrinal expositions emanating from ʿAkká and Haifa, but underlying these factors was the vivid sense of the obedience and devotion which were due to God's representatives on earth. Furthermore, with the passing of time and with the still extant example of the perceived rebellion of the Azali Babis, the Baha'i doctrine of the Covenant assumed a central importance. God had established a Covenant with his believers by which they were bound to recognize and obey not only the Manifestation of God for the age but whomsoever he might appoint as his successor. There could be but one Centre of the Cause and it was the bounden duty of all believers to recognize and accept that Centre. Those who rejected it and rebelled against it had not only ceased to be Baha'is, but had utterly placed themselves beyond the pale; they had, as ʿAbdu'l-Bahá's own will was to put it, 'rebelled against God' and were in consequence to be shunned.[3] Accordingly, whilst the Baha'i account stresses ʿAbdu'l-Bahá's love for his rebellious brothers and their associates, and his repeated attempts to reconcile them to his authority, ultimately, when their attacks on his authority had become extreme, they were totally rejected by those loyal to ʿAbduʾl-Bahá. Again, after ʿAbduʾl-Bahá had died, having explicitly changed the order of succession in his will to exclude Muḥammad ʿAlí, almost all Eastern Bahaʾis readily extended their allegiance to ʿAbduʾl-Bahá's own youthful nominee, his eldest grandson, Shoghi Effendi Rabbání, the first Guardian of the Cause (*valí-amr*).

Given such an intense emphasis on centralized authority, combined with the practical means of ensuring the unimpeded exercise of that authority, it is of no surprise to discover that the secondary Baha'i leaders, teachers and administrators living in Iran were far less significant than the leading disciples of the Báb had been. Great respect was accorded such men by the mass of the Bahaʾis, but they exercised no independent authority of their own. Indeed, it seems likely that one of the motives which led Baha'i teachers such as Burújirdí and Kheiralla to give their allegiance to Muḥammad ʿAlí was the very desire to exercise such independent authority. Muḥammad ʿAlí may well have been perceived as a potentially weaker leader who would exercise less central control.

SOCIAL REFORMISM, MODERNIZATION AND THE MILLENNIUM

The second major motif which permeated the Bahaʾi Faith in the 1866–1921 period represented a complex of religious and social concerns centring on the idea of the transformation of the world. These concerns involved both a clear millennial vision and a programme of more 'secular' social reformism. Both elements were strongly imbued with a religious ethos, however, and both formed part of what was regarded as the latest stage of God's plan for mankind.

Babi millenarianism may be said to have culminated in the establishment of Baháʾuʾlláh's authority over the Babi community as *Man-yuẓhiruhuʾlláh*. Fulfilment of the messianic promise did not entail the establishment of the millennium, however, and the clear religious focus was the theophanic presence of Baháʾuʾlláh rather than any hoped-for Babi theocracy. Not that the goal of establishing a theocratic state was abandoned; rather, it was reasserted in a radically different form. Fully in keeping with the Ismaʿili–Shaykhi view of history as the progressive unfoldment of the divine will, the establishment of the Bahaʾi millennium, the *sulḥ-i aʿẓam* or Most Great Peace, was projected into the future as the eventual culmination of human progress. It was no Iranian-based utopia

2. ʿAbduʾl-Bahá (portrait by Gertrude S. Käsebier, 1912)

which was to be established, although particular regard for the potentialities of a Bahaʾi regime in Iran was expressed. Rather, Baháʾuʾlláh's proclamatory message was to all the peoples of the world, and ultimately, it was the unification and pacification of the whole world which was his objective. To Edward Browne he summarized this aspect of his teachings as follows:

That all nations should become one in faith and all men as brothers; that the bonds of affection and unity between the sons of men should be strengthened; that diversity of religion should cease, and differences of race be annulled – what harm is there in this? . . . Yet so it shall be; these fruitless strifes, these ruinous wars shall pass away, and the 'Most Great Peace' shall come . . . Do not you in Europe need this also? Is not this that which Christ foretold? . . . Yet do we see your kings and rulers lavishing their treasures more freely on means for the destruction of the human race than on that which would conduce to the happiness of mankind . . . These strifes and this bloodshed and discord must cease, and all men be as one kindred and one family . . . Let not a man glory in this, that he loves his country; let him rather glory in this, that he loves his kind.[4]

As to how this universal peace was to be established, it may well be that Baháʾuʾlláh had two processes in mind. Thus, in his letter to Queen Victoria, he referred to two separate goals, which he termed the *ṣulḥ-i aʿẓam* and the, inferior, *ṣulḥ-i akbar*. These Shoghi Effendi has translated respectively as the 'Most Great Peace' and the 'Lesser Peace'.[5] Shoghi Effendi's interpretation of these terms was that the Most Great Peace represented the future spiritualization of the world and the unification of its peoples under Bahaʾi rule, whilst the Lesser Peace represented a reconciliation amongst the existing world rulers. Thus, in the letter to Queen Victoria, Baháʾuʾlláh referred to the union of all the world's peoples in 'one universal Cause, one common Faith' as being the 'sovereign remedy' for the healing of the world, whilst he then addressed the world's rulers, advising them: 'Now that ye have refused the Most Great Peace, hold ye fast unto this, the Lesser Peace, *that haply ye may in some degree better your own condition and that of your dependents*.'[6] Read in this light, much of Baháʾuʾlláh's and ʿAbduʾl-Bahá's writings on the 'reconstruction of the world' which they desired would appear to have been directed towards the establishment of this Lesser Peace. Whether or not this was the case, it is clear that, in a radically different sense from most expressions of the esoteric Shiʿi progressivist tradition, the attainment of the future millennium was regarded as a matter of *human* achievement guided and inspired by God. The purpose and causation were divine and the ultimate triumph of God's Cause (*amr*) was assured, but the speed and ease of its attainment now became a matter of human responsibility. In so far as the Bahaʾi leaders continued the traditional concepts of Shiʿi progressivism they did so in markedly secularized form.[7]

The kings

That part of the peace whose establishment was assigned to the kings and rulers of the world was very specifically detailed in Baháʾuʾlláh's various addresses to the rulers – particularly the letter to Queen Victoria – and in ʿAbduʾl-Bahá's *Risáli-yi Madaniyyih* (*Treatise on Civilization*). The kings were called upon to convene a 'general consultation' on the subject of peace and to seek to establish 'a Union of the nations of the world', bound by inviolable treaty, in which national frontiers and armament levels were fixed and the principles of intergovernmental relations laid down. Such a treaty should be guaranteed by a system of collective security in which any violator nation would be reduced to 'utter submission' by the remainder. By such means the huge and costly armaments race would be made unnecessary and the excessive burden this imposed on the populace removed.[8] A change in consciousness was also required, however. Thus, at the same time as stressing a change in international relationships, Baháʾuʾlláh stressed the importance of the world's rulers adopting a world language and script so that 'the whole earth will come to be regarded as one country' and an individual traveller might find all cities as his own home.[9]

Whilst the kings and rulers addressed by Baháʾuʾlláh were exhorted to establish world peace, and the high station of kingship was extolled, they were also warned not to transgress 'the bounds which the Almighty hath fixed', and to walk in the fear of God and obey his laws, treating their subjects with justice and regarding the poor as a divine trust upon whose treatment they would be called to account by God. They were to fear 'divine chastisement' if they refused to listen to these counsels. Whilst a 'Just King' was to be regarded as the shadow of God on earth, and any king who might arise to aid the Bahaʾi Cause would be 'the luminous ornament on the brow of creation', others were censured and their loss of power prophesied.[10] Ultimately, the kings of the earth were but the vassals of God and of Baháʾuʾlláh as his appointed messenger; their duty was to respond to their divine summons and detach themselves from the world over which they ruled but fleetingly. Rejection of that summons would lead to the expression of divine anger.

Modernization and the critique of civilization

This dual theme of exhortation and divine judgement also pervaded the writings of Baháʾuʾlláh and ʿAbduʾl-Bahá concerning the contemporary civilizations of East and West. In their critique of the societies of the East the Bahaʾi leaders, particularly ʿAbduʾl-Bahá, pointed to the prevailing fanaticism, superstition, ignorance and backwardness. Like Japan, it was necessary to adopt elements of Western civilization, particularly its educational system, commerce, arts, sciences and technological developments. Government should change also, with the introduction of rationalized codes and practices of legislation, the modernization of the army, the stamping-out of corruption, and the introduction of the checks on absolutism afforded by a constitutional monarchy and proper control of provincial governors. There was nothing wrong with thus borrowing from the West. Those ulama who taught that such borrowings were sinful were flying in the face of the Prophet Muhammad's own example when he adopted pre-Islamic Persian and Arabic practices, and, in any case, 'the major part' of European civilization had originally been borrowed from the Islamic countries during their Golden Age and there was nothing wrong in borrowing it back. Material change was in itself insufficient, however. Spiritual enlightenment, promoting a love of justice and freeing man from fanaticism and unreasoning religious zeal, was also required, and without it any modernization programme would flounder.

When judged from a spiritual standpoint, indeed, the 'much vaunted' civilization of the West was itself also found to be greatly wanting and its materialism was severely condemned. Thus Baháʾuʾlláh wrote that 'When the eyes of the people of the East were captivated by the arts and wonders of the West, they roved distraught in the wilderness of material causes, oblivious to the One Who is the Causer of Causes [i.e. God]', or again, when praising the virtue of moderation, 'If a thing is carried to excess, it will prove a source of evil. Consider the civilization of the West, how it hath agitated and alarmed the peoples of the world.'[11] In his anonymously published treatise on civilization, ʿAbduʾl-Bahá was considerably more denunciatory, dismissing European culture as 'a superficial culture, unsupported by a cultivated morality' which was thus no more than a 'confused medley of dreams'. 'Notwithstanding their vaunted civilization', the Europeans sank and drowned 'in this terrifying sea of passion and desire'. Engaged in the senseless desire for conquest and its resultant arms race, the staggering costs of which were borne by its hapless masses, Europe represented only a 'nominal civilization' which could in no wise bring about peace.[12] The prominent Bahaʾi scholar, Mírzá Abuʾl-Faḍl Gulpáygání (1844–1914), appears to have carried such feelings even further, anticipating the imminent millenarian destruction of much of the world, and that of Europe in particular.[13]

The Bahaʾis: self-discipline and political quietism

As to the Bahaʾis own role in the attainment of the Most Great Peace, this was to centre on the teaching of their faith, self-disciplined application of

Bahá'u'lláh's teachings in their own community and personal lives, and the stance of reformist advocacy combined with political quietism. From the beginning of his rise to pre-eminence within the Babi community, Bahá'u'lláh, by his own account, had sought to reconcile the Babis with the Qajar authorities, condemning the Babi attempt on the life of the Shah and explicitly rejecting the Islamic and Babi doctrine of *jihád* on the first day of his Riḍván declaration in 1863, a definite abrogation to this effect later being promulgated. Warned not to shed the blood of anyone – 'It is better that you should be killed than that you should kill' – Baha'is were bidden to 'Unsheath the sword of your tongue from the scabbard of utterance, for therewith ye can conquer the citadels of men's hearts.'[14] More than this, Baha'is were not only categorically forbidden to engage in sedition, but were positively enjoined to render their loyalty to the State and its ruler. Such an attitude was of general application and not just of relevance to Qajar Iran. Thus Bahá'u'lláh quoted with approval Saint Paul's Epistle to the Romans (13:1) to the effect that 'every soul' should be subject to 'the higher powers' which were themselves 'ordained of God'.[15] Again, the Baha'is were bidden to 'Forbear . . . from concerning yourselves with the affairs of this world and all that pertaineth unto it, or from meddling with the activities of those who are its outward leaders', for 'To none is given the right to act in any manner that would run counter to the considered views of them who are in authority.'[16]

In place of *jihád* Baha'is were bidden to engage in non-violent teaching (*tablígh*) to spread their religion, *tablígh* being 'dependent on the acquisition of moral qualities and the exercise of spiritual influence'.[17] Thus, in his *Risáli-yi Madaniyyih*, ʿAbdu'l-Bahá insisted that 'the Faith of God must be promulgated through human perfections, through qualities that are excellent and pleasing, and spiritual behaviour', adding that 'As for the sword' – as necessarily used against the pagan Arabs in the early spread of Islam – 'it will only produce a man who is outwardly a believer, and inwardly a traitor and apostate'. For ʿAbdu'l-Bahá Christian missionary enterprise clearly demonstrated the efficacy of non-violent propagandizing. Christianity had 'encompassed the whole earth', and yet its early adherents had never used violence to counter the terrible persecutions from which they suffered. Again, the rapid diffusion of Protestantism showed the potency of religious ideas which were 'demonstrably correct' when the 'proper means' were adopted for their promulgation.[18] As a corollary of this irenic attitude, selfless missionary activity was extolled more highly than martyrdom. Indeed the self-sacrifice of martyrdom could be manifested just as much in living for the faith as in dying for it.

As to the various teachings and principles which Baha'is were to seek to embody in their lives, these included not only such general spiritual principles as loving-kindness, truthfulness and trustworthiness, but also more specifically 'worldly' teachings. Thus, whilst preaching the need for detachment from worldly things, Bahá'u'lláh directed his followers not to withdraw from worldly involvement. The 'pious deeds' of Christian monks and priests were commended, but their duty was to abandon seclusion, to enter the 'open world' and busy themselves 'with what will profit themselves and others', and to marry so that 'they may bring forth one who will make mention of God'.[19] More drastically, those Sufis whose pattern of life led to 'idleness and seclusion' were severely condemned and compared to fruitless trees fit only for the fire. Mendicancy was forbidden – 'God hates most those who sit and beg' as was religious asceticism.[20] In contrast, it was incumbent on the Baha'is to engage in some form of useful occupation to support themselves and their families, such work being regarded as an act of worship.

Amongst other 'economic' injunctions Baha'is were forbidden to give to beggars and, contrary to Islamic law, were allowed to charge interest on loans and to use gold and silver vessels. Charity was encouraged, and Baha'is were required to give a certain portion of their wealth 'to God' or rather to His earthly representative. The Baha'i House of Justice (*bayṭu'l-ʿadl*) was to serve as 'a shelter for the poor and needy' and to be responsible both for the education of those children whose fathers were unable to finance their education (all others being required to set money aside for that purpose) and for the disbursement of funds in cases of intestacy, expending monies on such needy groups as orphans and widows.[21]

THE LEGALISTIC MOTIF

These Baha'i teachings were also tied to a wider system of Baha'i law. Bahá'u'lláh stated that 'For a number of years petitions reached the Most Holy Presence from various lands begging for the laws of God, but We held back the Pen ere the appointed time had come.'[22] Whilst providing his followers with various distinctive Baha'i ordinances during the period of his stay in Edirne (1863–8), it was not until the ʿAkká period that Bahá'u'lláh finally revealed the provisions of a separate Baha'i *sharíʿa*, thus emphasizing his claim to be a new Manifestation of God and lawgiver. These provisions were mostly embodied in his *Kitábu'l-Aqdas* (*Most Holy Book*), written in about 1873, but supplementary information was contained in a number of subsequent Tablets and more especially in the

Risáli-yi Suʾál va Javáb (Treatise of Questions and Answers), in which Baháʾuʾlláh expounded on his laws in response to questions posed by a learned Bahaʾi who had previously been a *mujtahid*, Mullá Zaynuʾl-ʿÁbidín Najafábádí. As with the Islamic and Babi holy laws, the laws of the Aqdas ranged widely over the field of human activity, detailing not only Bahaʾi personal religious obligations but the basis for the regulation of a future Bahaʾi state.

These laws were regarded by Baháʾuʾlláh as binding upon his followers, but beyond the future imposition of laws regulating the conduct of a Bahaʾi society, obedience to the law appears to have been largely a matter of individual conscience and commitment. There was no equivalent of the Islamic practice of communal regulation of behaviour, 'the bidding unto good and the rejection of the reprehensible'; rather, his followers were told to 'Observe My commandments, for the love of My beauty.'[23] In observing the laws, however, the Bahaʾis were counselled to exercise tact and wisdom, and to be prudent so as not to cause disturbance and dissension among the heedless. Thus, at least during the lifetimes of Baháʾuʾlláh and ʿAbduʾl-Bahá, Bahaʾis in Muslim countries, whilst seeking to abide by the provisions of their own holy law, generally appear to have endeavoured not to contravene the outward observances of the Islamic *sharíʿa* and so not to alienate themselves unnecessarily from the wider society.

At a more general level, emphasis was placed on the need for law-abiding behaviour. By itself, wrote Baháʾuʾlláh, 'Liberty must, in the end, lead to sedition, whose flames none can quench' for 'the embodiment of liberty' was the animal, and what 'beseemeth man is submission unto such restraints as will protect him from his own ignorance' and thus preserve the dignity of his own station. Men were like 'a flock of sheep that need a shepherd for their protection', 'true liberty' only being found in complete servitude unto God and 'submission unto My commandments'.[24] Complete subservience to the divine decree was necessary for the individual's spiritual progress (a point also made by Baháʾuʾlláh in his discussion of Sufism in the *Haft Vádí*, composed during his sojourn in Baghdad). Further, God was 'not to be asked of His doings' and was well able to change his laws (as they were revealed by successive Manifestations of God) and 'to decree as lawful the thing which from time immemorial had been forbidden, and forbid that which had at all times, been regarded as lawful'.[25] The law of God was not to be judged by human standards. Provision for future legislation was laid down in one of the later Tablets, the *Kalimát-i Firdawsiyyih*, in which Baháʾuʾlláh charged the Trustees (*umaná*) of the Baha'i House of Justice 'to take counsel together regarding those things which have not outwardly been revealed in the Book, and to enforce that which is agreeable to them', adding, 'God will verily inspire them with whatsoever He willeth.'[26]

UNIVERSALISM

Whilst the Báb had anticipated the expansion of his religion to the West, had commented favourably on certain European institutions and patterns of behaviour, and had been seen to be reading the Bible during his imprisonment in Tabriz in 1848,[27] there is no sense in which Babism as a religious system ever transcended the particular cultural locus of nineteenth-century Persian Shiᶜism. Furthermore, the exclusiveness and hostility displayed towards unbelievers, which is so characteristic of Shiᶜism, was carried over into Babism, and, indeed, in certain respects intensified. In all these respects, the religion promulgated by Bahá'u'lláh and ᶜAbdu'l-Bahá stood in marked contrast to its predecessor.

Particularly crucial was the Baha'i attitude towards non-Baha'is. In this regard ᶜAbdu'l-Bahá contrasted the central teaching of Babism, characterized as 'the striking of necks, the burning of books and papers, the destruction of shrines, and the universal slaughter of all save those who believed and were faithful', with the central teaching of the Baha'i Faith, which he characterized as an emphasis on compassion, mercy, association with all peoples, trustworthiness towards all men, and the unification of mankind.[28] As religious law, Bahá'u'lláh specifically abrogated the Babi ordinances on holy war, the destruction of books, and the shunning and extermination of unbelievers. Going further than this, Baha'is were bidden to 'Consort with the followers of all religions in a spirit of friendliness and fellowship', to be tolerant, to 'adhere tenaciously unto that which will promote fellowship, kindliness and unity' and not to become the cause of strife.[29] Combined with this, Bahá'u'lláh and ᶜAbdu'l-Bahá commended the adoption of an irenic attitude in teaching the Faith, condemning violent controversialism, fanaticism, and religious disputation. In the particular context of Persian Shiᶜism, and in great contrast to it, these injunctions to associate freely with people of other religions were also combined with the removal of any considerations of ritual purity in relation to interpersonal relations. This 'open' attitude towards non-believers was extended to the attainment of salvation, Bahá'u'lláh assuring his followers that at the hour of death the life-long 'devout believer' might err whilst the 'sinner' attained the essence of faith.[30] The believer then should not despise the sinful.

Beyond this general attitude of tolerance which the Bahaʾi leaders sought to inculcate in their followers were the specifically universalistic statements and claims made by Baháʾuʾlláh. Statements about the oneness and wholeness of the human race are found in both the Christian (Matthew 23: 8–9; Acts 17: 26) and Islamic (Quran 2: 209; 10: 20) scriptures, of course, but for Baháʾuʾlláh they assumed central importance: the world was 'but one country, and mankind its citizens'.[31] His followers were exhorted to 'Close your eyes to racial differences, and welcome all with the light of oneness' and were informed 'That one indeed is a man who, today, dedicateth himself to the service of the entire human race'. Unity was the goal that 'excelleth every goal'.[32] It was not just an end to racial, religious and national divisiveness that was sought, however. True religion was the surest means to establish world unity and amity – the union of all the peoples of the world 'in one universal Cause, one common Faith' – and Baháʾuʾlláh himself had come 'to unite and weld together all that dwell on earth'.[33] Accordingly, Baháʾuʾlláh specifically addressed the 'people of the world' in his writings, referring in particular passages to the clergy of the Zoroastrian, Jewish, Christian and Islamic faiths and to the rulers and kings of the world (particularly those of Europe). This proclamation of his Cause to the whole world was made, not only in abstract in a number of general 'Tablets', but in particular letters which were sent to certain reigning sovereigns and leaders (specifically Náṣiriʾd-Dín Sháh, Sultan Abdulaziz, Queen Victoria, Emperor Napoleon III, Czar Alexander II, Pope Pius IX and various Shiʿi clerics). Furthermore, Baháʾuʾlláh's own claims were extended to incorporate the millenarian traditions of other religions. Thus it was claimed that not only was he *Man-yuẓhiruhuʾlláh* to the Babis, but also the return of Christ 'in the Glory of the Father', the expected Sháh Bahrám to the Zoroastrians, and so on.

In the specifically religious sphere this attitude of universalism was combined with a knowledge and respect for non-Islamic religious books (most particularly the Bible) on the part both of Baháʾuʾlláh and ʿAbduʾl-Bahá and of a number of Bahaʾi teachers which was most untypical of even educated Iranian Muslims. In the case of Baháʾuʾlláh, biblical references, both in support of his own claims and to illustrate particular moral and spiritual teachings, abound throughout his writings from at least the later Baghdad period onwards, for example the biblical citations in the *Kitáb-i Íqán* (1862) and the somewhat earlier *Javáhiruʾl-Asrár* (*Essence of Mysteries*), in which Baháʾuʾlláh commented on the signs of Christ's second coming as recorded in the Gospels (Matthew 24: 29–31; Mark 13: 24; Luke 21: 25–8; and various passages in John), and the many later biblical and

Christian allusions in such writings as the letter to the Pope and the *Lawḥu'l-Aqdas*. Knowledge and respect for the Bible amongst Baha'is in Iran, together with a readiness to associate with Christians and other minority groups, was also noted by some of the European missionaries and, with regard to the Zoroastrians of Yazd, by E.G. Browne.[34]

THE ESOTERIC-GNOSTIC MOTIF

One of the most distinctive characteristics of the Baha'i religion as compared with Babism is the almost total absence or diminution of esoteric and gnostic themes. Certainly gnosticism, in the sense of a soteriology based on esoteric knowledge, is totally absent: salvation lies in recognition and emulation of the Manifestation of God for the age. Esotericism, in the sense of a concern with the inner reality which lies within external appearances, is present, but exists for the most part in a strongly rationalized and 'moderate' form, in which stress is also placed on the importance of exoteric meaning and the observance of divine law. Whilst certain elements from the 'gnostic corpus' were incorporated into Baha'i metaphysics, this represented more the importance of Aristotelian and Muʿtazalite rationalism than any continuance of the Hermetic tradition within Baha'ism. Again, the strongly marked tendency towards secrecy and caution in the early Baha'i communities of the East had more to do with the realities of continuing persecution than with any desire to guard esoteric truths.

Quasi-magical elements also largely disappeared, although the concept of talismanic protection remained (though in greatly diminished form), as in the Long Healing Prayer, where God is beseeched 'to protect the bearer of this blessed Tablet . . . and whoso passeth around the house wherein it is'.[35] At a popular level, too, ideas of *baraka* possession continued, again in greatly reduced form, as in the still current belief held by some Iranian Baha'is concerning the healing properties of *nabát* (sugar loaf), placed in Baha'i shrines by them specifically to acquire *baraka*. Miracles (especially involving prescience or mind-reading) were also plentifully ascribed to Bahá'u'lláh and ʿAbdu'l-Bahá by their followers, although as ʿAbdu'l-Bahá himself explained, whilst all the Manifestations of God were possessed of supernatural power, their performance of apparent miracles was not to be considered important and could not constitute a rational proof of their missions.[36] As in Babism there were non-believers who 'though they do not believe in His [Bahá'u'lláh's] manifestation, nevertheless believe Him to be a saint and have faith in His miracles'.[37]

Again, the belief in specific divine chastisement was continued, most particularly with regard to various of the kings and ulama addressed by Baháʾuʾlláh, specific prophecies in some cases being made as to their downfall and their country's military defeats.[38] All the Babi restrictions on certain forms of intellectual pursuit were abrogated.

6

THE IRANIAN BAHAʾI COMMUNITY, c. 1866–1921

IRAN IN CRISIS

By the mid-nineteenth century Iran had already experienced the first impact of Western political and economic power. Isolated, relatively unintegrated as a national economy, and maintaining its political and cultural independence in the midst of the rival imperialisms of Russia and Britain, Iran nevertheless still remained relatively unaffected by that impact. Only by the 1860s was Iranian agriculture substantially altered by Western market demands, the neglect of subsistence crops exacerbating the great famine of 1869–72, in which perhaps one-tenth of the population died and a further tenth emigrated. Chronic village food shortages occurred again in the 1880s, whilst in the early 1890s rapid rises in basic food prices were also linked to a prolonged depreciation of the Iranian currency, a depreciation which became so severe in the early 1890s that by the winter of 1894 the Tehran bazaar came to a complete standstill. Although these developments made their severest impact on the poor, even the wealthy were affected, their increasing discontent coinciding with a wide-ranging crisis in administration characterized by an escalation in the level of corruption and the effective abandonment of state affairs by the Shah.

A further locus for discontent was the increasing direct economic and cultural impact of the West. Invaded by 'concession hunters' and subservient to the Great Powers, Iran was no longer effectively independent, and whilst the process of compradorization personally benefitted many members of the wealthier classes, their feelings towards this newly established dependency were often ambivalent. Again, the spread of Western-oriented education and notions of reform introduced a definite division amongst the higher social groups as the various 'Westernizers' and 'modernizers' increasingly diverged from what the 'traditionalists' (the ulama and those most influenced by them) regarded as the norms for 'Islamic' codes of dress, behaviour and thinking.

Nevertheless, elements of both these groups entered into an uneasy alliance in opposition to Qajar policies from the 1890s through to the 'Constitutional Revolution' of 1905–11.

These various pressures and discontents found their primary expression in the multi-faceted political oppositional movements which shook Iranian society from the 1890s through to the 1920s. Co-ordinated national protests against aspects of Qajar rule began in 1891–2, with the Shi'i ulama successfully calling for a total boycott on the sale and use of tobacco until a foreign concession on that product was cancelled. Radical critics went further, calling for the Shah's deposition. In 1896, a follower of Jamálu'd-Dín 'al-Afghání' assassinated the Shah. Government unpopularity increased under Náṣiri'd-Dín's weak and vacillating successor, the strength of oppositional activity forcing the new Shah to accept the formation of a consultative assembly (*majlis*) in 1906. In 1908 the government of his successor moved against the radicals, executing some and closing the *majlis*. An armed revolt then deposed the Shah (1909), Anglo-Russian military action thereafter effectively partitioning the country into the two 'spheres of influence'. War, devastation, regional uprisings and famine ensued. By 1917 foreign troops occupied nearly all of 'neutral' Iran, and by 1918 the British were planning to impose what was effectively a protectorate over the whole country. Nationalist resistance stiffened and the British withdrew, a military coup giving power to Reza Khan (1921). In 1925 the Qajars were deposed and Reza Khan had himself proclaimed Shah.

THE EXPANSION OF THE BAHA'I COMMUNITY

Against the background of this increasingly unsettled situation, the new Baha'i community was consolidated and expanded. By the combination of correspondence and pilgrimages to Syria, the Baha'is in Iran and elsewhere established firm links with the centre of their faith – literally the centre, for Bahá'u'lláh, as *Man-yuẓhiruhu'lláh*, was himself their *qiblih*, the point to which they turned in prayer. On the basis of this linkage the Baha'i community received firm guidance and co-ordination. Stressing the non-political and non-militant nature of his religion, Bahá'u'lláh directed his followers to unite, to live a moral life and to teach their faith. Some individuals in particular were called upon to teach 'the Cause', being specifically designated as *muballighín* (teachers). Others were encouraged to travel to areas in which there were no Baha'is in order to establish new groups. Both within and outside Iran this new and enthusiastic propagation of the Baha'i religion, together with the appeal of its teachings, generated a significant expansion in the community. Faced with a combination of competent leadership, efficient communications, a reassertion of claims to charismatic leadership, and an appropriate ideology, the Babis rallied to Bahá'u'lláh. Most of those who had not abandoned Babism after its devastating defeats became Baha'is by perhaps 1870 or so. Thereafter their numbers were augmented by new converts, including several of great calibre and leadership abilities, such as Mírzá Abu'l-Faḍl Gulpáygání, a leading clerical philosopher who was converted in 1876, and Mírzá Muḥammad Ḥasan Adíbu'l-ʿUlamá', who was later appointed by Baha'u'llah as one of the small group of *ayádí-yi amru'lláh* (Hands of the Cause of God), leading Baha'is who superintended many of the affairs of the Cause in Iran.

Expansion and persecution in Iran

Some indication of the emergence of an active Baha'i community is provided by references by contemporary European visitors to Iran. During the 1860s the Babi remnant maintained a secret existence, one European traveller (Michele Lessona) reporting that, 'in Persia it is impossible to speak of the Babis or to learn something about their affairs. The terror which this name awakens is such that no one dares to speak, or even think, of it.'[1] In contrast, by 1871 the Christian missionary, the Rev. Robert Bruce, having come into contact with Babis in the Isfahan area, wrote that Babism was rapidly spreading, and later (November 1874) noted that it was specifically the Baha'i faction of the movement which was increasing in numbers.[2] Increasing Baha'i activity was more commonly noted during the 1880s, Samuel Benjamin – the first United States minister to Iran – commenting, in 1886, that the 'Babees' (i.e. Baha'is) were 'full of proselyting zeal, and gaining converts every day in all parts of Persia', and that 'just now there seems to be unusual activity among the Babees; emissaries or missionaries are secretly pervading the country'.[3] Mme Jane Dieulafoy, in 1887, also referred to the 'growing influence' of Bahá'u'lláh in the early 1880s, even suggesting that Náṣiri'd-Dín Sháh had sent an emissary to ʿAkká to attempt a reconciliation, but that this individual (a leading cleric) had himself been converted to the new religion.[4] Similarly, in 1889, a British diplomat in Iran wrote to E.G. Browne referring to the 'increasing multitudes' of Baha'is and the movement's recent 'extraordinary development', whilst the future Lord Curzon, who was visiting Iran at about this time, speculated that 'If

Babism [Baha'ism] continues to grow at its present rate of progression, a time may conceivably come when it will oust Mohammedanism from the field in Persia.'[5]

Although these latter comments greatly overestimated the significance of the Iranian Baha'i community, they do at least support the belief that the Baha'i community was increasing in size and importance at this time. A more oblique indication of the reanimation of the Babi community in Baha'i form was the recrudescence of persecution. Whilst the timing and incidence of such attacks often varied with local factors, and generally seems to have reflected the particular motivations of the leading ulama who directed most of the persecutions rather than any actions of the Baha'is themselves, the fact that the Baha'is were such ready targets for clerical fury indicates their increasing importance, whether actual or merely reputed. Persecution was particularly severe in the Isfahan area – a major Baha'i stronghold – where the most influential clerics were particularly antagonistic and the local governor willing for his own reasons to acquiesce in attacks on Baha'is. Accordingly, a whole series of murders, executions, tortures, imprisonments and despoilations of property were meted out to the Baha'is in Isfahan and the surrounding villages, particular waves of persecution occurring in 1874–9 and 1888–91. Elsewhere, persecutions were relatively rare until the 1890s, when wider political and economic factors became involved. In some areas, such as Shiraz and Bushire in the south, positive and effective action on the part of the local governors ensured the protection of the Baha'is against their religious opponents.[6]

From the 1880s through to the 1920s Iranian Baha'is appear to have been increasingly optimistic as to their future role and influence in Iranian society. Although remaining subject to persecution, the Baha'i community became an increasingly well-established element in society. Amongst many of the secular elite and the educated classes the Baha'is were at least tacitly accepted. The number of Baha'is continued to grow, perhaps to as many as 100,000 in the whole of Iran (an entirely credible estimate in this instance).[7] Of the population as a whole, the Baha'is represented over 1 per cent of the total, their representation amongst the educated urban classes being much greater. Undoubtedly, there was also a wider circle of sympathizers who would have been prepared to join the movement if there had been an end to persecution. Sympathizers included those of high rank.

Internally, the Baha'i community itself became increasingly well-organized and diversified in its concerns. With ʿAbdu'l-Bahá's encouragement organizing committees or Assemblies were established in the major centres to manage the affairs of the Baha'is, their authority supplementing that of the leading Baha'i teachers or of such dignitaries as the Hands of the Cause. Baha'i schools were established, both for boys and for girls. These schools taught secular and modern subjects and were open to non-Baha'is as well as Baha'is. Various service committees were appointed, as in Tehran, where by 1919 there were committees responsible for the management of the local Baha'i schools, poor relief, teaching the faith, training children, hospitality, publishing, international correspondence, and the adjudication of commercial and other disputes amongst the Baha'is. The Tehran Baha'i Spiritual Assembly (*maḥfil-i rawḥání*) also came to assume the role of the co-ordinating body for all Baha'i affairs in Iran.

International expansion

There was also an expansion of activity outside Iran, almost entirely as a result of the emigration of Iranian Baha'is, either for economic reasons, or as Baha'i teachers, or in order to escape the constant threat of persecution. Not that there were not reverses. In Ottoman Iraq, the community in Baghdad was successively reduced following the removal of Ottoman protection in 1868 and in preparation for Náṣiri'd-Dín Sháh's visit to the shrine cities in 1870, zealous Shiʿis taking the opportunity of Baha'i vulnerability to murder several. Ottoman intervention against the Baha'is and the compulsory transfer of a group of thirty or more leading Baha'is to Mosul led to the establishment of a strong new Baha'i community, however. Elsewhere in the Ottoman Empire a number of Baha'is (and Azalis) came to reside in Istanbul, whilst in Syria Baha'is settled in Haifa, Beirut and other locales. In Egypt the expatriate Iranian merchant community soon came to include a number of Baha'is, the local Persian consul using their discovery to imprison a number of merchants on the charge of being Babis and releasing them only on payment of large bribes, but also causing the exile of a few Baha'is to the Sudan, where afterwards they succeeded in establishing a small Baha'i community.[8]

Baha'is also established themselves amongst the Persian communities of British India (particularly Bombay), and of Russian Turkestan and Caucasia, in all of which they prospered and in which the freedom from religious persecution enabled them to assert their Baha'i identity more openly and to promote their faith. In 1871 Bahá'u'lláh commissioned Jamál Effendi to act as a Baha'i teacher in India, his work leading to the establishment of small Baha'i communities in several of the main commercial centres (notably Bombay, Calcutta and Madras) and in Burma, as well as to meetings with the Arya Samaj and the Theosophical Society. In Turkestan the major concentration of Baha'is was in the new city of Ashkhabad, close to the Iranian frontier. By 1890 about 1,000 Baha'is had settled in Ashkhabad, the community further expanding following the Russian authorities' punishment of a group of Iranian Shiʿi zealots who had murdered a prominent local Baha'i in 1889.[9] Bahá'u'lláh himself attached particular significance to this action as being the first occasion on which Shiʿis had received judicial punishment for an attack made on Baha'is.

The international expansion of the movement, which had begun during the lifetime of Bahá'u'lláh, became increasingly significant during the years of ʿAbdu'l-Bahá's leadership (1892–1921). The most remarkable aspect of this development, the establishment of Baha'i communities in North America and Europe, will be discussed separately (Chapter 7). In the Middle East the most sustained expansion continued in Turkestan. Whilst groups of Baha'is settled in more distant cities, the central community in Ashkhabad became increasingly large and prosperous. Enjoying the unique position amongst Baha'i communities of official recognition, the community constructed not only the first ever Baha'i House of Worship or *Mashriqu'l-Adhkár* (dawning-place of the remembrance of God), but also a meeting-hall, kindergartens, elementary schools and a clinic. Baha'i libraries, public reading-rooms, a magazine and printing presses were also established. The communities in Caucasia and India, which enjoyed a comparable freedom of action, also prospered to a degree, as did the Egyptian community under much less favourable circumstances. As in Iran, Spiritual Assemblies were established to coordinate the affairs of Baha'i communities.

Social composition

There is every reason to suppose that the Baha'is were drawn disproportionately from potentially more influential social groups. Certainly, European observers in Iran commonly supposed that the Baha'i religion had 'taken the deepest hold among the educated and intelligent', or the 'rich and educated', of whom it was said that 'perhaps one-third' were Baha'is.[10] This last figure is most improbable, but is in keeping with the overall sense of buoyant growth felt by many of the Baha'is, and which many European observers reflected.

We do not yet have any systematic study of the social composition of the Iranian Baha'i community in the late nineteenth century. As most of the Babis became Baha'is, that pre-existing network of urban communities, comprising ulama, merchants and craftsmen, would have provided a base for further expansion. Similarly, the various villages which had had large concentrations of Babis now gained large concentrations of Baha'is. Amongst the social groups of high status the merchants appear to have become a particularly significant element in the developing Baha'i communities. Merchant conversions continued, including several members of the Báb's family. Baha'i merchants increasingly assumed positions of prominence within the movement, particularly in the expatriate communities of Iranian Baha'is in Turkestan, Egypt and India. By contrast, the ulama became a less significant element within the movement. Baha'i ulama continued to exercise an important leadership role, whether they had converted during the Babi period or had recently converted, but conversions became fewer. Babism had represented a major and sudden challenge to faith which had evoked an urgent response amongst the ulama, whether in conversion or opposition. Now, with the passage of time, the clerical view of Babism–Baha'ism had become fixed and hostile. The movement was now unambiguously perceived as anti-clerical and heretical, new members of the ulama being socialized accordingly. Whether or not there were conversions from amongst the civil elite, some at least of its members were aware of the distinction between Babi militancy and Baha'i quietism and were prepared to tolerate Baha'i activity. Indeed, in the late Qajar period, a number of eminent Baha'is were incorporated into the civil elite as provincial viziers, financial administrators, and even governors.

As to the social groups of lower status, the Baha'i community probably continued to be disproportionately represented amongst the craftsmen, petty traders and shopkeepers. Effective missionary activity also appears to have broadened the network of rural Baha'i communities, but no significant contact was made with the nomadic tribesmen. Conversions were made, however, from amongst two of the religious minorities – the Jews and Zoroastrians – but not from the Christian minorities (Assyrians and Armenians). Women appear to have become an increasingly significant element within the Baha'i communities, although conversion probably still proceeded mainly on family lines, with men being the primary 'carriers' of the religion. Once converted, however, women ensured the effective religious socialization of their children, Baha'i belief and practice becoming a well-knit part of family life. More than any other factor, this 'familialization' of the religion contributed to the Baha'is' future survival as an established and self-perpetuating minority group.

CONVERSION AND APPEAL

The only systematic work on Baha'i conversions during this period is that by Susan Stiles relating to the conversion of Iranian Jews and Zoroastrians.[11] Stiles points to the clear contrast between the conversion of Iranian Jews and Zoroastrians and the non-conversion of indigenous Iranian Christians. Accordingly, what differentiated these groups was their self-perception *vis-à-vis* the Muslim majority. Whilst the Christians had a strong sense of superiority, nationalist aspirations and an early identity with the West, Iranian Jews and Zoroastrians had come to accept their despised inferiority, perceived themselves as Iranians, and were largely isolated from their non-Iranian co-religionists. For both groups this isolation was ended during the mid-nineteenth century as their foreign co-religionists sought to protect them from persecution and to elevate their social condition. No significant religious reform accompanied these changes, and for the now upwardly mobile members of both communities, traditional religion proved unsatisfying. Initial adventitious contacts with Baha'is led to widespread conversions. These conversions were facilitated by the Baha'is' friendship and non-observance of the divisive practices of ritual purity, by their respect for the minority religions and their ready use of Jewish and Zoroastrian eschatological prophecy to support their claims, by the religious dedication of the Baha'i teachers and the example of sacrificial martyrdom, by the appeal to Iranian and minority cultural symbols, and by the relative modernism, rationality and tolerance of Baha'i ideas when compared with the traditionalist Judaism and Zoroastrianism then prevalent in Iran.

This account may well be paradigmatic for other Baha'i conversions during this period. Only further research will tell. Certainly Baha'i conversions from amongst the ranks of Iranian Jews, Zoroastrians, and Shi'i Muslims appear to share some similarities in structural context and expression. Although already a popular religious movement with followers drawn from a wide variety of social locations, Iranian Baha'ism appears to have drawn a disproportionate number of its followers and new converts from amongst the better educated or upwardly mobile. Conversion accounts commonly refer to the appeal of a combination of traditional religious symbolism and modernistic or rationalistic argumentation. All three religious communities were experiencing a growing tension between traditionalist and modernist interpretations of their beliefs and practices. Although it is difficult to be precise about the occurrence of conversions, there appears to have been a similar pattern. Thus, whilst significant numbers of conversions from amongst the minorities began a decade later (the 1880s) than amongst the Shiʿis (the 1870s), conversions from all groups seem to have become more common as the century drew to a close, thereafter levelling off, and declining from the 1920s onwards.

Religious factors

One of the most significant aspects of the Western impact on traditional Iranian society was the diffusion of knowledge of Western technology, institutions, and scientific and political thinking. Given the context of Iranian subservience to Western powers, the potential strength and utility of Western civilization appeared to be validated. Many Iranians were thus attracted by the West, or at least wished to incorporate elements of its civilization into their own culture and society.

Although there were doubtless exceptions, the majority of the traditional custodians of religion do not appear to have made any satisfactory response to the ideological challenge posed by the West. Neither mullas, nor rabbis, nor priests, nor Zoroastrian *mobeds* and *dasturs*, either accommodated themselves to the 'new knowledge' or prepared an adequate rebuttal of it. Instead, as with the Shaykhi leader, Karím Khán, they merely denounced it and reasserted their own traditional authority.[12] For many Iranians this attitude appears to have been highly unsatisfactory, and demands for clerical reform or straightforwardly anti-clerical sentiment became a marked feature of Iranian religious life. Only amongst the Christian minorities did religio-nationalist sentiment mute such criticisms. Bahaʾism made a ready appeal in this context, presenting a strongly religious world view which nevertheless accommodated many aspects of Western knowledge. Moreover, Bahaʾi teachers became adept at reinterpreting the 'religions of the past' in a way which seemed to preserve their 'essence' whilst legitimizing change appropriate to the 'new age'. Thus all past religions were proclaimed to be valid, but to have been limited both by the receptivity of their original adherents (who had received the divine message from their prophet) and by the later corruptions introduced by worldly clerics. To accept the Bahaʾi teachings was a means of preserving all that was best in traditional religion whilst at the same time adding to it new religious teachings which were in conformity with modernity, or which even transcended it. More specifically, Baha᾿i teachers took pains to contrast what they perceived as the enlightened tolerance of their own religion with the obscurantist fanaticism of their clerical opponents.

The appeal of the Baha᾿i Faith as an expression of religious modernism may well have been a primary element in the religion's expansion during the late Qajar period. At a time when even relatively secularist thinkers chose to clothe their thoughts in religious language,[13] there was an evident attractiveness in an ideology which combined religious and modernist elements. In the early Qajar period such an ideology would have been unnecessary. In the Pahlavi perod (1925–79), the open schism between religious and secular–modernist thinking created a new context in which such an ideology was restricted in its appeal.

There were other major religious elements in the religion's appeal. For Shiᶜis, and for those who have been influenced by their thinking – such as Iranian Jews and Zoroastrians – important proofs of a religion's validity include the appearance of a prophet with a holy book, the fulfilment of prophecy, and the sacrificial witness of the prophet's followers. Baha᾿i apologists readily utilized these traditional proofs in their missionary endeavour, rapidly developing Baha᾿i exegeses of the scriptures of all the major groups in Iran. Moreover, in terms of religious status groups, the Baha᾿i Faith offered a ready vehicle for lay religiosity. It was not just that Baha᾿i ideas appeared to be in closer conformity with modernity than those of the traditional expressions of religion, but Baha᾿ism had jettisoned most of the supports for traditional clerical religiosity. Its scriptures were accessible to any educated reader and required no clerical intermediary. Its law and authority stemmed primarily from charismatic leaders, and secondarily from locally elected councils of laity. As in Islam, there was no sacramental role for clerics. Those who regarded the various traditional religious leaders as corrupt or ignorant (as many seem to have done) might well have found Baha᾿i attractive in this regard. It is of note here that in Yazd the Zoroastrian Baha᾿is played an extremely influential role on the local elected council of prominent laymen responsible for overseeing the Zoroastrian community. With their sympathizers these Baha᾿i Zoroastrians sought directly to reform the local practice of Zoroastrianism in opposition to the traditional *dasturs*.[14]

One religious factor which does not seem to have been significant is the impact of Christianity. Modern religious movements in the non-Christian world have frequently been interpreted as responses or reactions to the world-wide Christian evangelism which was so characteristic of the nineteenth century.[15] Such an interpretation was certainly applied by some contemporary Christian missionaries, who saw Bahaʾism as a form of Christianized Islam,[16] but this view was weakly founded. It is true that both Baháʾuʾlláh and ʿAbduʾl-Bahá read and cited the Christian Bible, but little specifically Christian influence is discernible in their writings. Rather, the Bible was appropriated by the Bahaʾis for their own missionary endeavour amongst Jews and Christians. Again, in nineteenth-century Iran, despite much effort on their part, Christian missionaries did not pose a religious threat to traditional religious practices and beliefs except amongst the indigenous Christians. It was Western secular thought which constituted a challenge to traditional religious conceptions, and not Western religious thought.

Social and economic factors

Some Marxist historians have interpreted the Bahaʾi Faith as a deradicalized and cosmopolitan form of Babism which largely reflected the interests of the comprador-bourgeoisie.[17] Merchants were certainly a prominent element within the Bahaʾi community, and the religion's liberal internationalism might well have been particularly attractive to Western-oriented merchants on the basis of 'elective affinity', but no simple class analysis seems altogether appropriate. Bahaʾism exercised an appeal to adherents of a wide range of social backgrounds and continued to exercise an appeal to new generations of Bahaʾis of different class positions. Furthermore, if Ashraf is correct and the circumstances of Iran in the late nineteenth century compelled all Iranian merchants to become compradors in order to survive,[18] then the supposed relationship between Bahaʾi and comprador interests seems far less distinctive and important.

If not directly expressive of class interests, the Bahaʾi movement in Iran, at least during the late Qajar period, represented more than just a reassertion of religious enthusiasm, however. In the context of the wider-ranging social crisis engendered by the Western impact and political unrest, the Bahaʾi Faith exercised more than just a 'religious' appeal. With its advocacy of a wide-ranging programme of social reform, Bahaʾi functioned as a potential 'ideology of modernization'. Its adherents promised that it provided the only solution to Iran's multi-faceted problems. It provided Iranians with a means of incorporating elements of Western civilization into their own culture, and yet at the same time it remained distinctively Iranian. The antagonism expressed by the Bahaʾi leaders towards certain aspects of Western culture may well have enhanced this appeal. 'Modernistic' Iranians may have wished to emulate the West, but they were also appalled by the Western impact on their country; the Baha'is affirmed Iranian spiritual independence and condemned Western materialism at the same time as they advocated modernization.

Rudimentary material and other interests may also have constituted a factor in the movement's appeal to its more peripherally attached members. Baha'is became known for their generosity to their fellow believers, and it is entirely possible that some of the poorer Baha'is may have been attracted for this reason (starvation being an all too vivid reality of the time). More specifically, Baha'is evidently became (or were rumoured to have become) dominant in certain areas of employment. Thus the postal and telegraph services were believed to be staffed almost entirely by Baha'is, and adherence regarded as almost a *sine qua non* of employment.[19] Again, within the fraternity of the Baha'i community, or at least within Baha'i meetings, divisions of status were sharply minimized. For those of lower status fraternization with their social superiors in an atmosphere of relative equality may have constituted an aspect of the movement's appeal. Specifically, for Iranian Jews and Zoroastrians to be treated as fellow and equal human beings by members of the dominant culture was doubtless an experience of profound significance for them.

POLITICAL CHANGE: THE BAHA'I AND AZALI RESPONSES

The Babis had challenged the traditional social order of Qajar Iran, but as part of his subsequent transformation of Babism, Bahá'u'lláh had sought to depoliticize Babism. Abrogating the Islamic–Babi injunction to engage in holy war, Bahá'u'lláh stressed that his followers should be loyal to their government and should absolutely avoid sedition and political violence. Informing various members of the Iranian elite of this commandment, he sought to effect a reconciliation with the Qajar regime. This policy had some success, with Qajar politicians such as Mírzá Ḥusayn Khán, chief minister from 1871 to 1873, recognizing the non-political nature of the Baha'i religion,[20] and both Muẓaffari'd-Dín Sháh (reigned 1896–1907) and Muḥammad ʿAlí Sháh (reigned 1907–9) affording the Baha'is a measure of protection. Muḥammad ʿAlí even included a number of Baha'is in his entourage, and under both monarchs Baha'is were appointed to regional administrative posts. This process of the gradual acceptance of the Baha'is by the political elite was severely complicated by the political disturbances at the turn of the century when the legitimacy of the established regime was forcefully challenged. The response of ʿAbduʾl-Bahá was unambiguous. Although the Bahaʾi teachings condemned injustice, bade kings to be equitable in their rule, and advocated constitutional monarchy as the ideal form of governance – all of which represented an implicit critique of Qajar rule – they also demanded strict loyalty to an established ruler. Without departing from that loyalty, the Bahaʾis were now bidden to avoid 'connection with any party', and to seek for reconciliation between 'court' and 'people'.[21] More generally, Bahaʾis were advised that they should not expect any 'political' solution to Iran's problems to be effective; only the wide-ranging and spiritually based reconstruction of society on Bahaʾi lines would be effective.

In practice the Bahaʾi attempt to remain uninvolved in the growing conflict proved to be exceedingly difficult. Although centred on popular demands for the introduction of parliamentary and constitutional limitations on autocracy, the conflict was multi-faceted, involving a wide range of traditional and ideological interests on both sides. Those opposed to the autocracy were a particularly diverse grouping and included large numbers of ulama and many of the Azali Babis who were antagonistic to the Bahaʾis. In these circumstances the Bahaʾis, along with other minority groups, found themselves becoming convenient scapegoats in popular disturbances led by the ulama. Thus in 1891, 1896–1903 and 1909, the Bahaʾis in various parts of Iran were subjected to bouts of persecution leading to the death of at least 100 of their number.[22] More insidiously, the Bahaʾis were accused (supposedly by the Azalis) of being directly in support of the autocracy, an accusation which was presumably designed to cast doubt on the Islamic credentials of the Qajar regime. However, the accusation of Bahaʾi ('Babi') linkage was also used by the Royalists as a means of discrediting the constitutionalists, as at the assault on Tabriz, and by various Royalist clergy.[23] Again, an individual Qajar governor – such as Jaláluʾd-Dawlih in Yazd – might turn from persecution to defence and again to persecution of the Bahaʾis as political exigencies changed.[24]

In general the Bahaʾis adhered strictly to ʿAbduʾl-Bahá's injunction that they should remain uninvolved in the conflict – though there was one prominent Bahaʾi constitutionalist (Abuʾl-Ḥasan Mírzá, himself a Qajar prince) and several Bahaʾis in court circles – but there was an evident problem of identification. The Bahaʾis had shown themselves to be seeking to be above politics, but by remaining obedient to a despotic government at a time when its legitimacy was being massively rejected, they gave the impression of at least tacit support. The Baha'is might wish to accomplish radical social change, but they rejected radical means of accomplishment. For the increasing number of Iranians who saw the solution to Iran's problems in secular political terms, the Baha'i stance was doubtless perceived as an irrelevance, or even as an impediment to structural change. The Baha'is might insist that theirs was the only solution to Iran's problems, but as the twentieth century progressed secularity became an increasingly dominant ethos. When a religious approach to structural change was again presented, it was of a very different temper.

The Baha'i response to Iranian political change exemplifies the modern dichotomy between 'religious' and 'political' action. Such a distinction had not been characteristic of the more traditional movement of Babism, and was not characteristic of at least some of the Azali Babis. Whilst Ṣubḥ-i Azal sought to preserve the traditional teachings of Babism, a number of his younger followers found in the movement the resources for a new and more secular critique of late Qajar society. For these men 'the ideal of a democratic Persia developing on purely national lines' seems to have replaced the early Babi theocracy as an object of religious endeavour.[25] Ultimately, of course, such an objective has little inherent religious meaning, and by and large these younger Azalis, all prominently involved in the anti-Qajar movement, appear to have become free-thinkers, retaining their Azali links and their public identification as Shiʿis (often as Shiʿi ulama) for reasons of expediency rather than faith.

PART III: THE BAHAʾI FAITH AS A WORLD RELIGION

7

THE EARLY AMERICAN BAHAʾI COMMUNITY

The emergence of small communities of Bahaʾis in North America and Europe during the 1890s marked a profoundly significant advance in the development of the Bahaʾi religion.[1] Although comprising no more than a few thousand individuals, these early Western communities represented a major expansion beyond the existing cultural boundaries of the Bahaʾi community, demonstrating the cultural adaptability of the religion and securing a fresh base for further expansion.

THE KHEIRALLA PERIOD, 1894–1900

The primary locus of early Bahaʾi activity in the West was the United States of America. It was in America that the first Western converts were gained and it was from America that the teachers of the new religion came when the European and later the Australasian and Far Eastern groups were established. In terms of numbers, activity and influence the American Bahaʾis were the predominant group within the body of early Western believers and it was in their midst that many of the institutional forms which later developed into the Administrative Order were founded.

The initial growth of the Bahaʾi movement in America was almost entirely the work of one man, Ibrahim George Kheiralla (1849–1929), a Syrian Christian who had been converted in Egypt in 1889. By 1894 Kheiralla had established himself in Chicago and begun to teach the new religion. He soon gained his first converts, seemingly through personal contacts. Thereafter he fixed upon the system of giving a series of graduated lectures, the earliest dealing with general religious topics, the later lectures with biblical prophecy concerning the second advent and the existence of a 'Greatest Name' of God by which the believer would enter into a special relationship with the divine.[2] Those who had by then showed themselves worthy were finally given the 'pith' of his message: that God had returned to earth in the person of Baháʾuʾlláh, and that his son, Jesus Christ (ᶜAbduʾl-Bahá), was now living at ᶜAkká. Those who believed were given the 'Greatest Name' (*Bahá*) and told to write to ᶜAbduʾl-Bahá confessing their belief. The introductory lectures were soon expanded and published, and by 1900 about 2,000 Americans had become Bahaʾis, situated mostly in Chicago, New York City and Kenosha, Wisconsin. The name of the new religion was not made public, and adherents were known as 'Truth-Seekers' or 'Truth-Knowers'. Diverging strongly from Bahaʾi orthodoxy, Kheiralla evolved a unique synthesis of Bahaʾi ideas and his own conceptions which proved to be immensely appealing. Himself practising spiritual healing and offering a means of coming into contact with mysterious personages and spiritual powers, Kheiralla combined metaphysical speculation with an appeal to an esotericized version of the adventist tradition, thus bringing together two powerful motifs of late nineteenth-century American religious life.

Initially exercising a strong central control over the fledgling movement both doctrinally and organizationally, Kheiralla's own success in gaining converts soon necessitated his appointment of other teachers to impart the message, whilst amongst the larger communities, Boards of Counsel also emerged. Some consolidation of the movement was required, and towards the end of 1898 Kheiralla and some leading converts proceeded to ᶜAkká to see ᶜAbduʾl-Bahá. Whilst during this pilgrimage the new converts were mostly confirmed in their faith – writing later of the staggering impact which 'the Master's' (ᶜAbduʾl-Bahá's) personality had had upon them – Kheiralla fell out with ᶜAbduʾl Bahá and on his return to America threw in his lot with the partisans of Muḥammad ᶜAlí.

The dispute became public in March 1900 and the American community was thrown into confusion. Kheiralla's original Bahaʾi teacher from Egypt, ᶜAbduʾl-Karím Tihrání, was quickly dispatched to the United States to counter Kheiralla's influence. Separate and mutually antagonistic organizations were soon established, but most of the American Bahaʾis appear to have abandoned the movement, at least on a temporary basis.

Many of these individuals later reattached themselves to the followers of ʿAbduʾl-Bahá, and by 1906 this group was able to report a membership of 1,280 to the United States Census of Religions.[3] By contrast, Muḥammad ʿAlí's American following (the 'Behaists') rapidly declined and by 1906 they had a reported membership of only 40 individuals. Ultimately, whilst Kheiralla had been their 'beloved teacher', it was not to him that the early American Bahaʾis had given their allegiance. His defection troubled and perplexed them, but most did not follow him. It was devotion to the theophanic and messianic figure of ʿAbduʾl-Bahá which had become their religious focus.

THE AMERICAN BAHAʾI COMMUNITY AFTER 1900

Contact with ʿAbduʾl-Bahá

The figure of ʿAbduʾl-Bahá dominated the American Bahaʾi community in the years following 1900. Baháʾuʾlláh might be the centre of theological considerations, but it was the living messianic figure of ʿAbduʾl-Bahá who was the emotional centre of the community, their source of guidance and authority. He was their 'Lord', their 'Master', and with increasing contact he became an awesome yet loving friend and counsellor to whom all could turn for guidance and to whom unquestioning devotion could be given. Not that American Bahaʾis generally understood ʿAbduʾl-Bahá's 'station' in orthodox Bahaʾi terms. For them he was more than merely Baháʾuʾlláh's designated successor. If Baháʾuʾlláh was the Manifestation of God, the 'Lord of the Vineyard', then surely ʿAbduʾl-Bahá was the returned son of God to whom management of the 'kingdom' had been entrusted. It was easy to see ʿAbduʾl-Bahá, the loving teacher from the East, in Christ-like terms, and despite ʿAbduʾl-Bahá's own denials some Bahaʾis clearly regarded him as Christ returned.

Whilst ʿAbduʾl-Bahá dominated the Bahaʾi community, serving as its absolute and ultimate source of authority and guidance, the American community was not subject to strong central control under his guidance, nor did it become a tightly knit cohesive unit. Although a charismatic leader with considerable authority over his followers, ʿAbduʾl-Bahá's own style of leadership was generally one both of loving encouragement and of tolerance for the views of his followers. On issues which he regarded as peripheral he rarely issued any reproof. This flexibility was augmented by the 'technical' problems of communication between the individualistically oriented American Bahaʾis and their leader, confined in a remote part of the Ottoman Empire several thousand miles away. For the most part such communication was through a vast interchange of correspondence, most of it addressed to individuals, and subject to individualistic interpretation and the uncertainties of translation. Beyond conveying general exhortations – to be united, to be firm in the Covenant, to teach the Cause and serve humanity – this mass of correspondence was of limited effectiveness in giving strong directive guidance to the community. Again, whilst a significant minority of American Baha'is undertook the lengthy and arduous journey to visit 'the prisoner of ʿAkká',[4] in the absence of any universally agreed and effective structure of organization and authority within the American community it was difficult for more than general inspiration to be conveyed to the American Baha'is. Far more effective, but of limited duration, was ʿAbdu'l-Bahá's eight-month visit to North America (April–December 1912), his example and teachings making a direct and forceful impact on the community which greatly facilitated its consequent change and development.

The stabilization and expansion of the community

The events of 1899 and 1900 placed the American Baha'i community under the most severe stress it was to experience. In the midst of bitter denunciations, the teachings of the Baha'is' former leader and mentor were discredited and the foundations of their faith questioned. Besides believing that ʿAbdu'l-Bahá was their Lord, what else were they to believe? Communication with ʿAbdu'l-Bahá was limited by the difficulties of language and distance, and apart from a few typewritten copies of prayers and scriptures they had no Baha'i literature on which they could rely.

Initially these problems were met by ʿAbdu'l-Bahá's dispatch of a succession of four Persian Baha'i teachers, the first arriving in April 1900 and the last departing in 1905, and together serving to provide ideology and leadership at a time when the American Baha'is had lost both. Countering Kheiralla's influence, and writing and lecturing on 'orthodox' Baha'i doctrine, these men served to incorporate the American Baha'i community into the Baha'i world as a whole and to provide an approved statement of Baha'i beliefs to the wider non-Baha'i audience of the West, thus aiding the movement's emergence from the pall of secrecy which had surrounded it prior to 1900.

A more permanent response to the problem of doctrinal uncertainty was the development of a substantial body of Baha'i literature in the years following 1900. By 1912 at least 70 books and pamphlets had been produced, and by 1917 this number had risen to more than 100. Of this stock of literature the largest single category was translations of Baha'i scripture, ʿAbdu'l-Bahá's writings being predominant. There were also an increasing number of expositions of the Baha'i teachings (mostly by Americans) and accounts of pilgrimages to ʿAbdu'l-Bahá. In addition a number of Baha'i periodicals were initiated, notably the Chicago-based *Star of the West/Bahai News* (1910–22).

The growing stabilization of the community was accompanied by an increasingly outgoing attitude towards its expansion. In sharp contrast to the secrecy initially maintained by Kheiralla, ʿAbdu'l-Bahá constantly encouraged his American followers to teach the Baha'i cause, to 'diffuse the Divine fragrances'. Many individual Baha'is responded to this appeal and, in addition to contacting their immediate circle of friends and family, sought for opportunities to 'give the message' to sympathetic groups, sometimes undertaking extensive travel in order to do so. Much teaching activity was concentrated in the semi-formal meetings which individuals held in their own homes – what later generations of Baha'is have come to term 'firesides' – where, in an atmosphere of drawing-room geniality, the enquirer might meet a group of Baha'is discussing their teachings, or perhaps reading the latest 'Tablet' from ʿAbdu'l-Bahá. As to the non-Baha'i organizations contacted by the Baha'is, various metaphysical groups (New Thought, Theosophy, Divine Science) seem to have been particularly willing to accept Baha'i speakers in the early years, the New Thought and Vedantaist haven of Greenacre (Green Acre) – the summer colony held at Eliot, Maine, since 1894 – being effectively taken over by the Baha'is. Later the broadening basis of appeal of the Baha'i teachings led to increasing contact with liberal Christian groups and various organizations concerned with social issues, including even the Montreal socialists in 1912.[5] The visit of ʿAbdu'l-Bahá in 1912 was particularly important in this regard, his stated mission as an apostle of peace and world unity, together with his advocacy of a programme of social principles, affording him contact with a wide variety of religious, humanitarian and cultural groups.

By his example and encouragement, ʿAbdu'l-Bahá's tour of North America provided a great impetus to Baha'i teaching endeavour. Further impetus was given by ʿAbdu'l-Bahá's warnings of the inevitability of a European war.[6] The sense of impending apocalypse made the Baha'is' task of promulgating their teachings seem all the more urgent. As the urgency of Baha'i teaching endeavour increased, the issues of sponsorship and organization came to the fore. Prior to ʿAbdu'l-Bahá's visit the

Baha'is had for the most part rigorously eschewed subsidization of Baha'i teachers, fearing that to pay the expenses of the teacher would foster the growth of a 'clerical' group within the community. Yet not to subsidize was to limit the teaching work that could be done, given the size of the United States and the fewness of those with appreciable private incomes. This dilemma was now faced. By 1915 a scheme to fund part-time itinerant teachers centrally had been approved. A further incentive was received in the following year with the receipt of the first five of ʿAbdu'l-Bahá's general letters on teaching, the *Tablets of the Divine Plan*, in which the Baha'is were called upon to embark on a systematic campaign to establish new centres in those parts of America in which there were few or no believers. Thereafter five regional teaching funds were established and increasing calls were made for national and regional teaching organizations to be formed, a call which finally found fruition in 1920 in the surge of post-war enthusiasm for teaching.

This increasing concern with teaching led to a renewed growth in numbers, although it was not until the time of ʿAbdu'l-Bahá's visit that there were again as many Baha'is in North America as there had been under Kheiralla. In 1916 the Baha'is were able to report to the Census a membership of 2,884, adding that this represented 'those distinctly enrolled', there also being 'large numbers all over the country who attend the Bahai meetings and are closely identified with the movement, but have not discontinued their connection with the churches'.[7] With this recovery in numbers there was also a marked dispersion in the distribution of the community, as a deliberate effort was made to spread the Baha'i teachings throughout North America.

Organization and leadership

An element in both the stabilization and expansion of the Baha'i community in America was the growth of a local and national leadership and organization. Not that such developments were not contested, for fundamental to the religious understanding of many American Baha'is was an attitude of what Wallis has termed 'epistemological individualism', that is an assertion that the ultimate locus of religious authority was the individual believer.[8] Thus, beyond the recognition of ʿAbdu'l-Bahá's overall (and distant) authority, many American Baha'is were distrustful of any sort of organization and leadership. Kheiralla as the original teacher had occupied a special position, but with him discredited, they were wary of accepting any individual or group amongst their American co-religionists as a secondary authority. Local co-ordination of the movement thus proved difficult. Several local Boards of Counsel were established, but 'the affairs of the Cause' were still largely administered by individuals 'in accordance with their own guidance'.[9] More divisively, various individuals also exercised an informal authority within a particular group or clique, whether on the basis of their reputation and activity as teachers, or their contact with ʿAbduʾl-Bahá by means of pilgrimage or the receipt of Tablets, or more controversially, their claimed possession of special spiritual or psychic gifts.

From 1909 onwards, however, the increasing tempo of Bahaʾi activities was seen to necessitate the introduction of some form of organization. Several local communities began to hold regular business meetings, often with some form of elected executive board responsible for the day-to-day running of community meetings and activities. At the same time, several national organizations came into being, one to co-ordinate a project to construct a Bahaʾi temple (1909), and others to promote publishing activities (1910, 1911) and contacts with the Bahaʾis of the East (1910). The first of these was particularly significant, for whilst the actual temple project (at Wilmette, near Chicago) proceeded extremely slowly, the Bahai Temple Unity, which was organized to oversee the work, assumed increasing importance. Legally established as a delegate assembly representative of all Bahaʾi groups, the Temple Unity met in an annual two or three-day convention, deliberated on all aspects of 'the work of the Cause', and selected a nine-member executive board. Generating its own spirit of enthusiasm and camaraderie, the Temple Unity conventions gradually came to provide the basis for a national American Bahaʾi organization and leadership.

ACTIVITIES OUTSIDE THE UNITED STATES

The initial expansion of the Bahaʾi Faith in the West was almost entirely confined to the United States. Two expatriate American ladies, resident in Paris and London respectively, accompanied the 'first pilgrimage' group of 1898–9 and established the first two European Bahaʾi communities on their return. Growth was slow, and in Paris the new Bahaʾi group appears to have been predominantly American. The geographical mobility of many American Bahaʾis led to further diffusion of the religion, Bahaʾis from the United States, or American Bahaʾis from the Paris group, being responsible for the establishment of groups in Italy (*c.* 1900), Canada

(1902), Hawaii (1902), Germany (1905–7) and Japan (1914). After 1919 these pioneer moves multiplied, but overall the response to the Baha'i message outside the United States was minimal. Several active Baha'i communities were established, but their numbers remained small, and the resident American Baha'is generally remained the centres of activity. There was little organization. Even ʿAbdu'l-Bahá's two visits to Europe (August to December 1911 and December 1912 to June 1913) did not lead to any expansion comparable to that in the United States.

Containing members of affluence and ability, the American Baha'i community rapidly assumed a significant role in the overall development of the Baha'i Faith. Besides the pioneer moves of individual American Baha'is, and the consequent establishment of Baha'i groups in Europe and the Pacific, the international travels of American Baha'is did much to express the unity of the entire 'Baha'i world'. Visiting their co-religionists in Europe, Egypt, the Levant, Iran, Central Asia, India, the Orient and the Pacific, American Baha'is demonstrated the brotherhood and 'universal' appeal of the new religion, as well as helping and encouraging the weaker groups in their activities. Some individuals did more, settling on a permanent or temporary basis amongst their Eastern co-religionists. These included several Americans who helped in educational and medical work with the Baha'is in Iran, a Persian-American Educational Society being established in this connection in Washington DC, in 1910.

DOMINANT RELIGIOUS CONCERNS

The American Baha'is had their own religious concerns and emphases which to varying degrees were distinctive to themselves and perhaps to some of their European co-religionists. These may be described in terms of five interrelated motifs: millenarianism, social reconstructionism, religious liberalism, the polar motif and esotericism.

Millenarianism

Early American Baha'i literature emphasized the millennial fulfilment represented by the Baha'i revelation.[10] This was the 'Day of God', when the 'Fatherhood of God and the Brotherhood of Man' would become an earthly reality. Bahá'u'lláh was the 'Lord of the Vineyard' who had come to establish the biblical 'Kingdom of God on Earth'. His way had been prepared by the Báb in 1844 (the year of Millerite Adventist expectation).

He was now represented by the Christ-like figure of ᶜAbduʾl-Bahá.

Kheiralla had taught that the Most Great Peace would be established in 1917. Although after 1900 no Bahaʾi publications referred to this prophecy, many Western Bahaʾis continued to believe that the end of the old order would soon be at hand. These expectations appear to have been revived by ᶜAbduʾl-Bahá's warnings of approaching war in Europe, and by 1917 the eschatological significance of the war proved to be 'the leading topic of discussion' at the American Bahaʾi Convention.[11] Expectations were sufficiently vague, however, for no crisis of faith to be engendered when 1917 passed without the millennium having been established. Expectations were easily extended into the future. Whilst hopes that the millennium would soon be established were still voiced, as at the 1922 Convention,[12] most Bahaʾis settled down to work patiently for the Most Great Peace, a peace which would be established in God's own time.

Social reconstructionism

As their own contribution towards the attainment of the Most Great Peace, the American (and European) Bahaʾis became increasingly concerned with ideas of social reconstruction. Stemming largely from ᶜAbduʾl-Bahá's annunciation of the Bahaʾi 'universal principles', the Bahaʾi concern with the reconstruction of American and world society on the basis of religious imperatives came to form one of the most distinctive features of the 'Bahaʾi message'.[13] This may have led to the criticism quoted by Alter that 'Bahaʾism is not a religion but a society for social welfare.'[14] Yet, whilst for a number of Bahaʾis, 'good works' of one kind or another were regarded as an integral part of their religiosity, overall such works of charity did not form a major part of Bahaʾi activity. Only in the very real example given by the Bahaʾis with regard to the 'racial question', did Bahaʾi action impinge strongly on social reconstruction. It may have taken time to integrate black Americans into the (predominantly white) Bahaʾi community, but in the context of early twentieth-century America the advocacy of racial equality and the holding of interracial meetings were highly distinctive.

If the Bahaʾis offered little in the way of social action, they did offer advocacy of an overall solution to the social and economic problems of industrial society. Economic justice, sexual equality, racial amity, world peace, a world language and universal education all formed part of this solution. More fundamentally, a spiritualization of human collective life was called for so as to provide the moral impetus towards change.

Religious liberalism

With its emphasis on human brotherhood transcending race, creed and class, on the primacy of moral behaviour over creedal affirmation, on its own purpose as a non-sectarian, inclusive movement of unity untrammelled by dogma and organization and free from a priestly class, on the necessity for freedom from prejudices and for the individual search after truth, on the evolutionary nature of religion, on the rejection of biblical literalism, and on the essential harmony between science and religion, the Baha'i teachings as promulgated in North America were pre-eminently liberal in theological terms. Again, the primary vision of the Baha'i Cause which ʿAbdu'l-Bahá gave to his followers was that of a broad inclusive movement:

> The Bahai Movement is not an organisation. You can never organise the Bahai Cause. *The Bahai Movement is the spirit of this age*. It is the essence of all the highest ideals of this century. The Bahai Cause is an *inclusive Movement*: The teachings of all the religions and societies are found here; the Christians, Jews, Buddhists, Mohammedans, Zoroastrians, Theosophists, Freemasons, Spiritualists, et. al., find their highest aims in this Cause. Even the Socialists and philosophers find their theories fully developed in this Movement.[15]

To be a Baha'i was simply 'to love humanity and try to serve it; to work for universal peace and universal brotherhood'.[16] It made no difference 'whether you have ever heard of Baha'u'llah or not . . . the man who lives the life according to the teachings of Baha'u'llah is already a Bahai. On the other hand a man may call himself a Bahai for fifty years and if he does not live the life he is not a Bahai.'[17]

This broad and liberal vision of ʿAbdu'l-Bahá was taken up by his followers. The Baha'i gospel was 'a spiritual attitude', 'not so much a new religion as religion renewed'.[18] To become a Baha'i was not to abandon one's previous religion, but to add to it, to cast off dogma and 'discern the true spirit of its founder'.[19] Similarly, non-Baha'i observers such as G.G. Atkins saw Baha'i as 'a leaven rather than a cult', reducing religion to 'simple and inclusive forms' and challenging the followers of each religion 'to be more true to what is deepest in their [own] faith'.[20]

Not that this was the whole picture, however. The inclusivity of the movement was clearly on Baha'i terms: the other religions were accepted *as precursors* of the Baha'i religion. The Baha'is might only desire 'to diffuse in existing churches and societies the spirit of universal love', but the fruit of this love would be unity of the various denominations within the Baha'i Cause. Again, Baha'is who retained their church connections were liable to use these as a means for teaching the Bahaʾi message to such 'prepared souls' as they might find.[21]

The broad appeal of Bahaʾi liberalism contrasted with what many early Bahaʾis seem to have perceived as the narrowness and 'sectarian outlook' of the churches. For such individuals Bahaʾi membership could provide a basis for combining religious belief with the autonomy of free thought. The existence of implicitly authoritarian elements within the Bahaʾi religion was not immediately apparent to them. Nor was it apparent to the wider circle of Bahaʾi sympathizers.

Devotion and obedience: the polar motif

Despite the liberalism which was characteristic of many aspects of the Bahaʾi movement, the essential claims of its central figures were extremely authoritarian: Baháʾuʾlláh's writings were regarded as the unerring Word of God and, as ᶜAbduʾl-Bahá himself stated, 'Any opinion expressed by the Centre of the Covenant is correct, and there is no reason for disobedience by anyone.'[22] Liberalism and authoritarianism coexisted within the same movement. That they were able to coexist was due at least in part to the unifying effect of personal devotion to the living charismatic figure of ᶜAbduʾl-Bahá.

Whilst in the Bahaʾi context the personal devotion which many American Bahaʾis initially gave to ᶜAbduʾl-Bahá was theologically questionable, emotionally, personal attachment and devotion to ᶜAbduʾl-Bahá remained of immense importance within the community as a whole and, for some Bahaʾis at least, constituted one of the most basic elements of their faith. The devotion to ᶜAbduʾl-Bahá as 'Lord' and 'Master' went beyond purely theological considerations: in 'His Presence' reality seemed transformed; the material world faded before the world of the spirit; and the devotee prepared to enter 'undreamed of worlds' and 'a new, a boundless, and eternal life'.[23] Whatever his theological status, devotion to him brought his followers into contact with what they regarded as the numinous.

From such a figure claims to authority were acceptable and its exercise might not seem an imposition. His commands were as those of a loving, almost divine, father. They were not those of some religious functionary. The simultaneous devotion to ᶜAbduʾl-Bahá and opposition to any form of 'organization', which many Bahaʾis combined, is an indication of this attitude. The attitude towards ᶜAbduʾl-Bahá's authority also reflected the way in which it was exercised: his sympathetic encouragement, combined with only the occasional reproof, was doubtless a fairly easy form of authority to bear amongst the often fiercely independent Baha'is. For individual, highly religiously liberal Baha'is, devotion to ʿAbdu'l-Bahá provided the link between their continued theological liberalism and their obedience to the commands of ʿAbdu'l-Bahá and the divine laws of Bahá'u'lláh. This link was reinforced by the characteristically liberal nature of many of those commands and laws.

Undergirding the devotion of many American Baha'is towards ʿAbdu'l-Bahá was a relationship of obedience based on the Baha'i doctrine of the Covenant.[24] This doctrine first received attention in the West after Kheiralla had been discredited, ʿAbdu'l-Bahá's first two emissaries placing great emphasis on it. As the threat posed by Kheiralla lessened, so the doctrine of the Covenant received less emphasis, the doctrine being portrayed more in terms of its 'positive' aspect (i.e. that ʿAbdu'l-Bahá was Bahá'u'lláh's successor) than its 'negative aspect' (i.e Covenant-breaking). Only after ʿAbdu'l-Bahá's visit to America in 1912 was the Covenant doctrine again stressed, ʿAbdu'l-Bahá himself referring to his father's written appointment of him as successor and of the dangers to the unity of the Baha'i community posed by Covenant-breakers.

Besides the excommunication of unrepentant dissidents, 'protection of the Covenant' also involved ʿAbdu'l-Bahá issuing letters of credential to those Eastern Baha'is who wished to visit the Baha'is of the West. Without such letters even members of ʿAbdu'l-Bahá's own family were not to be received.

Esotericism, the religious search and the metaphysical movements

The tension between liberalism and authority within the early American Baha'i community became particularly apparent with regard to various expressions of esotericism within the Baha'i community.

For many Baha'is their acceptance of the Baha'i teachings had been preceded by a religious search. Conversion accounts by early American Baha'is frequently describe a pattern of initial disillusionment or dissatisfaction with their 'inherited' religion, followed by some sort of religious search, which in quite a number of cases took the form of a safari amongst the wide range of new religious movements which had sprung up in the late nineteenth century, followed in turn by an encounter with, and acceptance of, the Baha'i teachings. For others, doubtless, their encounter with the Baha'i teachings was merely one more way-station in their continuing religious quest.

The intellectual independence represented by these quests reflected a wide-ranging dissatisfaction with established religion, which led not to the abandonment of religion altogether, but often to religious experimentation in that 'vast and highly diffuse' collection of 'metaphysical movements' which included Theosophy, Vedanta, Christian Science and New Thought.[25] Possessing a certain 'doctrinal kinship' in terms of esoteric and metaphysical concerns, and rebelling against the creedal authority of organized Protestantism, these movements generally represented extreme forms of both doctrinal liberalism and 'epistemological individualism' with its characteristic suspicion of external religious authority. With its doctrinal liberalism, its assertion that religion was progressively revealed and needed to be compatible with science, its rejection of biblical literalism and Trinitarianism, and its stress on the individual's own search after truth unconstrained by any clerical controls, the Bahaʾi movement in America had an initial affinity with this 'cultic milieu', gaining an appreciable number of converts from within its bounds.

In itself the fact that a good many Bahaʾis would seem to have held religiously unconventional ideas would not necessarily have caused much impact within the Bahaʾi community. Practices like spiritual healing, astrology and fortune-telling could doubtless have been tolerated. What was more serious was the authority which some of the more 'metaphysical' Bahaʾis claimed on the basis of psychic communications, visions and esoteric knowledge. More pervasively, the rejection of external religious authority – what one prominent early Bahaʾi termed the 'occultist attitude' – led to a situation in which no Bahaʾi doctrine or practice was sacrosanct, a situation which many of the more 'orthodox' and conventional Bahaʾis found intolerable.

EMERGENCE FROM THE CULTIC MILIEU

The divergent attitudes generated by the early Bahaʾi community's connection with the cultic milieu formed part of a wider set of tensions which gradually cut through all aspects of community life. These various tensions tended towards an increasing polarization around two rival conceptions of the Bahaʾi Faith. On the one hand, there were those who saw the 'Bahaʾi movement' as what Johnson has described as 'a loosely knit, inclusive, spiritual philosophy infiltrating the existing religions'.[26] Such individuals tended to oppose organization, to be attracted towards ideas drawn from the cultic milieu or at least to be permissive of their presence in Baha'i dialogue, and to be epistemologically individualistic in their conceptions of authority. On the other hand, there were those who saw the 'Baha'i religion' as an independent, and even exclusive, revealed religion, and who tended to favour organization, doctrinal controls, and 'epistemological authoritarianism'. Almost inevitably, individuals holding this latter conception dominated the various administrative bodies which gradually emerged and were in the forefront of those promulgating the doctrine of the Covenant. Moreover, it may well be that those who were most active in the movement, who were 'distinctly enrolled and not identified with any other religious body',[27] were more inclined towards the attitude of independent exclusiveness whilst those more peripherally involved were more inclined towards inclusiveness, but this is by no means certain. Certainly, outside observers such as Richardson, together with the Baha'is own report to the Census, suggest an effectively two-tier structure of membership, the more committed Baha'is necessarily being more inclined to accept the full authority claims of Bahá'u'lláh and ʿAbdu'l-Bahá.[28]

Only the lack of a specific creedal formulation or of membership qualifications, and the tolerant but emotionally charged leadership of ʿAbdu'l-Bahá, appears to have enabled these very divergent attitudes to coexist freely within the same religious movement. When contact with ʿAbdu'l-Bahá was cut off because of the war, these tensions became unmanageable. Even prior to the war, in the years following ʿAbdu'l-Bahá's visit to America in 1912, these tensions had been mounting, as the greater stress which was placed on teaching and the doctrine of the Covenant accentuated the more 'authoritarian' conception of the religion. Thus, as the extent and scope of the teaching work expanded, the need for organization became more urgent, and as a national organization came into being, it developed its own momentum. More traumatic than this steady expansion of organization, however, were the events centring on the Chicago Reading Room controversy of 1917–18. Originating in a local conflict between the Chicago House of Spirituality and a 'cultic' group associated with the local Bahai Reading Room established by Luella Kirchner, the affair rapidly acquired wider national importance, serving to articulate the underlying tensions generated by the variant attitudes towards the Baha'i Faith. In November 1917, a national Committee of Investigation was established which charged the Reading Room Baha'is with being violators of the Covenant, creating disunity and spreading false teachings. This judgement was endorsed by the 1918 Convention (though many delegates abstained from attending).

The Reading Room controversy marked an important watershed in the development of the American Bahaʾi community. A process of 'emergence' from the cultic milieu was definitely set in train, and the more authoritarian attitude towards doctrine and organization increasingly came to prevail. There were now moves in the direction of bringing some measure of control over what was taught as Bahaʾi doctrine. As early as 1913 Albert H. Hall had told the Convention that whilst some years previously no one had dared to raise the question of a test of doctrine, they now had such a test in the idea of 'firmness' in the Covenant.[29] In 1918 this idea found formal expression in the proposals to establish reviewing procedures for Bahaʾi books, both old and new, for the words 'approved by the Publications Committee' to be printed in the front of all new American Bahaʾi books, in the need expressed for a 'correct list' of Bahaʾi teachings, and in Remey's appeals to ensure doctrinal control at Green Acre.[30] Whilst much of the old liberalism still remained, it is clear that the post-1918 American community was already displaying signs of the greater control which was to characterize it in the period of Shoghi Effendi's leadership.

8

INSTITUTIONALIZATION IN THE FORMATIVE AGE

Shoghi Effendi divided Bahaʾi history into three great 'ages' of development: an Heroic, Apostolic or Primitive Age lasting from the Báb's declaration in 1844 until ʿAbduʾl-Bahá's death in 1921; a Formative or Iron Age, characterized by the institutionalization of the Faith and its world-wide expansion, and lasting from 1921 until the future establishment of the Most Great Peace; and the succeeding millennial Golden Age.[1] The first sixty or so years of this Formative Age form the subject of this present chapter.

THE ESTABLISHMENT OF THE ADMINISTRATIVE ORDER

The succession of Shoghi Effendi as Guardian

ʿAbduʾl-Bahá died peacefully in the early hours of 28 November 1921. The event came as a dreadful and unexpected blow to his family and followers. Shoghi (Shawqí) Effendi Rabbání, ʿAbduʾl-Bahá's eldest grandson and the addressee of his Will, was summoned from England, arriving in Haifa at the end of December. ʿAbduʾl-Bahá's *Will and Testament*, first read officially on 3 January 1922, surprised many of the Bahaʾis, not least amongst them Shoghi Effendi, who found himself appointed *Valí-amruʾlláh* (Guardian of the Cause of God) and head of the future Universal House of Justice.

Shoghi Effendi, together with many of the Western Bahaʾis, had expected that ʿAbduʾl-Bahá would have left instructions for the immediate formation of the House of Justice referred to by Baháʾuʾlláh, instead of which they found that a new institution – the Guardianship – had been created. As ʿAbduʾl-Bahá made clear in his Will, both the Universal House of Justice and the newly instituted line of hereditary Guardians were under the protection and unerring guidance of Baháʾuʾlláh and the Báb. 'Whatsoever they decide' was of God. Obedience to them was the same as obedience to God, opposition to either of them was opposition towards God and merited divine vengeance.[2] Whilst the House of Justice was 'the source of all good and freed from all error', and was empowered to enact and if needs be later to rescind 'all ordinances and regulations that are not to be found in the explicit Holy Text', [3] it was not yet elected. Whilst an outline for its election was given, it was clear that even with its formation the newly appointed Centre of the Cause would remain the first Guardian, the 'sign of God' on earth, Shoghi Effendi, and (by implication) after him his lineal descendants or such other member of the *Aghsán* (the male descendants of Bahá'u'lláh) as each Guardian in turn appointed as his successor. It was incumbent on all Baha'is 'to show their obedience, submissiveness and subordination unto the guardian of the Cause of God, to turn unto him and be lowly before him'.[4] The Baha'is were strictly warned that they must be faithful to this command. There was to be no excuse for any opposition of the type ʿAbdu'l-Bahá had encountered from his own family after the death of his father. The warnings and commands of the Will were to be taken absolutely literally and 'to none is given the right to put forth his own opinion or express his particular convictions. All must seek guidance and turn unto the Center of the Cause and the House of Justice'.[5]

Born in 1897, Shoghi Effendi was ʿAbdu'l-Bahá's eldest grandchild and the first of his male descendants to survive childhood. After completing a Bachelor of Arts degree at the American University of Beirut in 1918, Shoghi Effendi returned to Haifa to act as one of ʿAbdu'l-Bahá's secretaries and translators, leaving after two years of close association with his grandfather to go to the University of Oxford to perfect his English. Gaining admission to Balliol College to read political economy, Shoghi remained in England until the news of his grandfather's death, returning to Haifa in a state of shock. He was then a young man of 24 and was unprepared for either the death of ʿAbdu'l-Bahá, to whom he had been greatly devoted, or for the high office unexpectedly thrust upon him. It evidently took him several years to come to terms with these shocks, and for eight months in 1922 (April–December) and again for five months in 1923 (June–November) he totally absented himself from Haifa, leaving all direction of the affairs of the Baha'i world to ʿAbdu'l-Bahá's sister, Bahiyyih Khánum, the Greatest Holy Leaf (*Varáqi-yi Ulyá*), in consultation with the rest of the family and a newly elected Haifa Assembly. In 1922 he returned only in response to his family's pleadings. To the severe stress occasioned by these shocks was added the pressures and worries occasioned by the sheer volume of work which confronted him, together with a number of serious problems regarding the development of the Faith. When in Haifa he worked almost continuously, sleeping and eating little, but neither physically nor emotionally could such a pace be maintained for long. In 1924 he again absented himself from Haifa for six months or so, referring on his return to 'those sullen days of my retirement, bitter with feelings of anxiety and gloom' and deploring his 'forced and repeated withdrawals' and 'utter inaction'.[6] This time, however, he maintained contact with Haifa during his absence and attended to correspondence. A pattern of life was effectively adopted in accommodation to the pressures of office: months of sustained hard work in Haifa alternated with several months' absence in the summer, often spent in energetic walking and climbing expeditions in the Swiss Alps. Even as late as 1926, however, a devoted American Bahaʾi was to write from Haifa that Shoghi Effendi had again been forced to leave Haifa 'at an hour's notice' because of his chronic exhaustion and the threat of 'what in the case of an ordinary person might be called a nervous breakdown from overwork'.[7]

These personal difficulties of adaptation to his new role undoubtedly exacerbated the central problem confronting Shoghi Effendi at this earliest stage of his ministry: the gaining of wholehearted support for his leadership. Whilst there were a small minority of Bahaʾis who outrightly challenged his authority, their opposition does not appear in retrospect to have constituted so major a problem, however distressing for Shoghi Effendi it undoubtedly was at the time. The real problem lay in the fact that whilst most Bahaʾis had accepted the strongly worded and explicit statements of ʿAbduʾl-Bahá in his appointment of Shoghi Effendi, they had not necessarily all done so without reservation. ʿAbduʾl-Bahá had been seen as a venerable patriarch, a kindly and loving father, whose authority had been gladly accepted by the majority of Bahaʾis regardless of their particular interpretation of the Bahaʾi teachings. As events were to show, Shoghi Effendi was a very different kind of leader; furthermore, he was young, relatively inexperienced and not particularly well known. Worse, at least as far as some Western Bahaʾis were concerned, he was soon advocating policies which radically challenged many existing patterns of thought and behaviour. Thus, during the 1920s especially, Shoghi Effendi had to confront not only several overt attacks on his leadership, but also the more subtle and insidious challenges represented by patronizing acceptance of his role, attacks on his policies, and perhaps most dangerously, apathy.

The most immediate challenge to his authority came from the partisans of Mírzá Muḥammad ʿAlí. Even prior to the first reading of ʿAbduʾl-Bahá's Will, Muḥammad ʿAlí publicly addressed the Bahaʾis in the local

3. Shoghi Effendi

Arabic language newspapers, calling upon them all to accept his leadership in accordance with Bahá'u'lláh's declaration in the *Kitáb-i ʿAhdí* that after the *Ghuṣn-i Aʿẓam* (ʿAbdu'l-Bahá), he, the *Ghuṣn-i Akbar*, had been chosen, a call publicly rebutted by the Baha'i House of Spirituality in Cairo. Indeed, in Palestine and Egypt, ʿAbdu'l-Bahá's death appears to have strengthened the resolve of the Baha'is loyal to ʿAbdu'l-Bahá to completely shun the 'violators of the Covenant' (*Náqiḍín*), a resolve strengthened by the renewed stress on the need for vigilance in this matter which ʿAbdu'l-Bahá had made during the last months of his life and which was again emphasized in his Will. Of particular importance here was ʿAbdu'l-Bahá's emphatic statement that the 'Center of Sedition', Mírzá Muḥammad ʿAlí, had 'passed out from under the shadow of the Cause' and 'been cut off from the Holy Tree'.[8] From the standpoint of those loyal to ʿAbdu'l-Bahá, Muḥammad ʿAlí had, by his actions, totally forfeited such rights as he may have been accorded in the *Kitáb-i ʿAhdí*. In obedience to ʿAbdu'l-Bahá's previous statements and those made in his Will, the breakers of the Covenant were now to be utterly shunned and avoided. This was 'one of the greatest and most fundamental principles of the Cause of God'.[9] As one Baha'i stressed, whilst ʿAbdu'l-Bahá had had the prerogative to be 'loving and kind to his enemies', his followers could not allow themselves any such compromise.[10]

Whilst Muḥammad ʿAlí's 'Unitarians' continued their activities in various parts of the world for a while – including the inauguration of a short-lived *Behai Quarterly* in Kenosha in 1934[11] – they constituted little real threat to the loyalty of most Baha'is to Shoghi Effendi. Still regarding themselves as Baha'is, they were more effectively cut off from the 'Baha'i world' than ever before. Remaining as a number of extended and interrelated families, they continued to pose a persistent local problem to Shoghi Effendi, however, even after Muḥammad ʿAlí's death in 1937.

Of those loyal to ʿAbdu'l-Bahá the vast majority accepted Shoghi Effendi's succession without demur. This was perhaps especially the case in the East where the long-established Baha'i communities had grown used to vigilance in defence of the Covenant during the course of the extended struggles with the *Náqiḍín*. Loyalty to Shoghi Effendi was a straightforward extension of loyalty to ʿAbdu'l-Bahá and the Covenant. However surprised they may have been at the inauguration of a new form of leadership, most seem simply to have been pleased that the Cause once again had a leader, a living centre towards whom all could turn as an expression of their unity. Again, not only had ʿAbdu'l-Bahá already required the Baha'i properties in Iran to be registered in the name of Shoghi Rabbani,[12] but in the East the general principle of hereditary religious leadership was well known and understood, the example of the Imamate perhaps being seen as a ready parallel to the Guardianship.

In the East, then, there was little outright opposition to Shoghi Effendi's leadership or plans. With the exception of a short-lived opposition group in Egypt (the Scientific Society) established by an Armenian Baha'i in the early 1920s, those who came out in opposition to Shoghi Effendi remained solitary individuals, cast out completely from the Baha'i community and presumably still regarded with considerable suspicion by the Muslim majority.

In the West, however, the situation was different. The Baha'is were for the most part relatively new in the Faith, and were almost all first-generation converts who had chosen to become Baha'is as a result of their own, often highly individualistic, religious quests. Whilst there were a good many 'seasoned believers' whose loyalty to, and understanding of, the Covenant doctrine had already been well proven, they belonged to a movement which also included a great many people who were profoundly suspicious of anything suggestive of external religious authority. Shoghi Effendi's transformation of the pattern of leadership – particularly his stress on organization – readily engendered opposition which was ideological as well as personalistic in nature.

The development of the Administrative Order

The process of development of the Baha'i Administrative Order, which was so characteristic of the period of Shoghi Effendi's leadership, was begun within three months of his assumption of office. In March 1922, at his request, there gathered in Haifa a group of well-known Baha'is representative of the communities of America and Europe. Representatives of the Eastern communities only arrived later. At this meeting Shoghi evidently stressed the need for there to be functioning local and national administrative bodies throughout the Baha'i world before the anticipated Universal House of Justice could be established. He also gave priority to the consolidation of the movement before its further expansion.[13] Specifically, the Executive Board of the American Bahai Temple Unity was to change from being a merely executive body, implementing the Convention delegates' decisions, into being also a legislative one, guiding all national Baha'i affairs. This message was reinforced by a letter received shortly before the April Convention in which Shoghi Effendi called for the establishment of Local Assemblies wherever there were more than nine adult Baha'is, and directed that all Baha'i activities should be placed under the authority of Local and National Spiritual Assemblies, the national body being given responsibility for determining their respective spheres of interest, as well as for managing all national teaching, reviewing, publishing, temple and archival work, for receiving Orientals, and for identifying those who threatened the unity of the Cause.[14] Jurisdiction over the *Star of the West* and other national activities was straightaway transferred to the new National Assembly, new committees responsible for these various national activities being appointed.

In March 1923 Shoghi Effendi issued a second lengthy letter on the subject of administration, addressed to all the various Western Baha'i communities, including those in Japan and Australasia.[15] In this letter he detailed the responsibilities, powers and processes for annual election of these Assemblies (direct elections at local level, indirect elections through a system of delegates at national level), and called for the setting-up of local and national Baha'i Funds under the exclusive control of the Spiritual Assemblies. Subsequent elaborations of detail and guidance as to the general 'spirit' of Baha'i administration aside, such was to remain the essential system of Baha'i administration until Shoghi Effendi's appointment of the International Baha'i Council and of functioning Hands of the Cause in 1951.

The formation of Local and National Assemblies progressed as circumstances permitted. National Assemblies were only formed in the larger communities. The most marked administrative progress occurred in North America, where 43 Local Assemblies had been formed by 1925,[16] the year in which the full transformation of the old Executive Board of the Bahai Temple Unity into the new National Spiritual Assembly of the Baha'is of the United States and Canada was completed. Elsewhere the proper formation of Local Assemblies occurred more slowly, quite large local communities (as in some parts of Iran) being relatively unorganized. Nevertheless, National Assemblies were instituted in England, Germany and India in 1923, and in Egypt in 1924, whilst a system of central co-ordinating Assemblies was adopted in Iran, Iraq, Russian Turkestan and the Caucasus. The two Russian central Assemblies soon ceased to operate, following the severe restrictions imposed by the Soviet authorities from 1928 onwards, but the Iraqi and Persian Baha'is were afterwards enabled to form proper National Assemblies in 1931 and 1934 respectively. Also in 1934, the Baha'is of Australia and New Zealand formed their own

National Assembly. Thereafter no new National Assemblies were formed until 1948, after which there was a rapid rate of progress (see pp. 160–1).

Besides this formation of Local and National Assemblies with their attendant funds and committees, the most important administrative developments of the twenties and early thirties were the placing of this burgeoning administration on a definite legal basis and the adoption of specific membership requirements for those who wished to be part of the Baha'i community. These developments first occurred in America and were then adopted by the other National Assemblies. The preparatory step to national legal incorporation was accomplished in 1927 by the adoption of a Declaration of Trust and accompanying by-laws, the Department of State issuing the necessary certificate of incorporation in May 1929, thus enabling the National Assembly to enter into contract, hold property and receive bequests.[17] Most other National Assemblies followed suit in the thirties. The basis for local incorporation was provided in 1931 by the New York Baha'is drafting a set of local by-laws which soon became the pattern for all local Baha'i constitutions throughout the world.

The acquisition of a definite legal status also involved the delineation of specific membership requirements for voting members of the Baha'i community. These were taken from a letter of Shoghi Effendi in 1925 and were included in Article II of the National By-Laws.[18] Other administrative developments in America were the initiation of a National Assembly *Baha'i News Letter* (in 1924); the establishment of a National Baha'i Office (in 1925), the National Secretary becoming a full-time paid official; the preparation of a membership roll; the introduction of 'enrolment cards' on which to record the professions of faith of would-be new believers, and of 'credential cards' by which to validate membership; the acquisition of properties at which Baha'i summer schools might be held; and the restructuring of the regular Nineteen Day Feast so as to include a specific administrative section. These developments were, again, generally emulated by other National Assemblies. Western Baha'is were also introduced to a new Arabic term by which to describe the national or local Baha'i administrative headquarters, referred to by Shoghi Effendi as the *Ḥaẓíratu'l-Quds*, the Sacred Fold.

Opposition in the West

In America the accession to power and authority of the Local, and more especially of the National Assembly, could not but be tremendously controversial given the existing sentiments about organization. Initially, at least, the newly formed National Spiritual Assembly appears to have gained a fair measure of support, Shoghi Effendi himself expressing his surprise in December 1922 that 'the darkness of doubts, of fears and mistrust' had vanished so speedily.[19] That the National Assembly members themselves were well aware of 'some misapprehension . . . as to the need of organization in the Cause', however, was demonstrated by the appearance of a lengthy article on 'Bahaʾi Organization: Its Basis in the Revealed Word', which appeared in the March 1923 issue of *Star of the West*. Evidently seeking to assuage the fears of those 'liberal minded people' who 'rebel against the restraint to which they sincerely think organization subjects them', the authors cited ʿAbduʾl-Bahá's various references to the need for organization in the Cause as well as in the world in general, referred to ʿAbduʾl-Bahá's own qualification of his much quoted saying that 'the Bahai Cause can never be organized' as meaning that the necessary organization of the Cause can never be rigid, and stressed the flexible, non-exclusive and naturally evolving nature of Bahaʾi organization. Again, when the March 1923 directive from Shoghi Effendi first appeared in *Star of the West*, it did so in a heavily amended form which omitted all reference to administrative change, only giving Shoghi Effendi's appeal for the Bahaʾis to be united, to teach and to be steadfast in the Covenant.

As subsequent events were to demonstrate, there were a good number of American Bahaʾis who were not altogether happy with this increased stress on organization. At the present time, however, it is not possible to gauge the extent of this discontent. It seems that the level varied greatly: if there were some who were sufficiently discontented as to actually cease to be members of the community, there were others whose disquiet was no more than slight and temporary. Moreover, it should not be forgotten that for many American Bahaʾis, the further development of organization was to be welcomed, whilst for others it was at least tolerable given their commitment to the doctrine of the Covenant and their pleasure at once again having a leader. As Mountfort Mills reported to the April 1922 Congress and Convention in Chicago, shortly after his return from seeing Shoghi Effendi, the impression given in Haifa was that God was in his heaven and that 'all is well with the world'. Whilst there, they had lost their sense of sadness at their loss of ʿAbduʾl-Bahá:

> The Master is not gone. His Spirit is present with greater intensity and power, freed from bodily limitations. We can take it into our own hearts and reflect it in greater degrees. In the center of this radiation stands Shoghi Effendi. The Spirit

streams forth from this young man. He is indeed young in face, form and manner, yet his heart is the center of the world today. The character and spirit divine scintillate from him today. He alone can today save the world and make true civilization.[20]

Opposition tendencies amongst the Western Baha'is were at first somewhat inchoate. Indeed, Harrison Gray Dyar (1866–1929), the editor of the New York based Baha'i magazine *Reality* (1922–9) and the first person to mount an extended attack against the newly developing administration, expressed his views in a conceptual language so far removed from that which normally prevailed within Baha'i circles that it seems unlikely that he attracted more than peripheral support.[21] More effective was the extensive publicity campaign mounted by Ruth White from 1926 through to the 1930s.[22] Resolutely opposed to all forms of Baha'i organization and feeling that she was 'guided' by 'Higher Powers', White came to believe that ʿAbdu'l-Bahá's Will was a forgery, a notion which even opponents of Shoghi Effendi and of the Baha'i Faith have found unconvincing.[23] Generally unable to convince the American Baha'is of this assertion, she succeeded in gaining some support in Germany. As a result a small and short-lived breakaway Baha'i World Union was formed in about 1930. White renewed her campaign in the 1940s, but seemingly with no result. Whilst several of the German 'Free Baha'is' have remained active, White herself eventually found a new spiritual home, becoming a devotee of Meher Baba.

A far more sustained and serious attack on 'organization' came from ʿAbdu'l-Bahá's former secretary and interpreter, Mirza Ahmad Sohrab (1891–1958). Sohrab had long been a proponent of an 'inclusivist' conception of the Baha'i Cause, and had already come into conflict with those 'orthodox' American Baha'is whom he described as clinging to 'the dark ages of blind authority'.[24] Having moved to New York in 1927, he soon came into conflict with the local Baha'i Assembly when he began to lecture extensively on Baha'i without securing their continued approval. Matters reached a head in April 1929, when, feeling that the Baha'i Cause was making no progress whatsoever, Sohrab joined with others to form the New History Society, which was dedicated to the promotion of Baha'i ideals. Rapidly expanding its activities, the New History Society was quickly perceived by the Local and National Assemblies as a threat to Baha'i unity. When attempts to bring the Society under administrative control proved unavailing, the National Assembly, with Shoghi Effendi's subsequent approval, publicly announced to the Baha'is that Sohrab's New History Society activities were to be regarded as being 'independent of the Cause' and 'in no wise entitled to the cooperation of the Bahaʾis'.[25]

The immediate effect of this decision on the American Bahaʾi community is difficult to gauge. Whilst Sohrab's overt rejection of Bahaʾi administration had aroused intense indignation amongst some Bahaʾis, the liberalism and extensiveness of the Society's teaching work had aroused great admiration amongst others. In the short run at least, many Bahaʾis, particularly in the New York area, would appear to have been attracted by the Society's activities. Nevertheless, after the *de facto* excommunication of 1930, it seems likely that most of this support fell away, the Society recruiting new members and sympathizers from outside the Bahaʾi community. With a membership of 1,200 or so by June 1931, the Society continued to promote a broad and inclusivist conception of the Bahaʾi principles. It was more or less ignored by the Bahaʾis loyal to Shoghi Effendi.

The Society again came into prominence in 1939 when it opened a 'Bahaʾi bookshop' in New York. A public dispute ensued (1939–41), in which the National Assembly unsuccessfully sought to sue Sohrab for his unauthorized use of the name 'Bahaʾi'. Sohrab then gave lengthy vent to his feelings against Shoghi Effendi and the Bahaʾi administration, most notably in his book, *Broken Silence* (1942). Although this affair created unfavourable publicity for the Bahaʾis, the public conflict with Sohrab appears to have had little effect on the American Bahaʾis, beyond making them more concerned with defence of the Covenant. Shoghi Effendi, however, now took a far harder line with those who rejected his authority, a long-developing dispute with various members of his family – his brother, sisters, aunts, uncles and cousins – finding resolution in their excommunication in 1941–2.

The overall effect of these various attacks on Bahaʾi organization and on Shoghi Effendi's authority as Guardian is difficult to evaluate. At one level their effect appears to have been negligible in that few Bahaʾis actually transferred their allegiance from the Bahaʾi 'organization' to the various anti-establishment groups. More generally, however, the prolonged period from the early twenties to the early thirties during which the developing administration in America was subjected to almost constant attack by its opponents appears to have completed the process of polarization which was already evident in the period of the Chicago Reading Room affair. There was no longer an unequivocal common allegiance to a charismatic authority figure which could serve to unite the 'organizers' and the 'anti-organizers'. Shoghi Effendi himself plainly asserted that his leadership was part of an evolving system of administration and that obedience to that Administrative Order was an essential part of being a Baha'i. It was an exclusivist view of the Baha'i Faith which was now officially promoted, and those who still subscribed to the earlier inclusivism now found themselves increasingly out of step with the prevailing spirit animating the community. Ultimately, perhaps, they had but little choice, having either to change and adapt their own perceptions and relationship with the Cause or to grow away from it. Those who chose to assert a directly oppositional view were few, but those who became confused, dispirited or disaffected were more in number. Thus throughout the 1920s the National Assembly expressed its concern about the poor response to its plans, referring to 'periods of doubt and foreboding', to crisis or stagnation in support for its new National Fund – in which regard Shoghi Effendi himself referred to the 'feeble and uncertain' response – and to a general lack of growth, sympathizing with the 'indifference' towards 'the material side' of the Cause by those Baha'is who had originally been attracted by its 'pure spirituality', and rejoicing at a perceived transition 'from negative loyalty to positive devotion' and from 'irresolution' to 'exhilaration'.[26]

ADMINISTRATION AND SUCCESSION, 1950–85

Institutional developments, 1950–7

In his *Will and Testament* ʿAbduʾl-Bahá had referred to the two institutions of the Guardianship and the Universal House of Justice as jointly assuming authority over the Baha'i world after his death. Initially, Shoghi Effendi himself (as with many other Baha'is throughout the world) evidently anticipated the imminent formation of the Universal House of Justice, calling to Haifa early in 1922 a number of leading Baha'is for consultations. After these meetings, however, he appears to have become convinced that a firmer establishment of local and national administrative bodies was required prior to the election of the Universal House of Justice, these constituting the 'bedrock' upon which it could be raised. The possibility of election seems again to have been considered in the late twenties, but the opposition to organization expressed by some Western Baha'is, together with what his widow later felt sure was a paternalistic attitude displayed towards him by certain prominent individuals who aspired to be elected to the House of Justice, appears to have convinced him that he should postpone the election yet further.[27] In the meantime various interim institutions were considered, notably the possible establishment of an International Baha'i Secretariat in Haifa, but other events intervened and no such body was formed. The International Bahaʾi Bureau in Geneva (1925–57), however, with its tri-lingual (English, French and German) *Bahaʾi Bulletin*, was regarded as fulfilling some of its functions.

The necessary administrative 'bedrock' slowly emerged. By 1950 the 'present adequate maturity' of nine 'vigorously functioning' National Assemblies decided Shoghi Effendi to appoint eight members to an International Bahaʾi Council, the Council itself being seen as the forerunner of the Universal House of Justice. The formation of this body was announced to the Bahaʾi world in January 1951. In December it was followed by the announcement of the appointment of the 'first contingent' of Hands of the Cause of God twelve in number, three each being appointed in Asia, North America, Europe and the Bahaʾi World Centre in Haifa–ʿAkká. Both institutions were seen as evolutionary in concept, Shoghi Effendi subsequently further delineating their role and enlarging their memberships.[28]

In addition to their existing individual administrative and teaching tasks, the Hands of the Cause were charged with assisting the various National Spiritual Assemblies in their attainment of the goals of the Ten Year Crusade, and later with the 'primary obligation' of protecting (in collaboration with the National Assemblies) the Bahaʾi world community from the attacks of its external and internal enemies. In the prosecution of these tasks the Hands were directed to appoint Auxiliary Boards, whose members were to act as their 'deputies, assistants and advisers'. The first set of Boards, established in 1954, came to be concerned with the propagation of the Faith, whilst a second set, established in 1957, was concerned with its protection. From 1954 onwards, with the exception of those Hands resident at the World Centre, the Hands and their Auxiliary Board Members were organized on a continental basis, Continental Bahaʾi Funds being established to facilitate their work. In 1952 the 12 initial Hands of the Cause were augmented to 19 in number, this figure being further raised in 1957 to a total of 27 (3 × 9). In the same year the number of the Board Members, initially 36 (4 × 9), was doubled with the creation of the new Boards for Protection.

The International Bahaʾi Council, five of whose members came to be appointed as Hands of the Cause, was initially given the tasks of forging links with the authorities of the Israeli state, of conducting negotiations regarding matters of personal status with the civil authorities (presumably with a view to the establishment of a Bahaʾi court) and of assisting Shoghi Effendi in the completion of the superstructure of the Báb's Shrine.

Effectively functioning as an International Secretariat, the Council members worked at a wide range of endeavours under Shoghi Effendi's direction. Most became residents of Haifa. In 1955 a ninth member was appointed.

The Hands of the Cause, 1957–63

Shoghi Effendi died unexpectedly on 4 November 1957 during a visit to London and was buried there. Two weeks later all bar one of the Hands of the Cause gathered together in conclave in Haifa. This was the first ever meeting of the Hands as a whole group. A search was made for any document which Shoghi Effendi might have left in guidance as to what should be done in the event of his death. None was found, and as care had been taken to seal his room at the time of the first news of his death it seemed evident that the Guardian had left no Will, appointed no successor, nor given any definite instructions as to what was to be done. Still grief-stricken at their bereavement, the Hands were now plunged into bewilderment and despair as to the future of the Baha'i Cause. In his last general letter to the Baha'is of the world, dated October 1957, Shoghi Effendi had referred to the Hands as 'the Chief Stewards of Bahá'u'lláh's embryonic World Commonwealth, who have been invested . . . with the dual function of guarding over the security, and of insuring the propagation of [the] Faith',[29] and it was in their capacity as 'Chief Stewards' that the Hands now acted.

On 25 November, at the end of their Conclave, the Hands issued a Proclamation 'to the Baha'is of East and West' stating that there was no Will and no appointed heir; that due to the death or declared Covenant-breaking of all of Bahá'u'lláh's male descendants no successor could have been appointed by him; that the institutions of the Cause were firmly established and that the goals of the present plan were set; that the International Baha'i Council would, in the course of time, evolve into the Universal House of Justice, 'that supreme body upon which infallibility . . . is divinely conferred'; and that for the present, a body of nine Hands had been constituted to serve at the Baha'i World Centre to deal with the affairs of the Cause. The Baha'is were urged to be firm in the Covenant and to teach the Faith. As was implicit in the Proclamation and is clear from various legal and other documents that were drawn up at the time, the Hands now constituted 'the Supreme Body of the Bahá'í World Community', and, subject to their direction, the nine Hands serving in Haifa – the 'Custodians of the Faith' – were to exercise 'all such functions,

4. The Hands of the Cause of God, Haifa, 1963

rights and powers in succession to the Guardian' as were necessary to serve the interests of the Faith until the due establishment of the House of Justice.[30] All 26 Hands present in Haifa signed these various documents; all the National and Regional Assemblies officially recognized their authority, as did the various bank and government officials in the state of Israel with respect to the Bahaʾi properties and funds held at the World Centre.

At first it seemed that there would be no problem in this dramatic and totally unexpected accession of the Hands to the position of supreme authority in the direction of the affairs of the Faith. As they reported in various early letters, no challenge to their actions or decisions had been made by either the Covenant-breakers or other enemies of the Cause, and the Bahaʾis everywhere had stood firm in the Covenant. The Bahaʾi world seemed united in its grief and dedication. From their second Conclave, held in November 1958, the Hands announced that the Universal House of Justice should be established at the time of the Most Great Jubilee at Riḍván in 1963, so that 'once again a precious source of divine infallibility will return to the earth'. At their third Conclave, held in the autumn of 1959, a plan of action was adopted to accomplish this goal, with the call being made for the formation of 33 of the projected new National Assemblies in 1961 and 1962 so that there would be a 'wide and representative' base for the election of the Universal House of Justice. At the same time, it was announced that at Riḍván in 1961 there would be a postal ballot in which the members of all duly constituted National Assemblies would vote for the nine members of a new, elected International Baha'i Council to replace the existing appointed body and to serve as a preparatory step to the formation of the House of Justice. All the Baha'is in the world, with the exception of the Hands of the Cause, were to be considered eligible for election to this body. This new Council would work under the direction of the Hands resident in the Holy Land.[31]

Charles Mason Remey and his claims

Opposition to this move came from Charles Mason Remey, the veteran American Hand of the Cause and president of the International Baha'i Council. Apparently, Remey had already tried to convince his fellow Hands that the Guardianship had to be continued in order for the administration to survive and for the Faith to continue to progress. Unsuccessful in these attempts, Remey went into 'voluntary exile' after the 1959 Conclave. In 1960 he proclaimed that he was the Second Guardian of the Faith. As he was subsequently to explain, the idea that he might become Guardian had occurred to him at the time of the 1957 Conclave, but in the confusion of the time he had succumbed to the majority opinion and so signed the proclamation that no successor had been, or could have been appointed by Shoghi Effendi. In retrospect, however, he had come to realize that by appointing him as president of the International Council, Shoghi Effendi had covertly appointed him as his successor, for the Council would evolve into the Universal House of Justice, whose president, according to ʿAbdu'l-Bahá, would be the Guardian. The Baha'is of the world were called upon to accept him.

For the most part Remey's hopes for recognition were not realized. 'Almost the entire Baha'i world', as Remey himself admitted, 'endorsed the violation of the Hands of the Faith' in their repudiation of him.[32] Rejecting Remey's claims, the Hands had, by October 1960, declared Remey and those who followed him Covenant-breakers, expelled them from the Faith and forbidden all association with them.

They argued that as Remey had not only not received any written appointment from Shoghi Effendi to be his successor, but was not even a descendant of Bahá'u'lláh, there was no possibility of his claim being accepted. Whilst the vast majority of Baha'is accepted this judgement, Remey's widely circulated claims were taken seriously by quite a number of Bahaʾis who were disturbed by the absence of a 'living Guardian'. This was a crisis, albeit one that the Hands successfully defused. Those whose doubts were sufficient to cause them to follow Mason Remey into excommunication from the rest of the Bahaʾis may not have been many, but they were widely spread throughout the Bahaʾi world. According to one of Remey's leading followers there were, in 1963, 'Bahaʾis under the Guardianship' in some 15 countries of Latin America, Europe, Africa and the Indian Ocean, exclusive of the two larger (Remeyite) communities in the United States and Pakistan.[33]

Entirely cut off from the majority of the Bahaʾis, the group that followed Mason Remey (the self-termed 'Bahaʾis under the Hereditary Guardianship' or 'Orthodox Bahaʾis) was subject to its own complex development. There is a confusion of claims and counter-claims, but before his own death in 1974 (at the age of 99), Remey appears to have separately appointed various individuals to be his successor. As a consequence of this, even prior to Remey's death, his American followers, at least, divided into a number of separate groups, each following a different successor or claimant to supreme authority.

The election of the Universal House of Justice

For most Bahaʾis, Mason Remey soon became just one more in the succession of Covenant-breakers who had unsuccessfully sought to undermine the unity of the Faith. Almost the entirety of the national and international leadership of the Faith were united in their rejection of Remey's claims, and whatever worries may have existed as to the future of the Cause without a present living Guardian, the sense of the rapid progress of the Faith, the anticipation of the imminent election of the infallible House of Justice, and the personal affection felt for many of the Hands of the Cause militated in favour of acceptance of the Hands' decision. The plans for the election of the new International Bahaʾi Council went smoothly into effect in 1961, and in April 1963 nearly 300 of the members of the 56 National Spiritual Assemblies elected in 1962 gathered together in Haifa for the first International Bahaʾi Convention and the election of the Universal House of Justice. The election of that nine-man body having been accomplished, they travelled to London for the celebration of the Most Great Jubilee (28 April to 2 May 1963), the commemoration of Baháʾuʾlláh's declaration in Baghdad 100 years previously. The jubilant and emotional celebration in London, attended by nearly 7,000 Bahaʾis, marked not only the first large-scale gathering of

Baha'is on a global scale, but provided a reaffirmation of the unity and perceived continuity of divine guidance after the 'interregnum' following Shoghi Effendi's death. The assembled Baha'is, coming from a multitude of racial and religious backgrounds, offered to each other an impressive proof of the growing universality of the Baha'i religion, whilst the nearness of Shoghi Effendi's grave provided a further focus for a sense of renewed dedication.

Administrative developments under the Universal House of Justice

The establishment of the Universal House of Justice once again provided the Baha'is with what they regarded as a source of divinely guided authority. In terms of Shoghi Effendi's delineation of the structure of Baha'i administration, important theoretical and practical questions remained to be resolved, however. In particular, as the House of Justice soon stated, it could find no way in which the line of Guardians could be continued. This cessation of the living Guardianship represented a 'grievous loss', the significance of which could not be underestimated.[34] Only the Guardians were assured of interpretative infallibility. Without a continuing line of Guardians, there could be no further authoritative interpretations of doctrine. The existing interpretations of ʿAbdu'l-Bahá and Shoghi Effendi were extensive and detailed, but they could not now be supplemented. The continuing unity and progress of the Faith were not thereby imperilled, however. The Universal House of Justice was empowered to function independently of the Guardianship and was assured of infallibility in both its legislation and its protection of the Cause. It now represented the sole centre of divine guidance, delineating its powers in a written Constitution (1972) and establishing a series of subsidiary departments to further its various functions.

Without a living Guardian, the House of Justice concluded that it was not possible to appoint any further Hands of the Cause. However, it was possible to establish institutions which would continue the responsibilities and functions exercised by the Hands, particularly those functions concerned with the protection and propagation of the Faith. To this end, two new institutions were created. The first, the Continental Boards of Counsellors (est. 1968), was charged with the administration of the Auxiliary Boards and the general review of activities on a continental or sub-continental basis. By 1985 there were 5 such Boards and a total of 72 Continental Counsellors. The second institution was the International

5. The members of the Universal House of Justice, Haifa, 1983

Teaching Centre (est. 1973), a body comprising all of the Hands of the Cause and a number of specially appointed Counsellors (at present seven) to be resident in Haifa. The responsibilities of the Teaching Centre include the direction of the Continental Boards, liaison with the House of Justice, information gathering, and the preparation of teaching plans. The number of Board Members has also been greatly increased (by 1985 there were 622), and they have been empowered to appoint assistants to aid them in their work. As to the Hands of the Cause, only 9 out of the 27 alive in 1957 still remain. Freed now of all administrative responsibilities, these individuals are encouraged to devote their energies to the 'spiritual inspiration' of the Bahaʾi world.

AUTHORITY AND LEADERSHIP IN THE CONTEMPORARY BAHAʾI COMMUNITY

With supreme authority now vested in the Universal House of Justice, the Bahaʾi community has completed the process which Max Weber termed the 'routinization of charisma'.[35] The original charismatic power of one regarded as a Manifestation of God has become 'routinized' in an elected institution. Although regarded as providing infallible guidance for the development of the Bahaʾi religion, the institution of the House of Justice comprises individual human beings who bear no divine afflatus. Only as a collectivity do the members of the Universal House of Justice exercise their authority over the Bahaʾi world.

This depersonalization of authority represents a further stage in a process of progressive routinization earlier exemplified by the 'humanization' of supreme authority in the person of ʿAbduʾl-Bahá and by its institutionalization in the Guardianship of Shoghi Effendi. A further process of depersonalization has occurred at the level of secondary leadership within the Bahaʾi religion. During the lifetime of Baháʾuʾlláh the great teachers and Hands of the Cause exercised a considerable personal authority, albeit always strictly subordinated to that of Baháʾuʾlláh. Such individuals retained their importance under the leadership of ʿAbduʾl-Bahá, but increasing stress was placed on the newly instituted elective Assemblies. Under Shoghi Effendi, these Assemblies, formed at local and national level, were invested with all the powers and authority to administer the affairs of the Cause in their localities. Consequently, when the institution of Hands of the Cause was revived it was in a markedly different institutional context. Indeed, a clear distinction was now made between the institutions of the 'rulers' and the 'learned'.[36] Administrative authority rested with the Assemblies as 'rulers', whilst the 'learned' (the Hands of the Cause and their related institutions) assumed a more general role in the encouragement and assistance of the Bahaʾis. As individuals, the newly appointed Hands were doubtless very influential, but they had little direct power until the period of the unforeseen 'interregnum' of 1957–63. After 1963 the Hands returned to their former role, except that most now functioned as more or less full-time travelling Bahaʾi teachers. Those who now came to assume many of their functions, the Counsellors, were plainly of a different rank from the Hands. Possessing less individual authority than the Hands and being appointed to only five-year terms of office, the Counsellors again represent a more depersonalized form of leadership. More intangibly, whilst the Hands gained great respect and even devotion as the most prominent link with the vanished days of the Guardianship, the Counsellors occupy a more strictly functional role of more limited symbolic significance.

The formal structure of present-day Bahaʾi administration is illustrated in Figure 1. Under the supreme authority of the Universal House of Justice are the two institutional 'arms' of the Faith. To the left of the diagram are the 'rulers', the Local and National Spiritual Assemblies

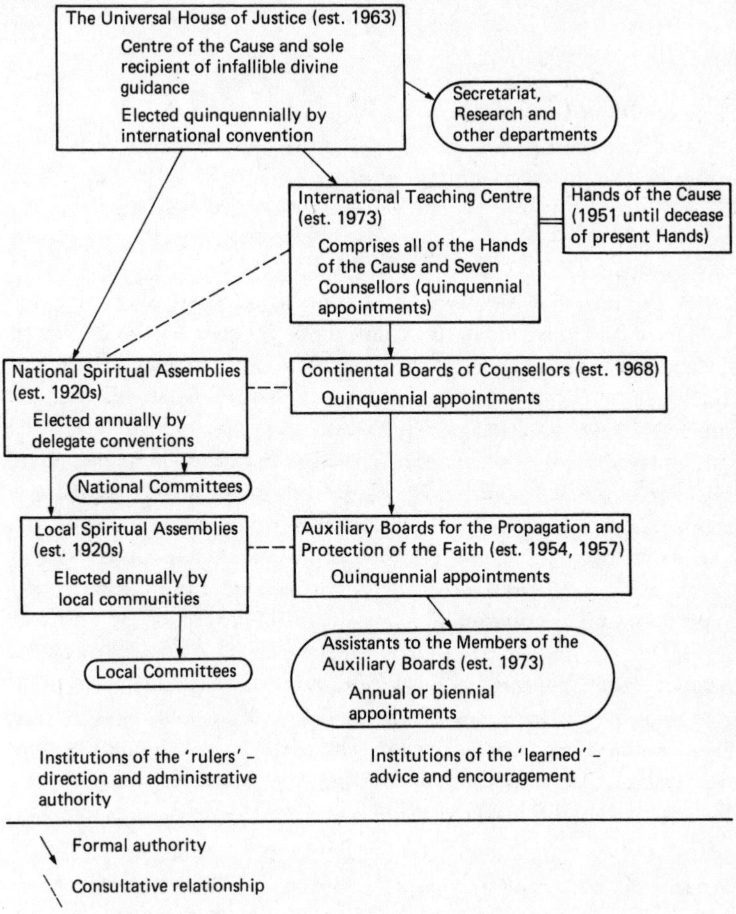

Figure 1. The present-day structure of Bahaʾi administration

charged with the direction of the affairs of the Faith in their respective areas. To their right are the institutions of the 'learned' (International Teaching Centre, Hands, Boards of Counsellors and Auxiliary Boards). Various departments, committees and assistants work under these institutions.

9

MODERN BAHAʾI MOTIFS

Given the relatively strong central control exercised over what are considered the most important elements of modern Bahaʾi belief and practice, it is appropriate to preface a discussion of the religion's present dominant motifs with an account of the writings of the Guardian and the Universal House of Justice, which, with the exception of material written on behalf of the Universal House of Justice by its various departments, are considered authoritative and generally binding on the mass of the Bahaʾis. It should be noted, however, that despite this strong central control – seen most explicitly in the present review of all literature published under Bahaʾi auspices and the clear distinction made between authoritative and non-authoritative material[1] – a considerable degree of flexibility is allowed, especially with regard to matters which are relatively peripheral to central Bahaʾi concerns (such as metaphysics). Indeed, in general, it is by sustained emphasis on official belief and practice, and by the relativization of non-official views rather than by any attempt at their suppression, that orthodoxy and orthopraxy are maintained. As the Universal House of Justice explained in May 1966:

> individual interpretation is considered the fruit of man's rational power and conducive to a better understanding of the teachings, provided that no disputes or arguments arise among the friends and the individual himself understands and makes it clear that his views are merely his own. Individual interpretations continually change as one grows in comprehension of the teachings . . . The friends must therefore learn . . . to express their own views without pressing them on their fellow Bahaʾis.[2]

Modern Bahaʾi authoritative literature

Most modern Western Bahaʾi literature – whether scripture, commentary, or introduction to the Faith – dates from the 1930s at the earliest. That this is the case is perhaps above all the consequence of the fact that Shoghi Effendi's leadership, his interpretation of the Faith, with all its differences from that which obtained in the West prior to the 1920s, has become the dominant vision which formal statements of Baha'i belief now reflect. Although there are strong continuities between the early Eastern and Western Baha'is and their modern-day successors, it is clear that to a considerable degree modern Baha'i 'ideology' is the 'creation' of Shoghi Effendi in both its overall balance and in many points of detail. This 'creational' element is present not just in those areas of belief and practice to which Shoghi Effendi devoted much of his own original writings – pre-eminently the administration and the concepts of 'world order' – but more subtly throughout most major areas of Baha'i thinking, where Shoghi Effendi in his role as interpreter of Baha'i scripture provided what Baha'is regard as authoritative translation and interpretation.

The matter of translation possesses a particularly subtle importance in this regard, for until very recently the majority of the major items of translated scripture available to most Baha'is were originally translated by Shoghi Effendi. Even now only the works translated by him (into English) are regarded as fully authoritative translations. Moreover, these translations have themselves now effectively become the original writings in that further translations into other languages are generally made, at Shoghi Effendi's instructions, not from the original texts, but from his translations. Even prior to Shoghi Effendi's appointment as Guardian the work of translation was one to which he attached a particular significance and he had gone to Oxford specifically to perfect his English for that task, later devoting considerable attention to it.[3]

Besides translations, Shoghi Effendi's main literary output consisted of an enormous number of letters written by him or on his behalf to the Baha'is of the world, together with one book, his interpretative survey of the first hundred years of Babi and Baha'i history, *God Passes By* (1944). This extensive body of writings provided the Baha'is with authoritative commentaries and statements which represented a formalization of orthodox doctrine and defined what was to be considered as canonical scripture.[4] Additionally, Shoghi Effendi's published and unpublished writings now constitute a primary source used by the Universal House of Justice in its deliberations.

In that the Universal House of Justice is essentially a legislative body rather than one concerned with the interpretation of scripture, Shoghi Effendi's interpretation and formalization of Baha'i doctrine remains largely as it was during his lifetime. However, in that one of the primary tasks which the House of Justice has set itself is the collection, preservation, collation and classification of Baha'i sacred texts and authoritative writings, the process of formalization continues, particularly symbolized by the publication of a 'synopsis and codification' of the *Kitábu'l-Aqdas* (1973), but also by a whole series of compilations on various Baha'i subjects taken from the writings of Bahá'u'lláh, ʿAbdu'l-Bahá and Shoghi Effendi.[5]

As to the collection of texts, as of 1983 over 60,000 original writings or copies had been collected, comprising some 15,000 from Bahá'u'lláh, nearly 27,000 from ʿAbdu'l-Bahá, and over 17,500 from Shoghi Effendi.[6] The Universal House of Justice has also had produced on its behalf fresh translations: a volume of Bahá'u'lláh's major writings from the post-Aqdas period (1978) and a volume of selected writings each from the Báb (1976) and ʿAbdu'l-Bahá (1978). Some of the House of Justice's own numerous letters have also been published (1969, 1976), as has its Constitution (1972).

It should be noted that whilst the primary languages of Baha'i discourse during the Heroic Age were Persian and Arabic, under Shoghi Effendi's leadership English effectively became the religion's working language, a development which has been accentuated under the Universal House of Justice. Whilst Shoghi Effendi wrote extensively in Persian and to a lesser extent in Arabic, it was his writings in English (together with his translations) which became normative for international Baha'i belief and practice. Under the Universal House of Justice decisions are made in English and may then be translated into Persian or Arabic.

THE POLAR MOTIF

Despite the absence of continuing theophany, the polar motif continues to be of crucial importance in modern Baha'ism. Its continuing centrality is demonstrated by the almost total allegiance given by the Baha'is to the successive centres of their Faith despite the change from strong charismatic leadership to various forms of rational-legal authority, and the considerable uncertainties involved in the initial successions to both ʿAbdu'l-Bahá and Shoghi Effendi. In the face of well-organized campaigns of opposition to the leadership of both Shoghi Effendi and the Hands of the Cause, the overwhelming mass of Baha'is chose to remain 'firm' in the Covenant and thus maintained the unity and much of the momentum of their religion (the 1920s 'doldrums' in the West notwithstanding). By contrast, those who followed the various opposition leaders appear to have been far less able to retain their unity and momentum, and neither the inclusivist New History Society nor the various factions of

6. The Seat of the Universal House of Justice

those who followed Mason Remey have remained viable threats to the Baha'i mainstream. Even the attempted alliance of various oppositional elements in the Baha'i World Federation in 1950 appears to have been totally unavailing, the component elements lacking any collective point of unity other than their common opposition to developments in the Baha'i mainstream.

THE LEGALISTIC MOTIF

According to the Baha'i concept of progressive revelation, not only does each religion represent a further revelation of divine truth, but within each religion the full implications of the divine teachings are only gradually revealed.[7] In keeping with this view, many of the provisions of Baha'i law still remain unimplemented, especially in the West. Shoghi Effendi, however, did seek to ensure that the fundamental elements of Baha'i law concerning acts of worship and the regulation of personal status were described and implemented. Thus throughout the Baha'i world the main elements of law concerning Baha'i obligatory prayer, fasting, marriage, divorce, burial and the prohibitions on political activity, homosexuality and the use of alcohol and non-medicinal drugs are emphasized either as spiritual obligations (as with prayer and fasting), or as community laws whose breach may occasion administrative sanction. Whilst these administrative sanctions are relatively severe, consisting of the temporary removal of the offending individual's rights to vote in Baha'i elections and to participate fully in Baha'i community life, they tend to be applied more *in extremis* than for casual breaches of the law. The National Spiritual Assemblies (the bodies responsible for determining membership status) are directed not to deprive Baha'is lightly of their voting rights but rather to induce them to rectify their conduct. In addition to the laws generally applicable throughout the Baha'i world, Baha'is of Middle Eastern origin are also charged with more detailed spiritual obligations concerning prayer, betrothal, personal cleanliness, and the payment of *huqúqu'lláh* (the right of God), an exaction of 19 per cent on capital gains, payable to the Centre of the Faith. Some initial codification of Baha'i law has been made, both in association with several unsuccessful attempts to establish Baha'i courts regarding matters of personal status in various Muslim countries during the period of the Guardianship, and, more recently, by the issuing of a synopsis and codification of the *Kitábu'l-Aqdas* (1973).

Baha'i law relating to the governance of the Baha'i community has been largely subsumed under the developing Baha'i Administrative Order, which has become such a characteristic feature of the Formative Age. In this regard considerable and detailed guidance has been provided by Shoghi Effendi and the Universal House of Justice and an extensive literature has developed concerning the operation of the administration. In general, however, Shoghi Effendi sought to discourage Assemblies from 'overadministering' and becoming bound by too much procedure and detailed regulation, encouraging them rather to be flexible in their approach.[8]

MILLENARIANISM

Prior to Shoghi Effendi's accession as Guardian it would seem that there was a distinct substratum of millenarian anticipation in both the East and the West, even though such ideas were rooted more in a framework of progressive human enlightenment than in any divine *Endzeit*. The 1914–18 war had been the Battle of Armageddon, and humanity was expected to suffer further before the Most Great Peace would be established, but the prevailing expectations were optimistic. Thus in 1922 Martha Root predicted that the millennium would soon be established, whilst J.E. Esslemont reported ʿAbdu'l-Bahá as predicting that the universal peace, the oneness of mankind and the promulgation of the Baha'i Faith throughout the world would all be achieved by 1957.[9] Again, as late as

1933 Horace Holley was interpreting Shoghi Effendi as predicting that the Most Great Peace would be established by 1963.[10]

Such optimism was gradually abandoned as the century progressed, and images of a far more protracted struggle to establish the Kingdom of God on Earth came to prevail. In the establishment of this modern Baha'i consciousness of millenarian ideas, the main basis was provided by Shoghi Effendi's systematized account of the Baha'i view of the historical process, an account which drew together and interpreted the main elements of Bahá'u'lláh's and ʿAbdu'l-Bahá's teachings on millenarian themes.[11]

In his role as Interpreter of the Word of God, Shoghi Effendi developed a complex metahistory in which the Baha'i interpretation of the historical process in general, of the 'destined' consummation of history, and of the Baha'i Faith's specific historical role, were described. The whole of human social and religious evolution led to the present age, to which Bahá'u'lláh – with the Báb, the fulfilment of the messianic expectations of all religions – had brought the teachings of the new era that was dawning. Acceptance of Bahá'u'lláh, and of the pivotal principle of the oneness of mankind, constituted the only means by which a suffering humanity might find rest in the age of transition between messianic fulfilment and the future establishment of the Most Great Peace.

The future Golden Age rested on the operation of two processes. The first was the indirect manifestation of the principle of the oneness of mankind in the gradual diffusion of the spirit of world solidarity. This was demonstrated by the establishment of such bodies as the League of Nations and the United Nations and would lead to the establishment of the Lesser Peace, that is the political unification of the world. The second was the Baha'is' own divinely guided endeavours to build a new world order. This would ultimately replace the decaying order which currently prevailed with the Most Great Peace. Opposition to these processes, whether in the form of the championing of unfettered national sovereignty or of the persecution of the Baha'i Faith, could only add to the tumult attendant upon the transformation of the world and to the threat of divine chastisement against a world which had both rejected Bahá'u'lláh's redemptive message and the elementary principles of religion in general.

There was a strong apocalyptic element in this analysis. Humankind would surely be assailed by a calamity that would punish and purify it. As a result, the barriers to world unity would be thrown down, the bankruptcy of materialistic civilization would be demonstrated, the nations would be welded into a unified world, and mankind would be prepared for the future unfoldment of 'God's struggling Faith'. Elements of God's display of anger and correction had already occurred, notably the downfall of those kings who had opposed, or failed to heed, Baháʾuʾlláh's summons. Heedless of its God, mankind had suffered two world wars which were stages in 'global havoc' and which presaged further sufferings. In one of his most specific references (dated April 1957) to the 'signs and portents' prophesied by Baháʾuʾlláh or ʿAbduʾl-Bahá that must either herald or accompany the retributive calamity' which would 'sooner or later' afflict the world, Shoghi Effendi referred to:

> The violent derangement of the world's equilibrium; the trembling that will seize the limbs of mankind; the radical transformation of human society; the rolling up of the present-day Order; the fundamental changes affecting the structure of government; the weakening of the pillars of religion; the rise of dictatorships; the spread of tyranny; the fall of monarchies; the decline of ecclesiastical institutions; the increase of anarchy and chaos; the extension and consolidation of the Movement of the Left; the fanning into flame of the smouldering fire of racial strife; the development of infernal engines of war; the burning of cities; the contamination of the atmosphere of the earth.[12]

This cataclysmic picture of the nearer future and present stood in marked contrast to Shoghi Effendi's vision of the future Golden Age. Out of catastrophe would emerge a consciousness of world citizenship on which world unity and peace could be established, leading to 'that world civilization' which would mark 'the coming of age of the entire human race'. Furthermore, mankind would be spiritualized, resident in a Bahaʾi World Commonwealth synonymous with the Christ-promised Kingdom of God on Earth, which would continue throughout a 500,000 year Bahaʾi Cycle.

According to his most detailed description of the promised Golden Age (contained in a letter dated 11 March 1936), that future civilization would be characterized by the unity of humanity's nations, races, creeds and classes; the safeguarding of state autonomy and individual freedom and initiative; a world legislature, executive, police force and tribunal; a mechanism of world intercommunication; a world metropolis, civilization, language, script, literature, currency and system of weights and measures; the co-operation and development of religion and science; a free and unmanipulated press; the organization and development of the world's economic resources, raw materials and markets; the equitable regulation of the distribution of its products; the disappearance or abolition of national rivalries, hatreds and intrigues, racial animosity and prejudice, of the causes of religious strife, of economic barriers and restrictions, of inordinate distinction between classes, and of both destitution and gross accumulation of ownership; and the consecration of the enormous energy wasted on political and economic war to the improvement of the physical, intellectual, moral and spiritual well-being of the entire human race.[13]

On the basis of this schema modern Baha'i millenarian expectation centres on three elements; an expected world-wide catastrophe and the establishment of the Lesser Peace – both of which are popularly expected to occur before the end of the twentieth century – and the far distant, but 'infinitely glorious', Most Great Peace. At the level of official belief the catastrophe occupies a subordinate but important role in relation to the fundamentally optimistic view of the future. It constitutes the 'messianic woe' prior to the establishment of the Lesser Peace. Popular concern with the expected catastrophe may ebb and flow relatively independently of this official position, in response to perceptions of the world situation, but in the absence of any official dogma on the subject such concern remains purely speculative. In the absence of any specific official dating of the events prophetic fulfilment remains vague, and there is no potential crisis of millenarian non-fulfilment.

Significantly, the idea that the present world sufferings are part of a general process of retribution and cleansing, and that they will be succeeded by something even worse *which can be mitigated* by the actions of wise governments and determined Baha'is, provides both an explanatory schema by which such sufferings can be understood, and thereby to some extent accommodated, and also a goad to 'sacrificial efforts' on the part of the Baha'is. Thus, during the Great Depression, some American Baha'is directly linked their own progress in the completion of the Wilmette temple with the idea of staving off some possible general disaster which they feared might befall their country;[14] or, again, repeatedly in the messages of both Shoghi Effendi and the Universal House of Justice, the Baha'is have been assured that the fate of humanity in large measure depends upon their efforts, that time is urgent, and that sacrificial efforts to teach the Faith, or raise its institutions, are called for. Such appeals have been particularly linked to the achievement of the goals of the specific seven-, ten-, nine- or five-year plans which have been such a characteristic part of Baha'i endeavour since the 1930s. To draw a parallel with certain aspects of the development plans of various socialist countries in their efforts to establish a secularized utopia is not unrealistic; in both cases human effort is given an important and guided role in the achievement of an 'inevitable' social transformation.

At both an official and a popular level the optimism engendered amongst Baha'is, both by the sense of living in an age of messianic fulfilment and by confidence regarding mankind's distant future, would seem to outweigh the apprehensions about the immediate future. The problems of the world are seen not as a reason for rejecting the world, but rather as an indication of the need for the Baha'i Faith as providing the only possible solution. Again, it may well be that many individual Baha'is see themselves as part of the leaven that will leaven humanity as a whole, and as part of the potential remnant that will undertake, or contribute towards, the task of reconstruction necessitated by the perceived disintegration of the present world order. In contrast to this general Baha'i optimism-in-the-face-of-catastrophe attitude, Mason Remey and his followers have displayed a far more vivid sense of impending catastrophe and suffering, which in the case of Remey himself seems like a direct continuation of the concerns he voiced during the First World War. According to Remey's doctrine of the 'great global catastrophe', cataclysmic movements in the earth's crust will lead to a universal inundation and the death of two-thirds of the earth's population. Initially expected in 1963, the catastrophe was later rescheduled for 1995.[15]

UNIVERSALISM AND LIBERALISM

The image of the Baha'i Faith as a broad, liberal and universal religion has continued during the Formative Age. As before, the stress on Baha'i universalism has incorporated two elements. Firstly, an injunction to Baha'is to be tolerant in their attitude towards other religionists (extending to the dedication of Baha'i schools and *Mashriqu'l-Adhkárs* to people of all religions, not just Baha'is), and secondly, an attempt to convey the Baha'i message as the fulfilment of all religions. In this latter regard the messianic expectations of all non-Baha'is have provided a fertile area of interpretation.

Prior to the extension of the Baha'i Faith to the West, explicit reference had been made to its claims to fulfil the messianic expectations of Islam, Christianity, Judaism and Zoroastrianism. With the spread of Baha'i to the West and to the non-Muslim Third World, the idea of messianic fulfilment could easily be extended: Bahá'u'lláh was the promise of *all ages*. Thus Shoghi Effendi referred to Bahá'u'lláh as being the messianic figure expected by not only Judaism, Christianity, Islam and Zoroastrianism, but also Hinduism and Buddhism.[16] More recently, Baha'i writers have extended their polemic to attempt to prove, for example, that the Baha'i Faith fulfilled the millenarian expectations of Buddhists, Mormons and North American Indians; that such groups as the Saint-Simonians, the

Millerites or the Romantic poets were in some way precursors of the millennial dawn; and even that Joachim of Fiore's prophecies regarding AD 1260 might instead refer to AH 1260 (i.e. AD 1844).[17] Whilst lacking orthodox sanction, such arguments undoubtedly reflect widely held views and are compatible with the overall Baha'i understanding of religious history. In general, claims of messianic fulfilment constitute a major element in Baha'i teaching endeavour and in the attempted validation of religious truth claims.

More recently, Baha'is have also begun to adopt more varied cultural styles, both so as to mediate their message to people outside the traditional thought worlds of Iranian Shiʿism and Western, educated liberalism, and, on the part of those Baha'is from outside those traditional thought worlds, so as to express their Faith in more culturally familiar terms. This is seen most clearly in the development of distinct Hindu–Baha'i forms of expression in which the Islamic title *Bahá'u'lláh* has become *Bhagavan Baha* and full reference is made to Hindu cultural symbols.[18] In this cultural mediation one major facilitating factor is the relative lack of concern displayed by Baha'is about metaphysics and theology, and their concentration instead on devotion to the Central Figures (Bahá'u'lláh, the Báb and ʿAbdu'l-Bahá), obedience to the Covenant, and acceptance of the various moral and social principles, all elements of the religion which 'travel' more easily across cultural barriers.

This extension of Baha'i universality has been accompanied by the development of a far more exclusivist conception of Baha'i membership. Prior to the Formative Age Baha'i membership often tended to be somewhat indistinct, whether as a result of Easterners seeking not to disrupt their precarious relationship with a hostile environing society or of Westerners interpreting their Faith as the inclusive spirit of the age. By contrast, a more exclusive interpretation was emphasized, and in many ways introduced, by Shoghi Effendi, who in 1925 for the first time established qualifications for true Baha'i belief:

> Full recognition of the station of the Forerunner [the Báb], the Author [Bahá'u'lláh], and the True Exemplar [ʿAbdu'l-Bahá] of the Bahá'í Cause, as set forth in ʿAbdu'l-Bahá's Testament; unreserved acceptance of, and submission to, whatsoever has been revealed by their Pen; loyal and steadfast adherence to every clause of our Beloved's [ʿAbdu'l-Bahá's] sacred Will: and close association with the spirit as well as the form of the present day Bahá'í administration throughout the world.[19]

This statement was later embodied in the 1927 American Baha'i National Assembly's By-laws, thus providing a definite legal basis for voting membership of the Baha'i community.

Membership rolls, enrolment procedures and printed credentials followed. Although recognizing that the 'process of becoming a Bahaʾi' was necessarily 'slow and gradual' and advising that 'the line of demarcation' should not be drawn too rigidly, Shoghi Effendi had now introduced a distinct division between those who were 'definitely enrolled' as Bahaʾis and the wider circle of sympathizers. This division was made even more marked in 1935 by Shoghi Effendi's instruction that Bahaʾis could not also be members of other religious bodies, apart from such general organizations as the World Fellowship of Faiths.[20] Eastern Bahaʾis were also strongly discouraged from dissimulating their faith in any way, and the 1925 Egyptian court decision denouncing Bahaʾism as a non-Islamic religion was hailed as an important development.

As to Bahaʾi liberalism, this continued somewhat as before, that is in the combination of liberal and humanitarian principles, with an emphasis on central authority. With the transition to a far less charismatic form of leadership, the importance of central authority became more evident, perhaps particularly up to the 1940s as the new leadership style was established. However, doctrinal liberalism also received more emphasis, particular stress being placed on such principles as world unity and the need for a modern and 'scientific' social religion.

SOCIAL RECONSTRUCTIONISM

Millenarian hope and doctrinal liberalism coalesced in the Bahaʾis' continuing advocacy of a programme of social reconstruction, an overall solution to the world's problems in terms of the spiritualization of human life and the implementation of the social principles extolled by Baháʾuʾlláh and ʿAbduʾl-Bahá. Comprising a wide-ranging series of policies on how government, the economy, social relationships and education should be restructured, such advocacy has been closely linked with Bahaʾi teaching endeavour. It has not, however, generally been linked with specific patterns of activism, and whilst individual Bahaʾis and Bahaʾi communities have on occasion involved themselves in various charitable and 'reconstructionist' activities, such participation cannot be regarded as having been central to collective Bahaʾi endeavour until recently.

Major factors in this lack of activism, and central to the developing Bahaʾi attitude towards social reconstructionism, have been the principles of strict abstention from political activities and of obedience to government.[21] Originally advanced by Baháʾuʾlláh and ʿAbduʾl-Bahá with reference to the Iranian Bahaʾis, these principles were emphasized and amplified by Shoghi Effendi, most especially in a number of communications with the American Baha'is in the early 1930s. Henceforth, Baha'is were bidden to avoid any activity which might be interpreted, 'either directly or indirectly' as interference in political affairs; to rise above particularism and partisanship; not to take sides in political controversies, discuss political affairs at their meetings, or make reference to political figures in their public talks; to be on their guard against any attempt to solicit their political support as a community; to abstain from membership of any political party; and when obliged to vote, to vote for political candidates as individuals rather than as members of this or that party. Only thus, it was felt, could the Baha'is demonstrate the supranational unity of their Faith. Those Baha'is who refused to disengage from political activity were subject to the removal of their voting rights.

Abstention from political activity was combined with the requirement that Baha'is should demonstrate their unqualified obedience and loyalty to the government of whatever country they resided in, strictly eschewing involvement in any subversive or seditious movement. Such a ban applied even if the government was unjust, and even to the extent of subordinating the operation and application of all but the most fundamental Baha'i laws and principles. Baha'is could, however, employ such means as were lawful, to petition for the changing of unjust laws, although even in this instance they were also warned against the precipitate adoption of a specific 'Baha'i' attitude or course of action.

One particularly acute focus for the operation of these principles was in the issue of military service. Although permitting limited self-defence, the Baha'i teachings were unambiguous as to the illegality and immorality of armed assault and homicide except for the maintenance of civil order. What then should Baha'is do when called upon to serve in their countries' armed forces? The policy laid down by Shoghi Effendi during the 1930s was that as Baha'is were obedient to governments and were not absolute pacifists they should accept enlistment, but apply, where possible, for non-combatant status, regardless of whether this exposed them to any physical danger.[22] Where non-combatant status was not available, Baha'is were bidden to obey the instructions of their governments, although in the last analysis 'it is for each believer, under pain of his own conscience, to determine for himself what his actions should be'.[23] By these standards, whilst voluntary enlistment was unacceptable, the Baha'is clearly distanced themselves from any perceived pacifist orientation. More generally, it was commonly maintained that work for the Baha'i Cause far outweighed work for peace movements as a means of striving towards peace.[24]

As with the insistence upon the independent nature of the Baha'i religion and the resultant distancing from other religious organizations, the stress on the religion's non-political nature led to a distancing from a certain category of reformist social movements, of which the peace movements were the most obvious example. Thus, whilst up to the early twenties, certain Western Baha'is had had extensive contacts with various peace societies, most dramatically perhaps in New York City in the aftermath of the First World War, where Baha'is had participated in the Peace Parade and held a large open-air meeting which had been dispersed by the police,[25] such contacts do not appear to have survived the thirties. Advocacy of world peace remained a central element in the Baha'i message, but such advocacy was now largely divorced from the endeavours of that wider circle of peace workers who were also advocates of pacificism and a political approach. This situation may well change, however, particularly following the initiation of a major peace campaign by the Universal House of Justice in October 1985.[26]

Contacts with 'socialistic' groups died away even more rapidly. Whilst prior to the war, the Baha'is had proclaimed that 'even the Socialists and philosophers find their theories fully developed in this Movement', and one of the Baha'is had presented the Baha'i teachings 'from the standpoint of the working class movement', any sense that socialism (in some form) and Baha'ism were parallel liberal movements was quickly eroded after the war.[27] Even prior to the strict prohibition on Baha'i political activity, the place of socialistic ideas in the American context had dramatically changed and placed them beyond the Baha'is' normal range of discourse, the Sedition Act and the post-war 'red scare' marking a sharp rightward swing in the public debate, whilst the Russian Revolution and the rise of American Communist parties marked a sharp leftward and revolutionary change in leftist circles. Moreover, for the Baha'is, established Communist regimes soon proved themselves implacable opponents not only of religion in general but of most religious groups, the Baha'i Faith amongst them. Ultimately for Shoghi Effendi, Communism was one of three 'false gods' of an irreligious world (with Nationalism and Racism), whose false and crooked doctrines merited 'the wrath and chastisement of God'.[28] Moreover, Communism and Capitalism were to be 'commonly condemned . . . for their materialistic philosophies and their neglect of those spiritual values and eternal verities on which alone a stable and flourishing civilization can be ultimately established'.[29] As with peace, Baha'is continued to advocate their ideas for economic change, but generally in isolation from other groups and organizations.

Other elements in the Baha'i 'programme' could be profitably pursued in association with others, however, and for many Baha'is their religion still remained above all 'a social religion in which is found the solution of present day problems'.[30]

Important *loci* for the advocacy of Baha'i principles have been the successive international organizations of the League of Nations and the United Nations, both seen by Baha'is as welcome stages in the creation of a political new world order. Only able to establish modest contacts with the League through the creation of the International Baha'i Bureau at Geneva (1925–57), the Baha'is have been far more successful with the United Nations, making initial contacts at the Allied Nations Conference in 1945 and later becoming a 'non-government organization', affiliated from March 1948 onwards as the 'Baha'i International Community'. In this role the Baha'i representatives have been able to present statements on a wide range of subjects, from human rights and racism to the environment and disarmament, and including a set of 'Proposals for Charter Revision', which advocate the considerable strengthening of the international body against 'unfettered national sovereignty'.[31] Baha'i involvement with the United Nations has particularly increased since the late 1960s, and since then they have gained consultative status with the UN Economic and Social Council (ECOSOC) – in 1970 – affiliation with the Environment Program (UNEP) and consultative status with the Children's Fund (UNICEF). There is also considerable Baha'i involvement with such allied groups as the United Nations Association, although always on a strictly non-political basis.

Contacts with 'other liberal groups' became a particularly characteristic feature of Baha'i activity in Europe between the wars – perhaps accentuated by the European Baha'is' relative lack of success in enlarging their communities and the greater persistence of the 'universalistic movement' conception of their religion. In England such groups included the Fellowship of Faiths, the Free Religious Movement, the New Commonwealth Society, the Quakers and the Unitarians. Everywhere the Theosophical Society provided a convivial home from home. In Europe as a whole, the most important liberal group contacted was the Esperanto movement, with whom extensive contacts were made throughout the continent during the inter-war period.[32] ʿAbdu'l-Bahá had specifically encouraged Baha'is to learn Esperanto and, at least during the inter-war period, it may have appeared to many European Baha'is that Esperanto could be the international auxiliary language referred to by Baháʾuʾlláh. Enthusiastic Bahaʾi Esperantists were thus able to work for a movement embodying one of their central teachings, at the same time as thereby gaining access to a large number of potentially sympathetic internationally minded individuals to whom they could present the Bahaʾi message. Especially to those Esperantists who might be attracted by the 'spiritual side' of the Esperanto movement,[33] the Bahaʾi vision of world unity and peace was presented as the necessary framework within which the Esperanto ideal of a universal world language could best be established. Accordingly Bahaʾis regularly participated in such meetings as the annual Universal Esperanto Congresses in various parts of Europe and in the organization of Esperanto societies. There was also an extensive production and distribution of Bahaʾi literature in Esperanto, notably by the German Bahaʾi Esperanto Society (Bahaa Esperanto-Eldonejo), an organization which also produced a regular Bahaʾi Esperanto magazine, *La Nova Tago* (*The New Day*), from 1925 until 1937. Whether or not these extensive efforts secured many actual conversions, there was certainly much interest generated thereby and at least one prominent convert, in the person of one of Dr Zamenhof's own daughters, Lidia, who became a Bahaʾi in 1926 and enthusiastically promulgated both movements in Europe and America. After the war, however, the Esperanto movement failed to recapture its former dynamic and Bahaʾi interest in the movement waned.

In America, by comparison, there seems generally to have been far less sustained contact with other liberal groups, as the Bahaʾi community increasingly sought to consolidate itself as an organized and independent religious group. One exception to this was the sustained contact with liberal organizations concerned with the advancement of black Americans, notably the National Association for the Advancement of Colored People and the Urban League. Whilst, as with these other groups, the Bahaʾis failed to make meaningful contact with the mass of poor rural blacks, they succeeded in the inter-war period in hosting a number of well-attended Racial Amity Conventions, which, rather than detailing the sufferings of American blacks, sought to 'lift the whole matter up into the spiritual realm and work for the creation of sentiment'.[34] A leading black Bahaʾi – Alain Locke, the first black Rhodes scholar – also made a major contribution to the Harlem Renaissance, an upsurge of black literary and artistic activity in the 1920s, but this cannot be regarded as a specifically Bahaʾi contribution. Although the Bahaʾis' stress on the urgency of the racial problem – 'a situation which, if allowed to drift, will, in the words of

ʿAbduʾl-Bahá, cause the streets of American cities to run with blood'[35] – and their advocacy of a far-reaching change of heart on the part of both blacks and whites has continued to the present day, the increasing politicization and radicalization of black activism (especially from 1966 with the growth of Black Power) has tended in recent years to distance American Bahaʾi 'race policy' from the mainstream of that activism. The massive influx of poor rural black converts is perhaps too recent and too geographically concentrated to enable us to judge whether the American Bahaʾis have been successful in integrating these neophytes with the existing community of mainly middle-class whites. It is of note, however, that of the 51 American Bahaʾi National Assembly members in the period 1925–74, 8 (15.7 per cent) were black, in itself some indication of integration, at least of the earlier generation of largely middle-class blacks.[36] Amerindians have also served on the National Assemblies of both the United States and Canada.

The advocacy of the principle of the unity of mankind, regardless of racial, religious or national background, has not been confined to the American Bahaʾis, of course. Whilst everywhere eschewing political action, the Bahaʾis have nevertheless asserted their principles and sought to diversify their membership ethnically, so that as of 1979 there were Bahaʾis representative of 1,820 tribes and ethnic groups.[37] In that all adult Bahaʾis with voting rights are enabled to participate in Bahaʾi elections, and sustained emphasis is placed on the need for freedom from prejudice, the world-wide expansion of the Bahaʾi Faith has in itself resulted in a measure of inter-ethnic integration and co-operation, also providing leadership opportunities for minority-group members. How successful the various Bahaʾi communities have been in rooting out the deep prejudices which often divide various groups is difficult to evaluate. Certainly it would be naive to assume that the mere acceptance of Bahaʾism in itself is sufficient to transform such ingrained attitudes, even on the part of those who already subscribe to liberal ideas. Where evaluation is possible, it would seem that the continuous emphasis on unity does have a progressive effect within the Bahaʾi community. Thus Gayle Morrison notes the gradual transformation of attitudes amongst the white Bahaʾis of Washington DC towards their black co-religionists,[38] whilst, on the basis of numerous conversations with Iranian Bahaʾis, I would judge that although in the earlier part of this century the Iranian Bahaʾis of Muslim, Jewish and Zoroastrian backgrounds remained largely separate subcommunities – the Jewish Bahaʾis at one point having a separate Spiritual Assembly in Tehran[39] – their inherited mutual suspicions have gradually been dispelled, so that at least since the 1950s intermarriage between these groups has become more common.[40]

As to the Baha'i principle of the equality of the sexes, besides general advocacy, the Baha'is have again sought more to 'lift the whole matter up into the spiritual realm and work for the creation of sentiment' than to engage in more concrete activity.[41] As with several other of their social principles, the Baha'is now find themselves separated from the main body of Western advocates of women's rights by their refusal to espouse militant action, and more particularly in the case of feminism, by the ideological division between the 'reformist', family-oriented attitudes towards women promulgated by the Baha'is and the radicalism of the Western women's movement. Again, as with the expansion of the Baha'i Faith among ethnic minorities, the prevailing structures and attitudes within the Baha'i community are conducive to a certain measure of female emancipation, although again not in themselves sufficient to transform more deep-rooted prejudices. How successful the Baha'i communities have been in changing their members' consciousness with regard to gender roles is a moot point, and it seems likely that consideration of the issue of sexual equality has been less central than that of racial equality. Nevertheless, by the crude measure of participation in the higher levels of Baha'i administration, whilst women have everywhere constituted a minority of administrators, they have at least constituted a significant minority, which would appear to be growing in size and assertiveness.

At an international level, whilst 18.8 per cent of the Hands of the Cause appointed in the 1950s were women, some 25.4 per cent of the Counsellors appointed in 1980 were women.[42] The majority of National Assemblies now have women members, especially those in the West, but also those in the Muslim and Third Worlds. Of 51 members of the American National Assembly in the period 1925–74, 16 (31.4 per cent) have been women.[43] Moreover, recent Baha'i official reports have noted the growing participation of Baha'i women of the Third World in the running of the Baha'i community, and attitudinal changes on the part of members of both sexes.[44] During the 1970s and 1980s there has been increasing stress on the fuller participation of women in Baha'i affairs, including an emphasis on literacy training for Baha'i women (regarded by Baha'is as the initial educators of children) in the Third World.

In contrast to the emphasis on attitudinal change in the pursuit of a limited form of sexual equality, one area of social reconstructionism in which the Baha'is might be judged to have made more concrete progress is in relation to education.[45] Understandably, apart from the general advocacy of the need for universal education, mass literacy and the spiritual training of children, the primary educational emphasis within the Baha'i community has been on the proper induction of its own children, a need which has usually been met by the holding of some form of special Baha'i classes analagous to the Christian Sunday School, but Baha'i educational endeavours have ranged more widely. Until very recently Baha'i children's classes achieved their fullest development in the traditional Baha'i communities of the East, where some equivalent of the Persian Baha'i *dars-i akhláq* (character-training) classes was usually instituted. Such classes generally concentrated on the learning of Baha'i prayers, moral precepts, and some knowledge of Baha'i history and doctrine. In Iran the system would seem to have been put on a more systematic basis in about the 1930s, primarily through the influence of ʿAlí Akbar Furútan, a Moscow-trained child psychologist. In the West, systematic classes for Baha'i children were generally a later development, the primary emphasis being upon the socialization of adults rather than children. To this end the holding of Baha'i summer schools became a major activity, properties often being acquired for this purpose. There was a growing realization amongst Western Baha'is of the importance of religious instruction for their children, however, and children's classes became an increasingly common part of Baha'i activity in the post-war period.

As to more secular educational activities, the strong emphasis on education has led in several instances to the foundation of specific Baha'i schools teaching secular as well as spiritual subjects. The earliest of these were started in the late 1890s, both in Turkestan and in Iran. These schools had a high academic reputation and attracted non-Baha'i children as well as Baha'is, but were all closed in the wake of political repression, those in Turkestan from 1928, those in Iran (some 24 schools in ten towns) in 1934. Later, in 1945, a Baha'i children's hostel was opened in India which eventually developed into a fully-fledged high school catering for children of all religious backgrounds and which it is intended will further develop into a junior college. Besides an academic education, the Indian school emphasizes community service and rural development projects, and in 1977 a second Indian Baha'i school was opened in the 'mass conversion' area of Gwalior, this one geared much more closely to rural development. Elsewhere in the Third World there are a number of Baha'i primary, secondary and 'tutorial' schools, these latter concerned with teaching basic literacy to children and adults, whilst even in the United States a Baha'i high school is now being established, again catering for people of all religions.

The practical involvement of Baha'i institutions in secular education seems to have presaged a far more extensive involvement in the various aspects of social and economic development.[46] With the increasing expansion of the Bahaʾi Faith into the Third World, the need for comprehensive systems of development has recently begun to be emphasized very strongly. Various local Bahaʾi initiatives in literacy training, health education and rural development became increasingly common in various parts of the Third World during the 1970s. More obliquely, the establishment of Bahaʾi radio stations in Latin America gave scope for wider rural educational activities as well as for the sponsorship of indigenous cultural activities. As such initiatives proliferated, the need for some measure of world-wide co-ordination involving both rich and poor Bahaʾi communities became apparent. Accordingly, in 1982, a Canadian Bahaʾi International Development Service was established, to be followed in 1983 by a Haifa-based Office of Social and Economic Development. To a greater extent than other Bahaʾi ventures in social reconstructionism these institutions are charged with stimulating local initiatives rather than formulating plans from the top downwards. As with Bahaʾi ventures in secular education, Bahaʾi development work is not confined to the Bahaʾi community alone, but is directed to all members of a local community regardless of race or religion. It is obviously premature to attempt even a preliminary assessment of the effectiveness of this new area of Bahaʾi work.

ESOTERICISM AND RATIONALITY

One of the distinguishing features of early Bahaʾism as it emerged from Babism was the importance which the Bahaʾi leaders accorded to rationality and 'common sense' reasonableness, eschewing much of the complex esotericism of the Shaykhi–Babi tradition and denying the importance of the miraculous as any form of religious proof. Much of this emphasis was transmitted to the new Bahaʾi communities which were established in the West, but at the same time, many of the new Western Bahaʾis were greatly influenced by the esotericism of the cultic milieu. It was only the supposed 'scientific' nature of that milieu, together with ʿAbduʾl-Bahá's permissive form of leadership that enabled these potentially contradictory emphases to coexist. In America, of course, this coexistence began to come to a fairly rapid end with the polarization over the issue of organization, the more esotericist-minded Bahaʾis generally supporting the 'anti-organization' stance, and the furore over the Chicago Reading Room marking a decided shift of opinion against esotericism.

This shift was accentuated and internationalized by the increasing emphasis on organization and administrative authority, and those Bahaʾis with esotericist tendencies either accommodated themselves to the new situation or drew away from the community. Contacts with esotericist groups – once frequent – gradually atrophied.

As to esotericism itself, Shoghi Effendi's attitude was quite clear: direct divine guidance was vouchsafed only to the Manifestations of God, and whilst all individuals were called upon to work for their own spiritual development, such development came not from any esoteric knowledge or experience, but from the purity with which they turned to God, the selflessness and dedication with which they served God's Cause, and the extent to which they modelled their lives on the divinely given ethical imperatives.[47] 'Truly mystical experiences based on reality' were very rare and derived from God's bounty and not any esoteric search; inspiration and guidance through prayers and dreams were possible but they were not infallible; the Bahaʾis should rigorously eschew meddling with psychic forces, which were, in most cases, indicative of deep psychological disturbance; those who wanted to communicate with Shoghi Effendi should do so in writing, for that, rather than via any supposed psychic intermediary, was how he communicated with them; there was often little to be gained by the Bahaʾis in teaching those who were more interested in 'mystery itself' than in genuine mysticism, or in 'this present world in which we live' and the solution of its problems; the Bahaʾis should be gently but determinedly reminded that the Bahaʾi teachings were not to be confused with astrology, numerology or the 'prophecies of the pyramids', and should be encouraged not to waste their time with such pseudo-sciences and superstitions; spiritual healing could complement physical healing, but it could not be a substitute for it.

Combined with this strong anti-esotericist stand was a strong assertion of the 'scientific' and 'commonsensical' nature of the Bahaʾi teachings. Whilst the ultimate source of authority was divine revelation, the discoveries and principles of science were regarded as being of complementary authority. There are obvious ambiguities in such a stance, and it may well be argued that until now the 'scientific' nature of Bahaʾi thought has rested more on the lack of opposition to such traditional scientific 'anti-religious' assertions as evolutionary theory and the impossibility of the religious 'proof' of miracles, than on any more far-reaching philosophical linkage between science and religion. In the absence of any dogmatic assertions regarding issues in the physical sciences, the Bahaʾi Faith has escaped one of the main areas of tension between science and religion. It is not yet possible to say whether it will escape the tensions engendered by the application of 'scientific' principles in what, from a Bahaʾi point of view, are the more sensitive areas of historical analysis and textual criticism.

10

WORLD-WIDE EXPANSION

In the East the Báb, Bahá'u'lláh and ʿAbdu'l-Bahá had all encouraged their most eminent followers to engage in missionary activity so as to broaden the geographical extent of their religion and to consolidate and strengthen the newly emergent Babi and Baha'i communities. Thus the Báb's disciples had established the new religion throughout the Iranian heartland and Iraq; Bahá'u'lláh had directed leading followers to establish and strengthen Baha'i communities in the Levant, Asiatic Russia and India; and ʿAbdu'l-Bahá had co-ordinated a successful expansion of the Faith to North America and Europe, which, towards the end of his life, was in turn expanding even further afield.

Throughout the expansion in the East the prime agents of activity were certain prominent teachers of the Faith, often of clerical background, who provided much of the leadership and co-ordination required and to whom other Babis and Baha'is fairly readily deferred. The situation in the West differed quite considerably in two respects. Firstly, given the independent attitudes of many of the Western Baha'is, the role and authority of those who became prominent teachers and leaders was extremely circumscribed; secondly, it was in the West that the emerging system of Baha'i administration was most extensively developed. Interrelating with both of these factors was the essential difference between the hostile social environment of the East and the relative freedom of religious expression in the West.

SYSTEMATIC PLANS FOR EXPANSION AND CONSOLIDATION

Collectively organized teaching activity was slow to develop in the West, only really beginning in 1916 after the receipt of the first of ʿAbdu'l-Bahá's general letters on teaching, the *Tablets of the Divine Plan*. Addressed to the Baha'is of North America, these Tablets directed the Baha'is to establish new centres throughout the continent and throughout the world. Although foreign tours by individual Baha'is thereafter became more systematic, the American Baha'is as a whole at first concentrated their endeavours on domestic expansion, and more particularly on the development of the Baha'i administration and the completion of the Wilmette temple. Only in 1936, when Shoghi Effendi judged these latter projects to be well advanced, did he initiate sustained, systematic and specific teaching plans. The building of the administration was to be seen as the creation of the necessary agency for the prosecution of the Divine Plan.

Systematic plans now became one of the most characteristic features of Baha'i activity, detailed goals being established for the expansion and consolidation of the community. A strategy of world-wide expansion was developed. Initially only the North American Baha'is were assigned such plans, but as other Baha'i national communities became better organized, they too were assigned plans and goals. Thus, in the first American Seven Year Plan (1937–44), the Baha'is were called upon to establish permanent residence in all of the states and provinces of North America and in each of the Latin American republics. Then, after a two-year respite to consolidate their accomplishments, they embarked on a second Seven Year Plan (1946–53), in which they were required to further their expansion in the Americas (including an attempt to widen the movement's social base), to create new National Assemblies in Canada and in the Central and South American regions, and to initiate a systematic teaching campaign in Europe. During the two plans they were also required to complete the ornamentation of the Wilmette temple.

Following the initiation of these American plans, all the other National Assemblies either set, or were given, plans of their own, mostly calling for a 'self-strengthening' of their communities by an increase in their numbers and in the numerical and geographical extent of their administrative base (the Local Assemblies). Goals were also set for the translation and publication of Baha'i literature and the settling of overseas pioneers. In these plans the Baha'is of India, Pakistan and Burma (1938–44, 1946–50, 1951–3) were directed towards South and South-East Asia, those of Iran (1946–50) and Egypt (1949–53) mainly towards various parts of the Middle East and North Africa, the Canadians (1948–53) to Newfoundland and Greenland, and the British (1944–50 and 1951–3) towards Africa, where they co-ordinated an Inter-Assembly Collaboration Project. The weaker Germano-Austrian (1948–53), Iraqi (1947–50) and Australian-New Zealand (1947–53) Assemblies were only assigned internal goals, although even here long term 'spiritual destinies' were specified.

These various national plans were followed by a ten-year Global

Crusade (1953–63). This involved all twelve existing National Assemblies and called for a whole series of building, publishing, institutional and administrative developments throughout the world. The holding of world-wide plans involving all Bahaʾi communities was continued by the Universal House of Justice, their first Nine Year Plan (1964–73) being followed in turn by Five (1974–9), Seven (1979–86), and Six Year Plans (1986–92), all of which have both called for further massive expansion and institutional development and have stressed the need to foster certain qualitative aspects of Bahaʾi community life.

The results of these plans have been impressive and appear to indicate that, at least where external circumstances permit, the combination of reasonably efficient organization and specific operational goals is an extremely effective means of furthering the expansion of a religious movement. Whilst not every single objective of these plans has been achieved, it is clear that overall the attainments have far surpassed the goals set. This has been particularly the case with regard to specific numerical and concrete objectives such as the formation of Assemblies or the construction of buildings. Thus, for example, during the course of the Nine Year Plan, the goal of almost 14,000 Local Assemblies was surpassed by 3,000 and that of over 54,000 localities by over 15,000.[1]

Central to the plans has been the concern with the expansion and consolidation of the Faith. Expansion has primarily involved the reiterated appeal to all Bahaʾis to teach their religion, together with appeals for pioneers to establish residence in goal territories and travel teachers to make fresh contacts and visit existing Bahaʾi communities. Consolidation has entailed both the constant emphasis on the establishment of the local and national elements of the Bahaʾi Administrative Order and the attempt to increase the understanding and enthusiasm of the Bahaʾis. Expansion has clearly involved a deliberate policy of dispersion and diversification, the various plan messages stressing the need to open every territorial area and island group to the Faith, to expand the Bahaʾi administrative network within each National Assembly area so as to avoid undue concentrations of Bahaʾis (frequently in effect an emphasis on outlying rather than central areas), and to broaden the social base by attracting Bahaʾis from all strata of society.

Expansion has also involved a deliberate policy of attracting individuals from as wide an array of tribal and ethnic groups as is possible. The resultant diversity is regarded as illustrating the Bahaʾi teaching of unity, and detailed enumerations of the groups represented are often published in *Bahaʾí World*. This diversity is also aided and emphasized by the accompanying goal of the translation and publication of Baha'i literature into a growing number of languages. Thus, from being available in eight or so languages in 1928, by 1985 Baha'i literature was available in some 739 languages. From being available only in the major languages of Europe and the Middle East in the early part of the century, Baha'i literature is now available in an ever-increasing range of national, tribal and minority languages throughout the world. Whilst many of these are represented by little more than an introductory booklet or some prayers, a number of them are beginning to develop quite a substantial literature. Nevertheless, the major European, Middle Eastern and Indian languages continue to possess the largest literatures, with English now, even more than during the period of Shoghi Effendi's leadership, as the pre-eminent language of Baha'i international communication and publication.

As to actual numerical increases in the number of Baha'is, it is difficult to be precise. The Baha'i World Centre in Haifa referred in 1985 to a world total in the region of four million Baha'is, but a more detailed breakdown of figures is not yet available from official sources. Prior to the citation of this figure Baha'i sources generally refused to issue membership statistics, preferring instead to provide figures for the number of Assemblies and localities. The global distribution of Baha'is will be commented on below, but it is clear that from being a predominantly Iranian-based religion with a small but significant Western following, the Baha'i Faith has now developed into a world-wide movement with followers representative of most major ethnic and national groups and established in almost all of the countries of the world (the exceptions are Albania, the Vatican City, Sao Tome, Western Sahara, Mongolia and North Korea).

As regards growth and administrative consolidation, the most salient statistics are those giving the total numbers of Local and National Assemblies and of localities in which Baha'is reside (see Table 1), the total number of Baha'i localities rising from 579 in 1928 to over 111,000 in 1985, whilst in the same period the number of Local Assemblies has increased from 102 to over 30,000, and of National Assemblies from 9 to 148. In that these figures quite closely reflect (or exceed) Plan objectives, the detailed breakdown of figures in Table 1 indicates the great stress on the establishment of Local Spiritual Assemblies prior to the commencement of the Ten Year Crusade in 1953, the great increases in the numbers of National Assemblies and of localities only taking place after that date. Further administrative consolidation has occurred with the legal incorporation of most National Assemblies and of some Local Assemblies. Most National Assemblies have also acquired their own *Ḥaẓíratu'l-*

Table 1. *Selected Baha'i administrative statistics, 1928–85*

	NSAs		LSAs		Localities	
	no.	% incr.	no.	% incr.	no.	% incr.
1928	9		102		579	
1935–6	10		139	(36)	1,034	(79)
1945–6	8		505	(263)	1,895	(83)
1952–3	9		611	(21)	2,425	(28)
1964	56	(522)	4,566	(647)	15,186	(526)
1973	113	(101)	17,037	(273)	54,323	(258)
1985	148	(31)	30,304	(78)	111,092	(105)

Note: The figures in parentheses represent the percentage increase over the preceding time period. The 1928 figure for LSAs includes 5 in Germany, undifferentiated in the 1928 directory but assumed to have existed at that time (see the 1930 directory, *Bahá'í World*, vol. III, pp. 218,222), and 17 for Iran, which represents the total number of 'administrative divisions' rather than of LSAs, for which at that early stage of administrative development in the East figures are unobtainable.
Sources: Calculated from *Bahá'í International News Service*, 144, p. 14; *Bahá'í World*, vol. II, pp. 189–91; vol. VI, pp. 505–24; vol. X, pp. 551–82; National Spiritual Assembly of the Bahá'ís of the United Kingdom, *The Opening Phase of the Seven Year Plan*, mimeographed (London, 1979); and Shoghi Effendi, *The Bahá'í Faith, 1844–1952: Information Statistical and Comparative* (London, Bahá'í Publishing Trust, 1953).

Quds (the Sacred Fold, the Baha'i administrative headquarters), and many hundreds of local *Ḥaẓíratu'l-Quds* and district institutes have been constructed or are projected. Again, to cope with the growing diversity of publications, a number of Baha'i Publishing Trusts have been established, the two which had existed in 1953 (Britain and the United States) being joined by a further seven in Europe, three in North-East Asia, two each in South Asia, the Middle East and Latin America, and one each in Africa and the Pacific, thereby raising the total number to 20 by 1985.[2]

Besides expansion and consolidation, the various plans have also laid great stress on an extensive and developing programme of building and land acquisition. The most obvious elements of this programme have been the *Mashriqu'l-Adhkárs* and the Baha'i 'World Centre', but there have also been substantial constructions or acquisitions of national and local *Ḥaẓíratu'l-Quds*, district institutes, and temple and endowment lands.

The first *Mashriqu'l-Adhkár* had been built in the early 1900s at Ashkhabad in Russian Turkestan. This building was later appropriated by the Soviet authorities (1928), so that by the completion of the Wilmette temple in 1953 it was the only Baha'i House of Worship in the whole world. Thereafter, Shoghi Effendi determined that the increasing world-wide expansion of the Faith should be marked by the construction of one temple in each continent. These edifices were to be both smaller (and cheaper) than the Wilmette temple, the construction of which had constituted such a prolonged concern for the American Baha'is (1920–53). Accordingly, three new *Mashriqu'l-Adhkárs* were constructed for the Ten Year Plan, these being in Uganda, Australia and West Germany. Under the direction of the Universal House of Justice, small temples have also been built in Panama (1967–72) and Western Samoa (1979–84), whilst a large *Mashriqu'l-Adhkár* is due for completion in India in late 1986. In the case of the Third World temples in particular, a conscious attempt has been made to evoke indigenous architectural forms in their design. A start has also been made on the construction of the philanthropic 'dependencies' which are eventually intended to encircle the various Houses of Worship, one home for the aged having been built at Wilmette (1957–9), whilst a second is projected for the German temple near Frankfurt.

There has also been an ambitious building and land acquisition programme at the Baha'i 'World Centre', as Shoghi Effendi termed the Baha'i establishments and properties in the area of Haifa and ʿAkká. Houses and lands associated with Bahá'u'lláh and ʿAbdu'l-Bahá have been acquired – notably the mansion of Bahjí, in which Bahá'u'lláh spent the last years of his life and near which his shrine is located. Under Shoghi Effendi's direction memorial tombs were constructed near the Shrine of the Báb (in Haifa) for the mother, sister, brother and wife of ʿAbdu'l-Bahá. The Shrine of the Báb was also extended (1928–9), and later surrounded by an elaborate golden-domed superstructure (1948–53). A Parthenon-like International Archives building was also constructed near the Shrine of the Báb for the display of Baha'i relics and scriptures (1955–7). Extensive gardens were also established to border each of these buildings. These developments have continued under the Universal House of Justice with the construction of a large and stately building to serve as the seat of the House of Justice (1975–83).

GEO-CULTURAL EXPANSION AND CHANGE

The great expansion in the extent and administrative presence of the Baha'i community world-wide which has occurred since the 1920s has not been at all evenly distributed, the pattern of expansion being linked to the more general pattern of Baha'i geo-cultural development.

Taken overall, the history of Babi and Baha'i expansion may be seen as a series of cultural breakthroughs whereby the determination to engage in

7. Bahaʾi House of Worship, Wilmette, Illinois

8. Bahaʾi House of Worship, Apia, Western Samoa

missionary expansion was such as to transcend the limitations of the immediate socio-religious milieu. Thus, whilst Babism emerged as a sectarian movement with Shaykhism, its partisans succeeded in engaging the wider Shi'i world and even in attracting a number of non-Shi'is. Later, after Bahá'u'lláh's transformation of Babism, the new religion was able to expand its appeal, not only within Shi'ism, where the traces of specifically Shaykhi connections were almost entirely lost, but also beyond it by the inclusion of numbers of Sunnis, Jews, Zoroastrians and Levantine Christians. The early Baha'i Faith also expanded its extent geographically, albeit still largely within the confines of the various communities of Iranian migrants.

Whilst the breakthrough beyond Iranian Shi'ism remained limited in the Middle East, a far more decisive extension was achieved in the 1890s by the establishment of the Western Baha'i communities. Small though these were, they demonstrated the wider cultural adaptability of Baha'ism and also its logistical strength as its leaders co-ordinated the affairs of its adherents in two widely different socio-cultural worlds. Moreover, from its new geo-cultural bases, the religion was able to draw resources for yet further diffusion and at the same time to employ the context of religious freedom in the West to seek to safeguard the persecuted Baha'i community of the East. In terms of social location, diffusion throughout this 'second world' was predominantly amongst the minority of educated and middle-class urbanites. Diffusion from the West was multi-faceted, the primary diffusion from the strong American community to the culturally cognate territories of Europe and the areas of overseas British settlement being accompanied by a more subtle and progressive diffusion to what might almost be described as Western 'cultural enclaves' throughout the world, that is to those Westernized and educated urbanites whose cultural orientation was such as to make them amenable to conversion to a 'modernistic' world religion and who were thus almost necessarily in some sense alienated from the wider traditional societies in which they lived.

Breakthrough beyond this second world of cultural bases was slow in coming and only occurred from the late 1950s onwards as contact with what might be described as a third 'cultural world' was established. This Baha'i 'third world' comprised those societies or parts of societies which, at a cultural level, stood at the periphery of the world-historical process of modernization, consisting predominantly of tribal and rural groups in the socio-economically underdeveloped Third World, but also of groups such as the rural blacks in the south of the United States.

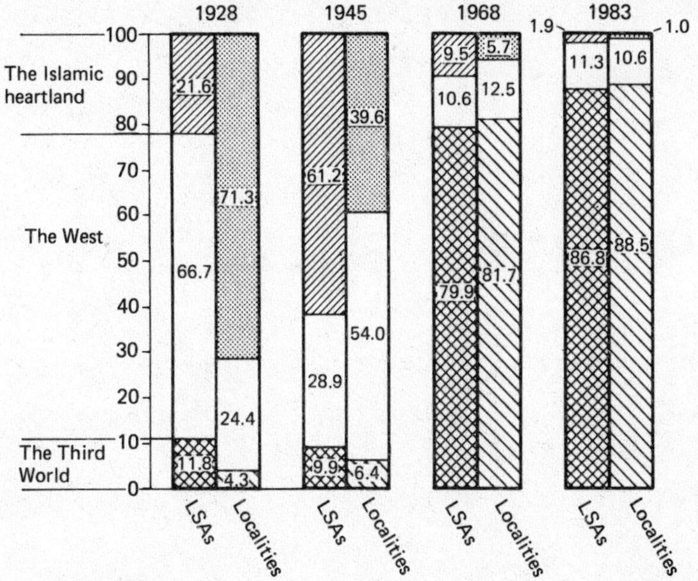

Figure 2. World distribution of Baha'i LSAs and localities (percentages)

These three 'cultural worlds' – the traditional Middle Eastern milieu within which Babism and later the Baha'i Faith first emerged, the wider and historically dominant world of the West and its cultural enclaves, and the Third World of peripheral modernity – occupy what is obviously a complex of spatial and historical location. In particular, the boundary between the modern 'West' and the modern periphery is fluid and changing.

Some indication of the relative importance of the three 'worlds' of the Baha'i community as a whole may be gathered from Figure 2, as well as from the selected Baha'i administrative statistics shown in Tables 2 and 3. Although the areas defined in these tables are not identical to the geo-cultural division outlined above, they substantially reflect it. The overall change from an essentially Middle Eastern community to one that is predominantly 'Third World' in composition is clearly revealed.

Thus, in 1928 the overwhelming majority of Baha'is lived in the Islamic heartland of the Faith, mostly in Iran, but also in other parts of the Middle East and North Africa as well as in Russian Turkestan and the Caucasus. This predominance was reflected in the area's share of the total number of Baha'i localities in the world (71 per cent). This compared with only 24 per

Table 2. *Selected Baha'i administrative statistics by area, 1928 and 1945*

Geographical area	1928					1945				
	NSAs	LSAs	(%)	Localities	(%)	NSAs	LSAs	(%)	Localities	(%)
The Islamic Heartland										
Iran	1	17[a]	16.6	346[a]	59.8	1	291	57.6	693	36.6
Middle East and North Africa (excl. Iran)	2	5	4.9	33	5.7	2	18	3.6	55	2.9
Turkestan and the Caucasus	2	0	–	34	5.9	0	0	–	2	0.1
Subtotal	5	22	21.6	413	71.3	3	309	61.2	750	39.6
The West										
North America	1	47	46.0	67	11.6	1	134	26.5	907	47.9
Europe	2	12[b]	11.8	65	11.2	2	6	1.2	93	4.9
Anglo-Pacific	0	9	8.8	9	1.6	1	6	1.2	24	1.3
Subtotal	3	68	66.7	141	24.4	4	146	28.9	1,024	54.0

The Baha'i Third World										
Latin America and the Caribbean	0	1	1.0	1	0.2	0	24	4.8	44	2.3
Africa (excl. the North)	0	1	1.0	1	0.2	0	0	–	6	0.3
South and South-East Asia	1	7	6.9	15	2.6	1	26	5.1	65	3.4
East Asia	0	3	2.9	6	1.0	0	0	–	5	0.3
Oceania	0	0	–	2	0.3	0	0	–	1	0.1
Subtotal	1	12	11.8	25	4.3	1	50	9.9	121	6.4
Total	9	102		579		8	505		1,895	

Notes: The 'Middle East' comprises Afghanistan, Turkey and the Arab countries of Asia; 'North Africa' comprises the countries of the Mediterranean littoral, Sudan and the former Spanish Sahara; the 'Anglo-Pacific' comprises Australia, New Zealand and Hawaii; and 'Africa' includes the islands in the west of the Indian Ocean but excludes the Arab north.
a The Iranian figures for 1928 represent regional administrative divisions and component localities.
b Includes a presumed figure of 5 for Germany (see *Baha'i World*, vol. III, p. 218).

Sources: Calculated from *Baha'i World*, vol II, pp. 181–91; vol. X, pp. 551–82.

Table 3. *Selected Bahaʾi administrative statistics by area, 1968 and 1983*

Geographical area	1968					1983					LSAs (1983) per 1m population
	NSAs	LSAs	(%)	Localities	(%)	NSAs	LSAs	(%)	Localities	(%)	
The Islamic Heartland											
Iran	1	574	8.4	1,539	4.9	1	355	1.4	709	0.6	9.5
Middle East and North Africa (excl. Iran)	6	78	1.1	237	0.8	12	113	0.5	373	0.3	0.5
Turkestan and the Caucasus	0	0	–	7	0.0	0	0	–	0	–	–
Subtotal	7	652	9.5	1,783	5.7	13	468	1.9	1,082	1.0	1.8[a]
The West											
North America	3	500	7.3	2,661	8.4	3	2,016	8.2	8,716	7.7	8.2
Europe	15	178	2.6	1,047	3.3	19	593	2.4	2,637	2.3	1.7
Anglo-Pacific	3	45	0.7	235	0.7	3	185	0.7	545	0.5	9.8
Subtotal	21	723	10.6	3,943	12.5	25	2,794	11.3	11,898	10.6	4.6[b]

The Baha'i Third World											
Latin America and the Caribbean	23	621	9.1	3,469	11.0	35	3,743	15.1	16,276	14.4	17.1
Africa (excl. the North)	11	2,039	29.8	6,173	19.6	34	4,616	18.7	27,385	24.3	13.7
South and South-East Asia	13	2,648	38.7	15,384	48.7	12	12,576	50.9	53,044	47.0	10.2
East Asia	3	100	1.5	442	1.4	4	148	0.6	1,216	1.1	0.9[c]
Oceania	3	57	0.8	342	1.1	12	369	1.5	1,875	1.7	72.4
Subtotal	53	5,465	79.9	25,810	81.7	97	21,452	86.8	99,796	88.5	10.2[c]
Total	81	6,840		31,536		135	24,714		112,776		8.3[d]

Notes: Geographical areas as in Table 2.
a Excludes Turkestan and the Caucasus.
b Excludes Eastern Europe and the USSR.
c Excludes mainland China, Mongolia and North Korea.
d Excludes most of the Communist block (as per *a*, *b* and *c*).

Sources: Calculated from Universal House of Justice, *The Bahá'í Faith: Statistical Information, 1844–1968* (Haifa, [Bahá'í World Centre], 1968); and Universal House of Justice, Department of Statistics, *The Seven Year Plan, 1979-1986, Statistical Report, Riḍván 1983* (Haifa, Bahá'í World Centre, 1983). Population figures for LSAs (1983) per million taken from the UN, *Demographic Yearbook, 1980*.

cent in the West and 4 per cent in the Third World, this last figure mostly representing the Iranian expatriate community in India (South and South-East Asia). The area's relative lack of administrative development was shown by its low share in the total number of Local Spiritual Assemblies (22 per cent). By contrast, the small communities in the West formed most of the Local Assemblies.

The situation had changed quite markedly by 1945. Although the Islamic heartland undoubtedly still contained most of the world's Bahaʾis, the extensive teaching campaigns in the West had led to a great diffusion of Bahaʾis, such that 54 per cent of Bahaʾi world localities were now in the West. Even so, only 14 per cent of these localities (146 out of 1,024) contained the minimum of nine adult Bahaʾis to form a Local Assembly. By contrast, following an intensive programme of Local Assembly formation in the Islamic heartland, 41 per cent of its localities (309 out of 750) now had Assemblies, constituting 61 per cent of the world total. The Third World remained an area of relative insignificance, the Assembly and locality figures being below 10 per cent of the total.

The transformation which underlies the modern distribution of Bahaʾis began in the 1950s with increasingly large-scale enrolments of new Bahaʾis in the Third World. The pattern is already shown in the 1968 figures and has been accentuated in those for 1983. Despite continued growth in the Islamic heartland and the West, their proportional share of Assemblies and localities had declined sharply in 1968, their combined total representing in the region of only 20 per cent of each. Despite sustained growth in the West, its world share of Assemblies and localities was still only 11 per cent by 1983. By contrast, the Islamic heartland now had less than 2 per cent of each, a decline which was accelerated by the persecutions in Iran (from 1979 onwards), which led to a net fall in the number of Assemblies and localities. It is the Third World which has come to predominate, and by 1983 some 89 per cent of world localities and 87 per cent of Local Assemblies were located in this area.

A similar, though less dramatic, pattern of change is revealed by the figures for National Spiritual Assemblies (Tables 2 and 3). In 1928, five out of nine NSAs were in the Islamic heartland, three were in the West, and one (India) was in the Third World. This situation was largely unaltered by 1945, even though persecution had led to the disbandment of the Assemblies of Turkestan and the Caucasus and an Australian–New Zealand Assembly had been formed. Marked increases in the number of NSAs only began in the 1950s. By 1983 the majority of NSAs (97 out of 135) were in the Third World, this figure exceeding the combined total for the West (25) and the Islamic heartland (13).

Expansion within each of these world areas has not been even. In the Islamic heartland Iran has always been overwhelmingly predominant, whilst the formerly significant Baha'i communities of Turkestan and the Caucasus collapsed under the pressure of persecution. Again, in the West, North America has shown a marked preponderance over Europe and the Anglo-Pacific. Finally, in the Baha'i Third World, South and South-East Asia has always been the leading area, although Latin America and Africa have also become significant areas. By contrast, East Asia and the thinly populated area of Oceania have had relatively few Assemblies and localities.

Population densities must also be taken into consideration, however. In this regard some measure of the relative success of Baha'i expansion is provided by the quotients of the number of Local Spiritual Assemblies per million total population. These are given in the final column in Table 3. Excluding most of the communist block (Eastern Europe, the USSR, Mongolia, China and North Korea), in which such Local Assemblies as there were have long since been disbanded, there were in 1983 approximately 8.3 Baha'i Assemblies for every million people in the world. The lowest quotients were for the Middle East excluding Iran (0.5), East Asia (0.9) and Europe (1.7). Quotients at or above the world average obtained in North America (8.2), Iran (9.5) (greatly reduced, in 1968 it had been approximately 21.2), the Anglo-Pacific (9.8), and South and South-East Asia (10.2). The highest figures obtained for Black Africa (13.7), Latin America and the Caribbean (17.1) and Oceania (72.4). In part, the small size of the host populations in the islands of the Pacific account for the exceptionally large figure for Assemblies per million, but even in terms of the total Baha'i population, the Baha'is on several of the island groups represent over 1 per cent of the total population.[3] By contrast, despite the large number of Assemblies in southern Asia, the massive size of the host population gives them relatively far less significance. Overall, the relative success of Baha'i expansion in the three world areas is reflected in the quotients for each, the Islamic world now being reduced to 1.8, the West having a figure of 4.6, and the Third World a figure of 10.2.

The internationalization of Baha'i leadership

One aspect of this changing balance between these three geo-cultural areas of Baha'i expansion has been the internationalization of Baha'i leadership. When the first Western Baha'i communities were established, various Western Baha'is readily assumed a leadership role in the international development of the religion. Possessed of relatively high levels of wealth, education and organizational experience, the Western Baha'is were also members of a culture and civilization which was exercising an increasing dominance over the whole world. Although the basis for the Baha'i administration had first been established in the East, it was the Western Baha'is, most particularly those from North America, who were the primary agents in its subsequent diffusion and establishment throughout the world. Notably, many National Assemblies in the Third World initially included a significant number of non-indigenous pioneers, and of the 36 individuals who were appointed by Shoghi Effendi as Hands of the Cause (1951–7) or as members of the first International Baha'i Council (1951–61), 23 (64 per cent) were from the West, 12 (33 per cent) were Iranian, and only one (a Ugandan) was from the Third World.[4] Again, of those 15 individuals elected to the second International Baha'i Council (1961–3) and to the Universal House of Justice (1963–83), 12 were from the West and 3 from the East. Of these, most of the Westerners (10) came from the United States (the other two from Britain), and all three of the Iranians had strong links outside Iran, two of them having been pioneers in the Third World.

Since 1963, however, the extensive expansion in the Third World has been rapidly and increasingly reflected in the composition of Baha'i leadership groups. As experience in administration has grown, most National Assemblies in the Third World have undergone an 'indigenization' of membership. Similarly, the Counsellors and Auxiliary Board members have been increasingly drawn from the ranks of the indigenous Baha'is. Thus of the 67 Counsellors appointed in 1980, whilst Westerners still comprised the largest group (26, or 39 per cent), Third Worlders were the second-largest group (24, or 36 per cent), Iranians being the smallest group (17, or 25 per cent). This compares with figures for the world distribution of Local Assemblies in the three areas of respectively 11, 87 and 2 per cent.

THE MIDDLE EAST

The main developments in the first of these three geo-cultural areas during the period – the traditional Islamic heartland – may be summarized as follows. The early years of the period were in some ways quite encouraging. In Iran the final years of the Qajar regime, which nominally lasted until 1925, and the opening years of Pahlavi rule were ones of relative expansion and freedom. Although still subject to occasional bouts of persecution and killing, the Baha'is at this time were still relatively confident of their success, freely publishing their own literature and holding public meetings. Whether because the Baha'is were overconfident – one Baha'i account in the late 1920s referred to 'the fact' that 'any progressive measures undertaken to rehabilitate Persia along the lines of modern liberalism and progress would have to be based upon the Baha'i community'[5] – and hence too assertive, or whether an increasingly well-established authoritarian regime could not brook the existence of a well-organized and influential religious movement independent of its control, the situation began to change in the early thirties, and in 1934 the Baha'i schools throughout the country were closed, Baha'is later being purged from high-ranking government and army posts and a general atmosphere of official harassment continuing until Reza Shah's overthrow by the British and Russians in 1941.

In Turkestan and the Caucasus the initial aftermath of the 1917 Revolution created conditions of unprecedented freedom of expression and organization for the Baha'is, and for the first time ethnic Russians joined the community, the Baha'i youth organization proving itself a serious competitor to the Komsomol.[6] From 1928 onwards, however, there was a build-up of anti-Baha'i activity, including the arrest and exile of leading Baha'is, the disbanding of their organizations, the closure of their schools and libraries, and the expropriation of their *Mashriqu'l-Adhkár*. In 1938 there was a further wave of mass arrests, internal exiles and deportations, and the Baha'i communities of Asiatic Russia – once the most flourishing in the entire Baha'i world – were all but destroyed.

In the Arab world the Baha'is of Egypt and Iraq were at first able to conduct a modest programme of activities and were even able to establish new groups outside the large cities. Toleration was always precarious, however, and in 1922 control of the Most Holy House, the building formerly occupied by Bahá'u'lláh in Baghdad, was taken from the Baha'is, a successful appeal to the Permanent Mandates Commission of the League of Nations being unavailing in securing its return. Again, in 1925, a provincial court in Upper Egypt set in motion a train of events by which the Baha'is were nationally proclaimed unbelievers. Both of these events had useful international repercussions for the Baha'is, the appeal to the Permanent Mandates Commission attracting considerable world attention to their claims, whilst the Egyptian court decision that 'the Baha'i religion is a new religion, with an independent platform and laws', provided an invaluable argument in support of their claim to be a new religion independent of Islam.[7] In Palestine, although the Baha'is secured a considerable degree of recognition from the mandatory authorities, no programme of expansion was undertaken, a policy which was later continued by the Bahaʾis in relationship to the new state of Israel, which was established there in 1948.

After the Second World War, the Bahaʾis' situation in the Middle East was uneven. In the Arab world some new centres were established and for a brief period the Egyptian community flourished, even though by their activities they attracted increasing opposition from Muslim activists, which in some cases even led to physical assaults. Considered suspect by Muslim activists and certain nationalists alike, however, and now in the politically compromising situation of having their World Centre in what had just become Israel, the Bahaʾis in the Arab world were increasingly beleaguered. In 1960 all Bahaʾi activities in Egypt were banned by presidential decree and numbers of Bahaʾis interrogated and arrested; in 1962 the newly emergent Moroccan community was subjected to severe harassment and several Bahaʾis sentenced to death (the sentences later being commuted after international appeals had been made); and in 1970 all Bahaʾi activities were banned in Iraq.

In Iran, meanwhile, the Bahaʾis had been able to renew their campaign of expansion in the confused aftermath of the war, but encountered increasing harassment by the members of the Fidáʾíyán-i Islám, an underground Muslim activist organisation. Several Bahaʾis were murdered as a result. Then in 1955, after another apparent improvement in their situation *vis-à-vis* the authorities, the Bahaʾis were subjected to a fresh campaign of persecution led by the ulama, but this time with the active co-operation of the Pahlavi regime, a campaign which led to government orders for the suppression of the 'Bahaʾi sect' and the expulsion of Bahaʾis from government employ. During this campaign the Bahaʾis were subjected to a sorry tide of physical assaults, rape, murder, abduction, food boycott, attempts at forcible recantation, looting and destruction of homes and property, attacks on holy places, and the destruction of Bahaʾi graves and corpses. After widespread international protests, the Iranian authorities took steps to end the physical persecution of the Bahaʾis, without, however, allowing Bahaʾis back into their employ, or granting them the recognition to contract legal marriages or assemble for worship. Thereafter the situation gradually improved until the period of turmoil which led in 1979 to the overthrow of the Pahlavis and the institution of the revolutionary Islamic republic. Under the Islamic republic the Bahaʾis have been subjected to a campaign of persecution of great severity leading to the execution of over 180 Bahaʾis combined with numerous unofficial attacks. Fearing mass slaughter, thousands of Bahaʾis have left Iran.

The modern Iranian Baha'i community

As a religious movement within Iranian society, the Baha'i Faith appears to have reached its zenith during the troubled years at the beginning of this century. Thereafter, whilst retaining its internal dynamism, it has apparently ceased to gain significant numbers of new adherents. Instead, the Iranian Baha'i community has come to rely on natural increase and the successful socialization of its children in order to maintain its existence. Whether or not the Baha'i fertility rate is lower than that of the general Iranian population (reflecting emerging middle-class norms), or whether there has been a net outflow of members, the percentage of Baha'is in the general population appears to have marginally declined over the course of the century, so that now, with about 300,000 members, the Baha'i community represents less than 1 per cent of the total population.[8]

The combination of a cessation of significant growth with the maintenance of a hostile external environment has led the Baha'i community to gain a precarious niche in Iranian society as an unrecognised 'minority Church'.[9] Fostering an attitude of expansionist universalism and tolerance amongst the adherents, Baha'i leaders have neither sought to impose a sectarian exclusivity on the Baha'is, nor to introduce any definite distinction between the committed and the relatively uncommitted. In contrast to the Babis, who drew a sharp distinction between themselves as true believers and the wider world of unbelief, the modern Iranian Baha'is have become separated from wider society by an externally imposed boundary defined by the custodians of traditional belief. Although membership remained theoretically voluntary, 'being a Baha'i' has come to assume a quasi-ethnic status.[10] Apart from those consciously leaving the religion, membership of the Iranian Baha'i community has now become largely ascriptive, both on the basis of family ties and external definition. Correspondingly, whilst Iranian Baha'is appear to be more likely than the general population to marry outside their immediate kinship networks, they are inclined to marry co-religionists and thus reinforce their identity as a separate socio-religious community.[11] Significantly, the distinction between Baha'is of different religious backgrounds has become much less important, and intermarriage between these different groups, and between Iranian Baha'is and their Western co-religionists has become relatively common.

No study of the social composition of the contemporary Iranian Baha'i community has yet been made. Certainly there remain Baha'i peasants and others of lower social status (including sedentarized nomads), but the overall impression gained is of a community that is disproportionately middle class. Growing up in a religion in which religious value is placed on literacy and modern education, Baha'is were likely to benefit from the modernization programmes initiated by the Pahlavis. Forbidden to engage in politics by their own leaders and restricted in their involvement in government employment, many Baha'is were, until recently, found in commerce and industry, or were independent professionals (perhaps particularly in medicine and engineering). Under the Islamic republic Baha'is in government employ have been sacked, and many others have been forced into unemployment or have had their means of livelihood expropriated or destroyed.

Various possible factors may be identified as contributing to the cessation of Baha'i growth in Iran. One of the most important has probably been the changing context of 'modernization'. In the earlier part of this century, at a time of widespread discontent with the established order, those who favoured modernization may well have found the Baha'i programme for social and religious change attractive. Under the Pahlavis (1925–79), by contrast, a strident secular nationalism became the official ideology of modernization. The regime itself became the main agency of modernization, seeking to monopolize and control all aspects of social change. Alternative (and hence rival) ideologies of modernization were allowed no institutional expression (Baha'i schools being closed, for example), and groups embodying such ideologies were either suppressed or restricted in their operation. More generally, for both supporters and opponents of the regime, modernization became a secular issue, and the appeal of a religious programme of modernization correspondingly declined. In any case such aspects of the Baha'i programme as were more widely known – such as the belief in female emancipation – were no longer regarded as particularly novel. Increasingly the main religious responses to Iran's problems took the form of a conservative Shiʿi fundamentalism, and it was only towards the end of the Pahlavi period that a religio-social programme of modernization again made a popular appeal, and then in the form of the anti-imperialist Islamic humanism of men like ʿAlí Sharíʿatí (1933–77).[12]

A second factor in the cessation of Baha'i growth was the logistical weakness of the Baha'i community. Despite being the largest religious minority in Iran, the Baha'is were accorded no official recognition by the Pahlavi regime (Thus, even at a personal level, Baha'i marriages were invalid and official employment problematic). As long as they engaged in no overtly 'public' expressions of their religion, the Baha'is were tacitly tolerated and generally protected from persecution, but they were given no freedom to publish their ideas. Not only were they thus unable to defend themselves against popular prejudice and the increasingly well-organized anti-Bahaʾi propaganda of Islamic activists, but they were unable to present their own ideas of social and religious change to a wider audience. Moreover, on occasion, the Pahlavi regime was willing to condone or even to encourage persecution of the Bahaʾis, whether as a sop to Islamic militants (as in 1955), or as an attempted means of diverting public discontent with the regime (as in 1978).[13] Again, possibly for tactical reasons, SAVAK, the secret police, readily countenanced the anti-Bahaʾi activities of the Tablíghat-i Islámí organization.[14]

A third factor was the developing political 'image' of the Bahaʾi community. Enjoined to be obedient to any established government, but forbidden to engage in political activity, the Bahaʾis came to be seen by opponents of the Pahlavi regime as having provided it with more than tacit support. Certainly they had failed to oppose it (but then so had most Iranians). However unjustly, the presence of several Bahaʾis amongst the non-political elite, and of several individuals with Bahaʾi forebears amongst the political leadership helped consolidate an image of complicity. Moreover, the known internationalist attitudes and linkages of the Bahaʾis lent support to the belief that they were unpatriotic, or worse, the agents of foreign powers. The Bahaʾis might deny such allegations, but in a society which had been the victim of repeated foreign interventions and in which the political process was generally covert and often conspiratorial, they were not believed.

A fourth factor was the symbolic cultural role of the Bahaʾis as internationalists and Westernizers. During the Pahlavi period the earlier tension between 'traditionalists' and 'modernists' had become a cultural schism of major proportions. Whilst the Pahlavi elite and large sections of the middle class adopted (or adapted) 'Western' or 'modern' styles of behaviour, the mass of Iranians became increasingly ambivalent or hostile towards the erosion of traditional mores. Moreover, the defence of certain aspects of traditional culture assumed significance not just as a reaffirmation of traditional certainties, but as a statement of opposition to both the dominance of the West over Iranian society and the actual rule of the Pahlavi regime. In this context – culminating in the neo-traditionalism of the Islamic revolution – the hostility towards 'modernism' was readily directed against the Bahaʾis (especially as they were relatively unprotected politically). The Bahaʾis were well suited to the role of symbolic modernists. Disproportionately middle class, they favoured Western education, were assumed (wrongly) to be anti-Islamic, enjoyed extensive contacts with their non-Iranian co-religionists (particularly in the West), and had their world headquarters in a land that had come to symbolize Western penetration into the traditional world of Islam. Perhaps particularly crucially, the Baha'is favoured female emancipation, with all of the profound destabilization of traditional Iranian mores which that represented.

Contemporary persecutions in Iran

In February 1979, after widespread popular agitation, the Pahlavi regime was overthrown and a revolutionary Islamic republic established in its stead. As the Islamic regime consolidated its position, the Baha'is found themselves increasingly beleaguered. Regarded by many Islamic activists as worse than heretics, the Baha'is were subjected to a mounting campaign of persecution. National Baha'i leaders, Local Spiritual Assembly members and others were executed. Hundreds of Baha'is were arrested. Baha'i properties were confiscated. All Baha'i institutions were closed down. All Baha'i activities were banned. Thousands of Baha'is were summarily discharged from employment. The assets of many individual Baha'is were seized. Many Baha'is were made homeless. Baha'i students were expelled from universities. Baha'i children were denied entry to schools. Even the corpses of Baha'is were disinterred and Baha'i burial grounds desecrated. No redress was offered other than for apostasy. No petition to those in authority was heeded, and even extensive international humanitarian appeals on behalf of the Baha'is were ignored.

Given the evidently popular nature of these persecutions amongst many non-Baha'is and the participation of at least some leading governmental figures in their encouragement, the question of motivation must be raised.

Doubtless for some of the most dedicated Islamic activists, Baha'is are simply heretics and apostates whose blood may therefore be shed with impunity, but at a popular level other factors also apply. Thus, in at least some cases, the appropriation of Baha'is' properties seems to have been a factor.[15] More generally, for many Iranians the Baha'is have come to represent national scapegoats, enemies within, who can be blamed for the loss of traditional culture and national independence. The political and cultural image which the Baha'is in Iran have come to acquire is highly relevant here. The accusations against them vividly illustrate the 'deep structures' by which, according to Harvey Cox, minority movements are commonly caricatured and condemned.[16] Thus the Baha᾽is are said to be subversive and immoral, their leaders adepts at devious misrepresentation, whilst the rank and file are ignorant dupes.

Reflecting common human uncertainties, these are all standard accusations which are levelled at 'heretical' groups. They say more about the accusers than the accused. That in the case of the Baha᾽is they are so firmly believed by many contemporary Iranians, despite what might be taken as a mass of evidence to the contrary, is perhaps indicative of the extreme stress placed on traditional Iranian society. It should be noted that the last two of Cox's deep structures are of the nature of non-falsifiable statements: if the heretic is automatically assumed to be lying or deluded then nothing that he or she may say need be taken at its face value. There is no escape. Certainly, this is the impression given by much of the argumentation against the Iranian Baha᾽is: they are assumed to be guilty whatever evidence they may use to defend themselves.

The accusations of subversion and immorality are more specific. In the case of the former the Baha᾽is are commonly alleged to be acting as spies, usually for some combination of the British, American and Israeli governments. The Baha᾽i Faith is also said to have been established by the British and/or the Russians as a means of colonial subversion. This account is unsupported by documentary evidence, is (at the least) historically and logistically unlikely, and is vehemently denied by the Baha᾽is. Nevertheless, the style of thinking which it exemplifies is readily understandable given the actual extent of foreign meddling in Iranian affairs. As to the accusation of immorality, it should be said that Baha᾽i standards of sexual morality are at least as high as those of other religions in Iran. What is more at issue here is the extent of female emancipation. The official non-recognition of Baha᾽i marriages and the greater freedom of Baha᾽i women (in terms of their abandonment of the veil and their participation with men in religious meetings and organization) may well provide a pretext for charges of immorality, but one suspects that underlying these charges are masculine uncertainties regarding the role of Iranian women. Even in the last century the Shaykhi leader, Karím Khán Kirmání, linked the threat of 'Westernization' to the threat of female emancipation,[17] and the reassertion of the traditional role of women became a significant element in the movement of neo-traditionalist revolt that culminated in the Islamic revolution. Even the modest assertion of female emancipation which has been made by the Baha᾽is may be taken by traditionalists as profoundly threatening.

The future for Iranian Baha᾽is seems bleak. A regime fundamentally antithetical to their aspirations seems firmly established in power. None of the groups in political opposition to the present regime has spoken publicly in their favour or defence. Whichever group rules in Tehran, the best the Bahaʾis might hope for is bare toleration. More fundamentally, a century of hostile propaganda, feeding upon the anxieties of Iran's international subjugation, has created what may best be described as a venomous popular attitude towards the Bahaʾis. There is little likelihood of their gaining the means of offering effective counter-propaganda. Personal contacts with non-Bahaʾis may mitigate hostility, but the Bahaʾis are in any case overrepresented amongst social groups that are unlikely to engage in religious persecution.

If the social environment remains unpromising, the cohesion of the Iranian Bahaʾi community may well have been increased.[18] Less committed members of the community may well seek to pass as Muslims or even apostasize,[19] but it seems likely that even if the level of persecution were to increase, a substantial section of the Bahaʾi community would seek to maintain their separate religious identity and to resist forcible recantation even to the point of martyrdom. Indeed, for the faithful, the threat of martyrdom doubtless represents a continued linkage with the idealized tradition of religious sacrifice which is so fundamental in Iranian culture. This is a basis for commitment and survival as a religious community: *sanguis martyrum semen Ecclesiae*. Moreover, the Bahaʾis now possess a comprehensive and well-established belief system of their own which makes genuine conversion to Shiʿism extremely unlikely. Again, the system of Bahaʾi administration is depersonalized, flexible and well-established amongst the community. Emotionally, idealistically and structurally the Iranian Bahaʾi community has considerable resources to ensure its survival in the midst of an extremely hostile society. Under present circumstances the hopes of Islamic activists for the destruction of the Iranian Bahaʾi community seem as unrealistic as the hopes of some Bahaʾis for an ending to hostility and the widespread conversion of their countrymen.

THE WEST

In terms of the development of the Bahaʾi Faith as a world religion, its growth as a religious movement in the West has been a profoundly significant one, marking the decisive breakthrough by which the religion's independence from Iranian Shiʿism was established; providing a new and crucial geo-cultural base from which a world-wide evangelism could be conducted; and providing both the locus and, to a considerable extent, the personnel by which the modern Bahaʾi administrative system could be developed. For the most part remaining comparatively small in numbers, the Western Baha'i communities have had an impact on Baha'i development out of all proportion to their size.

Although highly uneven, the growth of the various Western Baha'i communities has been distinguished by a notable similarity of development. Most of the older Western communities appear to have passed through what might almost be regarded as four 'stages' of development. Thus, initially, the Baha'i teachings generally appear to have exercised a particular appeal on the basis of their universality as the perceived expression of the 'spirit of the age'. As a corollary, many of those who became Baha'is were inclined to regard the Baha'i movement as inclusive in nature and to disfavour the development of more than a minimal level of organization. By contrast, in the second 'stage', those Baha'is who regarded Baha'i as being not just a universalistic movement, but as a revealed religion with its own specific teachings, increasingly predominated. Increasing stress was placed on organization and, whilst the Baha'i communities became more exclusive in their memberships, the establishment of a relatively stable and efficient administration seems to have initiated a long period of slow but steady growth. In the third stage, the developing administration was increasingly employed to pursue systematic plans of expansion and administrative consolidation. Baha'i activists at this time achieved considerable geographical diffusion of their communities, but were still generally unable to achieve high rates of growth. The fourth stage (starting in most of the Western world in the late 1960s or early 1970s) was marked by significantly higher rates of growth and a greater social diversity amongst those who became Baha'is. A certain broadening of cultural styles and religious interests has accompanied these later developments.

Universalistic individualism

During the early development of the Western Baha'i communities the religious appeal of the movement for many of its adherents centred on the broad and inclusive universalism of its teachings. Correspondingly the individual believer was perceived as a prime locus of authority. In the United States this view was increasingly challenged in the late 1910s and the 1920s, the resultant tensions marking the rise of what might be termed 'organizational exclusivism' as the dominant attitude within the community.[20] Elsewhere, 'universalistic individualism' persisted far longer. Thus, despite the formation of National Spiritual Assemblies in Britain and Germany (1923) and the initial attempt to form one in Australia and

New Zealand (1926), Baha'i activity remained largely a matter of individual or local initiative.

Not that individualistic action could not be highly effective. As in the early American Baha'i community, the combination of energetic Baha'i initiative and a favourable socio-religious milieu could lead to quite impressive results. This was especially true in Weimar Germany. In a period which, for some Germans at least, was one of considerable religious uncertainty and social idealism, the Baha'is met with relative success. Many new Baha'i groups were established. By 1925, of the 38 localities in Europe in which Baha'is resided, 26 were in Germany.[21] Publishing activities were expanded, the increasing number of items written in German rather than being translated from English indicating the emergence of a new and indigenous intellectual leadership. A monthly Baha'i magazine was started (1921); a Baha'i Esperanto Society was established, forging extensive links with the then flourishing Esperanto movement; and in 1931 the first German Baha'i summer school was held, modelled on the American Green Acre. Again, in Australia, the energetic labours of an American Baha'i couple (who arrived in 1920) soon established Baha'i Assemblies in five of the major cities. An Assembly was also established in New Zealand and plans made for the formation of a National Assembly for the two countries. As in Britain, much use was made of American Baha'i literature, but a locally based international Baha'i magazine was also started. As in the United States, the Australian Baha'is initially found the various New Thought groups productive locales from which to gain new members.[22]

Where initiative was lacking, or where the socio-religious milieu was thought to be unresponsive, results were meagre. Thus, although both the British and French Baha'i groups had been amongst the first established in the West, neither experienced any marked growth. The situation in France was particularly unproductive. There were few activities outside Paris; many of the Baha'is were not French; and, apart from the formation of a Local Assembly in Paris, there was no administrative development.

Nor was the situation much better in Britain. Apparently regarding the British as being too conservative to respond readily to their message, the Baha'is were generally restrained and unobtrusive in their presentation of their faith. When 'opportunity occurs' public lectures were given, but the movement was given 'no advertisement in the ordinary way'.[23] Attempts by some of the Manchester Baha'is to adopt a more dynamic approach received no wider support. Even with the acquisition of a London Baha'i centre (1929) and the commencement of a national Bahaʾi *Newsletter* (1929), there was little change. Meetings might be devotedly continued 'regardless of the number present', but few people became Bahaʾis, and as late as 1932, Shoghi Effendi's secretary was still encouraging American Bahaʾis to visit England, as the Cause there was 'at a standstill'.[24]

Organizational exclusivism

The acceptance of the need for an efficient and authoritative administration of the Bahaʾi community proceeded slowly. Those who favoured greater organization were generally able to initiate, maintain and control a range of administrative bodies with relative ease. It was more difficult for them to convince the rest of the Bahaʾis of the necessity for the change. Indeed, for many of these other Bahaʾis, 'organization' implied a loss of the earlier universalism of the movement. Others either adapted to it or ceased to be actively involved. Apathy and inertia rather than outright opposition were probably the main impediments to change. Furthermore, a significant part of the earlier universalism *was* lost. For many Western Bahaʾis the view that Bahaʾi was an independent revealed religion disturbed their traditional conceptions. Similarly, the new exclusivity of membership was profoundly disturbing.

Outright opposition to this transformation surfaced in both North America and Germany, the two largest and most dynamic of the Western communities. In North America the tensions of transition occupied the late 1910s and most of the 1920s. Although only a tiny minority, those Bahaʾis who actively opposed the developing administration were indicative of a wider sense of unease within the community. Other indications were the new administrative bodies' inability to gain wholehearted support for their plans, and an actual decline in membership.[25] By the late 1920s, however, there was increasing acceptance of organization, and from 1929 onwards a distinct increase in the numerical growth of the community can be detected. Whether or not the change in the national religious mood brought about by the Wall Street Crash (1929) contributed to this increase, it is ironic that it should have coincided with the peaking of the anti-organizational activities of Ruth White and Ahmad Sohrab. A decisive consolidation of the organizational stance within the American Bahaʾi community had occurred. In its wake the pace of Bahaʾi activity accelerated. After years of delay, sufficient funding was found for the construction of the superstructure of the Bahaʾi Temple at Wilmette (1930–1); a more sustained endeavour was made to establish

Bahaʾi groups and Assemblies throughout North America; and, from 1937 onwards, the American Bahaʾis embarked on a series of international teaching plans which demanded significant deployment of human and material resources. Although remaining small in scale, the American Bahaʾi community was able to sustain a steady rate of growth, averaging about 8 per cent per annum from 1926 until 1942, thereafter declining to about 4 per cent (1942–64). By the early 1960s there were about 10,000 Bahaʾis in the contiguous United States, a further 1,100 in Canada, and 200 in Alaska (with a separate Bahaʾi administration). Of the various regions, only the south-eastern United States had proved unamenable to the establishment of a widespread network of Bahaʾi Assemblies, although there were isolated states elsewhere – notably Mormon Utah – with few Bahaʾis.

In Europe the leading community of the 1920s had been Germany. As in America, the rising tide of organized activity produced its critics, and it was in Germany that Ruth White's attack on the administration produced its only tangible results in the form of Wilhelm Herrigel's Bahaʾi World Union (1930–7). Most German Bahaʾis remained loyal to Shoghi Effendi, however, and again, with the growing acceptance of the need for organization, there was a perceptible increase in the level of activity both in Germany and the surrounding countries. Supported by a succession of touring American Bahaʾi teachers, Bahaʾi activities throughout central and eastern Europe peaked in the mid-1930s, a particularly marked response occurring in Bulgaria and Hungary. Again, in Britain, the gradual acceptance of the need for organization ended the long period of stagnation which the Bahaʾi community had experienced. Thus from about 1936 onwards there was a distinct increase in the level of activity, with the adoption of a more outgoing approach to teaching, the initiation of a yearly summer school (from 1937), the establishment of a Bahaʾi Publishing Trust (1937), and the opening of several local Bahaʾi centres. Similarly, in Australia and New Zealand, the election of a National Assembly (1934) marked an increasing acceptance of the need for organization, even though there appears to have been no marked increase in the level of activity until after the war. As in Britain, there had been no overt opposition to the development of a more authoritative administration, but rather a lack of positive enthusiasm for it.

Political constraints and post-war planning

The acceleration of Bahaʾi activity which occurred in much of Europe during the mid-1930s was rapidly brought to an end by the changing political situation. In May 1937 all Baha'i activities and institutions in Germany were banned by order of the Gestapo because of the Faith's 'international and pacifist teachings'; Baha'i books, archives and records were confiscated; and a number of Baha'is were later tried and imprisoned. With the outbreak of war in 1939 all Baha'i activities in occupied Europe came to an end. As in Germany, numbers of Baha'is of Jewish background were sent to concentration camps and murdered, most prominently Lidia Zamenhof, the Baha'i daughter of the founder of Esperanto. Only in Britain were Baha'i activities able to be continued and the dynamism of the 1930s sustained.

In the aftermath of the war the proven advantages of systematic Baha'i expansion plans were applied to Europe. Already, in 1944, the British Baha'is had initiated a Six Year Plan of their own (1944–50) and had succeeded in raising their total numbers from 120 to 370 and the number of their Assemblies from 5 to 24.[26] On the Continent, systematic planning was adopted as soon as some recovery had been made from the enormous devastation and confusion caused by the war. The German Baha'is were fortunate in this regard, in that, as 80 per cent of them lived in the American zone of occupation,[27] they were able to receive the assistance of German-speaking American Baha'i servicemen in gaining permission to reorganize (in August 1945), thereafter recommencing public meetings, youth groups, printing and publishing, and, in 1946, the National Assembly and summer school. In 1948, a Five Year Plan was adopted (1948–53) and subsequently a European Baha'i House of Worship constructed near Frankfurt. Elsewhere in Europe, despite initial political opposition in Spain and Portugal, an influx of American Baha'i pioneers during their second Seven Year Plan (1946–53) initiated sustained and widespread teaching activities in all the countries of Western Europe. During the international Ten Year Plan (1953–63) National Assemblies were established in most of these countries, so that whilst prior to the war there had been only 2 National Assemblies, by 1964 there were 15. Again, during the same period, the number of Local Assemblies was raised from 15 to 181.[28] These developments were confined to Western Europe. Whilst there had been a brief period of activity in Eastern Europe immediately after the war, the Baha'is, along with several other smaller religious groups, found their activities proscribed by the newly emergent Marxist regimes.

One significant factor to emerge during this establishment of 'planification' was the importance of administrative independence. All of the long-established Baha'i national communities originally included small groups in adjacent countries. As long as these groups remained part of the larger communities, they experienced little growth. Thus, despite being established in the early 1900s, the Canadian Baha'i community remained but a tiny outlier of the United States community until the 1940s. Even by 1931 there were still only 30 Baha'is in Canada,[29] and it was only when it strove towards, and then (1948) attained, its Baha'i administrative independence that the Canadian community experienced a more marked increase in numbers. A similar pattern seems to have occurred in Alaska (1957), Hawaii (1964) (both ex-USA), Austria (1959, ex-Germany), and the Irish Republic (1973, ex-Britain). Only in New Zealand (1957) does 'independence' not seem to have had this result.

Recent growth and the period of 'mass teaching'

Despite sustaining steady growth, the Western Baha'i communities had remained minute. In terms of absolute numbers, by the late 1940s there were about 5,300 Baha'is in North America and Hawaii, about 1,400 in Europe and 200 or so in Australia and New Zealand.[30] Even by the early 1960s it is probable that there were no more than 16,000–17,000 Baha'is throughout Europe, North America and the Anglo-Pacific, 10,000 of these being in the United States alone, and Britain and Canada having about 1,000 each.[31]

This situation began to change from the late 1960s onwards. In most Western countries dramatic changes in the almost autonomous youth culture led to a sudden efflorescence of interest in social reformism and religious experimentation. Successfully adapting their styles of presentation, many Baha'i communities were able to gain significant numbers of neophytes from this volatile milieu. Where this mass influx of youth was successfully integrated into the existing Baha'i communities, important changes were engendered. From being an often neglected minority, young Baha'is suddenly became the most dynamic element within their communities, spearheading further teaching activity. In some communities they became the majority. The cultural styles of Baha'i activity changed, becoming more varied and experimental, and making more prominent use of music. By the early or mid-1970s, however, the youth culture had again begun to change. In common with other minority religious movements the Baha'is found that their influx of new young believers was slackening off. Moreover, in some countries successful integration of the young converts had not been achieved, many of them abandoning active Baha'i involvement.

Although significantly larger after the years of the 'youth boom', several of the Western Baha'i communities appear to have returned to something of their former state, experiencing steady but very slow growth. This would seem to have been the case in most of Western Europe, where sustained growth raised the total number of Local Assemblies from 178 in 1968 to 593 in 1983 (an increase of 233 per cent), but in which the quotient of Local Assemblies per million people remained one of the lowest in the world (1.7). By contrast, the Anglo-Pacific (9.8) and North America (8.2) attained much higher quotients and appear to have been more successful in retaining the dynamism of the early seventies. In the case of North America this was also due to a second mass influx of new Baha'is which accompanied or followed the youth influx. Although involving various minority groups, this second influx mainly comprised large numbers of Afro-Americans resident in the rural areas of the south-eastern states of the United States, over 20,000 Baha'i enrolments from these areas being recorded during 1970 and the early months of 1971 alone. Often poor and poorly educated, this mass of new Baha'is undoubtedly presented major problems of integration and socialization to the American Baha'i community. Nevertheless, successful Baha'i involvement of a significant number of these neophytes appears to have been achieved. Not only had the American Baha'i community undergone a significant expansion in numbers – from about 20,000 in 1969 to perhaps 100,000 in 1982 – but the social base of the community had undergone a major transformation.[32]

Social composition, religious background and the elements of attraction

As in their development, so in their social composition, the various Western Baha'i communities appear to have been remarkably similar until quite recently.[33] Thus, throughout their history, the Western Baha'i communities appear to have predominantly comprised relatively well-educated members of the urban middle classes. Professional rather than business or commercial groups have been particularly well represented, with the medical, legal, educational and artistic professions well to the fore. During the early period of Baha'i expansion in the West a number of individuals of high social or financial status became Baha'is, but this upper-middle-class group appears not to have been subsequently replicated. Lower-middle-class elements on the other hand appear to have become more significant, many perhaps being socially upwardly mobile. Educationally, large numbers of contemporary Baha'is have received university or college educations. Ethnically, most Western Baha'is have, until recently, been drawn from dominant white groups (Anglo-Americans in the United States and Canada, English in Britain), but in North America in particular this has now changed dramatically with the influx of Afro-Americans, Amerindians and other minority groups. There are also now large numbers of Iranian Bahaʾis in many of the Western Bahaʾi communities.

In terms of religious background most Western Bahaʾis were traditionally drawn from the various Protestant churches, especially from the more 'liberal' rather than 'fundamentalist' groups. There has also been a substantial minority of Bahaʾis of Jewish background in certain local communities, and in the early years, of Bahaʾis from the various metaphysical groups. Roman Catholic groups were until recently more resistant to Bahaʾi teaching endeavour, and it is only since the 1960s that the Bahaʾis have been able to gain a significant following in the Catholic countries of Europe. A substantial minority of Western Bahaʾis were not previously active members of any religion, but many were, including a small number of converted clergymen (mostly Unitarians).

As to those factors which first attracted Westerners to become Bahaʾis, there is remarkable similarity between the responses elicited by Peter Berger in his New York Bahaʾi survey of 1953 and those which I elicited in my sample surveys of Bahaʾis in Britain and Los Angeles in 1979 (Table 4).[34] In all three cases the Bahaʾi social principles emerged as a major factor of initial attraction, most notably those concerned with the advocacy of world unity and peace. Bahaʾi 'religious' doctrines were considerably less prominent, especially in the later surveys. Again, of these religious doctrines, it was the more general schema of progressive revelation rather than the more traditionally religious sense of prophetic fulfilment which was most often referred to. Of course, this prominence of doctrinal formulations may reflect a patterned response, the initial attraction of the Bahaʾi religion being retrospectively interpreted in terms of particularly characteristic Bahaʾi teachings. On the other hand, the belief in the Bahaʾi social teachings and in progressive revelation may be a more deeply rooted expression of idealistic aspiration and the general quest for meaning in a world in which wide-ranging social and political disunities and the coexistence of widely divergent systems of religious belief may themselves present profound problems of meaning. That the provision of a coherent and all-encompassing system of meaning represented an important attractive element was directly supported by many of the responses both in Berger's study – although not separately tabulated – and my own, respondents referring to the common sense practicality of the

Table 4. *Elements of the Baha'i religion regarded as initially attractive (sample surveys)*

	New York 1953 (%)	Los Angeles 1979 (%)	United Kingdom 1979 (%)
Aspects of the Baha'i principles			
World unity and the social principles	38.9	32.2	29.1
Progressive revelation	27.8	11.0	11.3
Prophetic fulfilment	13.3	2.5	2.6
Progressive and scientific	13.3	2.5	2.6
A sense of and approach to meaning			
Logical, commonsensical, 'confirmed what I already knew'	–	13.6	15.2
Practical answer to the world's problems	–	9.3	7.3
Independent investigation of truth	–	3.4	2.6
Everything	–	3.4	2.0
No ritual, dogma or clergy	–	4.2	4.6
Religious experience			
The Baha'i writings and prayers	4.4	6.8	7.3
The lives of the central figures and the history of the Faith	3.3	3.4	7.9
Search and religious experience	11.1	5.9	5.3
Sense of overwhelming truth	–	4.2	4.0
Social experience			
The Baha'is and the sense of community	14.4	17.8	30.5
Baha'i administration	3.3	1.7	2.6
	(N=90)	(N=118)	(N=151)

Note: Many respondents gave multiple answers, so the frequency percentages do not add up to 100.

Sources: Berger, 'From Sect to Church', pp. 134–6 (adapted); Smith, 'Sociological Study', pp. 442–4. See note 34.

Baha'i teachings, to their all-encompassing nature, or to their resonance with previously held attitudes to life. Only a few individuals particularly listed the presumed lack of dogma and the Baha'i doctrine of the independent investigation of truth, a paucity which may possibly indicate the absence of that epistemological individualism once so prominent in the Western Baha'i communities. As Berger noted, religious experience – the response to the Baha'i writings, to the persons of Bahá'u'lláh or ᶜAbdu'l-Bahá, or to mystical experiences – was not generally a major factor of attraction, although it is notable that whilst the religious 'quest' and general religious 'needs' were a significant factor amongst Berger's respondents, the Baha'i writings represented a more important element for my respondents. Again, in contrast to Berger's study, the two 1979 surveys elicited a greater response in terms of the attractiveness of the Baha'i community, over 30 per cent of the British respondents listing this as a significant factor. A few individuals listed the Baha'i administration as a factor of initial attraction.

THE THIRD WORLD

The growth of Baha'i communities in the Third World has become one of the most significant aspects of the religion's development, vastly changing the social composition of its adherents and realistically establishing its claims to be a world religion. This growth has been both complex and uneven, and no attempt will be made here to portray it adequately. Suffice it to say that the earliest Baha'i settlements beyond the religion's cultural heartlands were in cultural 'outliers' of those heartlands; thus the Baha'i community established in India from the 1870s onwards initially drew its main support from a tiny Persianized minority, whilst the small groups later established in the Far East and Latin America were at first drawn almost exclusively from sections of the Western-oriented urban middle classes. Through great ingenuity and endeavour, these groups were established widely and efforts were soon made to secure their consolidation through the formation of Assemblies and the translation of Baha'i writings into the indigenous languages. Necessarily, however, such groups made little impact on the mass of their fellow countrymen and were almost entirely confined to territories in which the appropriate cultural outliers existed. Outside such territories there were few or no Baha'is. In 1950, for example, there were probably not more than a dozen Baha'is in the whole of Black Africa, and the only areas in which any extensive Baha'i teaching work had been undertaken were

South Africa (from the United States) and Ethiopia (from Egypt), whilst in Oceania (that is excluding the Anglo-Pacific) there were no resident Bahaʾis whatsoever. During the period in which Bahaʾi expansion was confined to such outliers, Bahaʾi teaching techniques were almost entirely addressed to establishing contact with liberal and educated religious and social groups, often with meetings sponsored by the local Theosophists or Esperantists, or, on occasion, by a sympathetic university professor.

The 'break-out' from these confines occurred variously, but always followed the conscious attempt to teach the Bahaʾi message to 'the masses', be they tribal minorities or rural illiterates. A lack of sufficiently detailed information precludes even the exact description of those elements of the Third World 'masses' to which the Bahaʾis thus successfully extended their teaching endeavours. Indeed the situation clearly varies from one part of the world to another. Those detailed accounts which are available suggest that, at least initially, the 'masses' contacted were overwhelmingly rural, rather than from the urban poor, but this situation may well have begun to change with the increasing flight from the land in many Third World countries, combined with deliberate endeavours by the Bahaʾis to teach in the shanty towns and urban slums. To say that the massive influx of new Bahaʾis in the Third World was predominantly from rural locations suggests that these Bahaʾis were from peasant backgrounds, but lack of sufficient information prevents any definite assertion in this regard. Whatever the case, such groups were dramatically less affluent and educated than those groups who had hitherto comprised the bulk of the Bahaʾi populations in these countries.

In many cases less uncertainty attaches to the ethnic composition of the converts, the Bahaʾis making special and generally successful endeavours to attract individuals from indigenous minorities, as, for example, in Latin America where, even as early as 1963, the majority of the Bahaʾis were Amerindians.[35] Significantly, the Bahaʾis in those countries which lacked appropriate minority groups and which enjoyed a relative affluence were generally unable to achieve this expansion to the masses – for example Japan, Taiwan and Argentina, all relatively wealthy, with high literacy rates, and containing only tiny tribal or racial minorities, have remained 'underdeveloped' from a Bahaʾi standpoint, possessing some of the lowest quotients in the world for Assemblies per million population (the 1983 figures being 0.3, 1.2 and 1.7 respectively, as compared with Western Europe's 1.7). Correspondingly, whilst there is no simple correlation between these factors, it seems clear that those poorer countries whose populations contain a relatively high proportion of minority group members have often been amongst the most responsive to the Baha'is' attempts to broaden their social base. Bolivia and Ecuador, for example, both with over half their populations Amerindian peasants from the Altiplano and with two of the lowest GNPs in Latin America, had two of the very highest rates of Baha'i Assemblies per million population (143.6 and 35.9 respectively). However, the actual composition of the Baha'i community may in some cases also overrepresent any minority groups, thus making correlations on the basis of general and incomplete information suspect. In Panama, for example, which is a relatively affluent Latin American country with a tiny (5.5 per cent) minority population of Amerindians, approximately 32 per cent of the Baha'i community are Indian.[36] Correspondingly, even as early as 1968, the figure for Baha'i Assemblies per million (32.1) was one of the highest in Latin America.

The mere existence of what might appear to be a potential convert population does not of course of itself enable a religious movement to gain the potential converts; the movement's existing adherents must themselves mobilize to establish meaningful contact with the group in question. In the case of the Baha'is residing in Western cultural enclaves in the Third World there were a number of major barriers which had to be overcome before such contact could be established with the rural masses and tribal or other minorities. These difficulties were both cultural and logistical. Separated from these 'masses' both geographically and in their social networks, the existing Baha'i communities – mostly middle-class – had to make a deliberate effort to cross these barriers and to gain acceptance amongst people who were often, in terms of any social hierarchy, their inferiors. Accustomed to a religious movement which was intensely literate in its orientation, it was necessary to learn how to portray its teachings in a way that was meaningful to those who had little or no experience of a literate culture. There were often formal linguistic barriers to be overcome. Once these barriers were overcome, however, 'mass conversions' often readily occurred, the report of one Korean village where the inhabitants wanted to convert *en masse* seeming to be not untypical.[37]

If gaining new Baha'is by 'mass teaching' often proved to be relatively easy – and its occurrence throughout so much of the Third World suggests that this was and is the case – then ensuring that these new Baha'is all remained firm in their new-found faith was not. The problems of sustaining these new local Baha'i communities and of consolidating the faith and knowledge of those who generally lacked the literacy and organizational skills to consolidate their own faith and knowledge easily, often presented a considerable challenge to the existing Bahaʾi community. Far more intensive contact was required, and ultimately only by the establishment of rural teaching teams and training institutes do the various Bahaʾi communities appear to have brought their burgeoning rural expansion under full and proper control.

India

Various of these comments may be illustrated by reference to India, the largest and longest-established of the Third World Bahaʾi communities, and also the best researched.

Whilst there had been a number of Indians amongst the ranks of the Babis – including one of the Letters of the Living, four of those who fought at Ṭabarsí, and one of the claimants to spiritual leadership after 1850[38] – there is no evidence that Babism ever became established in India. Again, whilst during the period of Baháʾuʾlláh's rise to pre-eminence, there were Babis and Bahaʾis who migrated to join the already established Iranian communities in India, it was not until the 1870s that any active propagation of the new religion began. This was the result of the activities of Sulaymán Khán Tunakábuní, known as Jamál Effendi, who had been directed to India as a missionary by Baháʾuʾlláh in 1871. Remaining in India from 1872 until 1878, Jamál Effendi appears to have concentrated his attentions on the native elite and the immigrant merchant community, making particular use of the Imperial Durbar of 1876–7 to approach many dignitaries. Though converts were few, a small but energetic community developed, drawn mostly from those of Persian or Persianized background, whether Muslim or Zoroastrian. These Indian Bahaʾis were concentrated almost entirely in the cities of northern India, especially Bombay, Calcutta and Poona. In addition a very active community was established in Burma, initially amongst the Muslim minority of Mandalay (mostly merchants and shopkeepers and including *émigré* Iranians), but later on a communal basis in the village of Daidanaw.

From the 1870s through to at least the 1930s the Bahaʾi community of India appears to have remained substantially unchanging in its social composition and methods of teaching. Whilst over the years individual Ahmadiyyas, Sikhs and even Hindus became Bahaʾis (some of them very prominently so), the core of the community remained a Persianized Muslim or Zoroastrian section of the urban middle class. Whilst American international travel teachers came increasingly to supplement those from Iran, the primary method of teaching remained elitist, particular emphasis coming to be given to public lecture tours, with talks being given in universities and business association meetings and under the auspices of fellow 'liberal' organizations such as the Theosophical Society (a far more energetic entity in India than in the West), the universalistic and modernist Brahmo Samaj, and perhaps somewhat surprisingly, the 'fundamentalist' Hindu reform movement, Arya Samaj. Growth was very slow, and whilst there was doubtless a wider circle of sympathizers, even as late as 1961 there were still less than 900 Baha'is in the whole of India.[39] With only a small community, administrative development proceeded more slowly than in America and reflected what appears to have been a more 'inclusivist' understanding of the religion. Nevertheless, with the assistance of two American ladies, a systematic teaching campaign was attempted as early as 1911 and a 19-member teaching council elected, whilst in 1920 the first All-India Bahai Convention was held, attended by nearly 175 Baha'is,[40] its executive committee being transformed into the National Spiritual Assembly in 1923. The formation of Local Spiritual Assemblies was also slow, and even as late as 1939 there were still only five Assemblies in India, one of these in the area that was later to become Pakistan; there were also three Assemblies in Burma. Thereafter a greater emphasis on pioneering led to a marked increase in Assemblies, so that by 1961 there were 58 in India itself and (by 1963) 17 in Pakistan and 11 in Burma.[41] The first summer school was held in 1938.

Amongst the barriers to expansion were India's complex of linguistic and religious divisions and the Baha'is' own community roots and style of presenting their Faith. In 1923 Shoghi Effendi had referred to the few Indian Baha'is who were 'as yet unfamiliar' with the Persian language,[42] and whilst much subsequent Baha'i activity in India was also conducted in English, it would seem that the only Indian language which was commonly used by the Baha'is was the Arabic-scripted Urdu, as for example in a number of their publications and in their magazine *Kaukab-i Hind*. Only in the thirties and early forties did this situation begin to change, and at Shoghi Effendi's insistence translations were made into other Indian languages (initially almost entirely North Indian). Despite these measures and the increased tempo of teaching in the forties, the Baha'is remained circumscribed by their background – even in 1952 Hindu-background Baha'is were a minority in a country which after partition (1948) was overwhelmingly (85 per cent) Hindu – by the continued concentration of their endeavours on the educated urban population, and by their continued employment of a teaching style in which the cultural symbols were essentially neo-Islamic in theology and, we might add, Western modernist in many elements of social ethics.

The decisive breakthrough which transformed this state of affairs occurred in 1961, when at the instigation of an Iranian Hand of the Cause with extensive experience of 'mass teaching' in South-East Asia, a village conference was held in the Malwa area of Madhya Pradesh. Whilst not the first contact with rural Hindus, the resultant scale of activities was unprecedented. For the first time effective measures were taken to adapt Baha'i teaching techniques to a rural audience; Baha'i activists went and taught in the villages, making use of local social networks to broaden their missionary contacts. In dealing with a largely illiterate audience, use was made of visual aids, music and singing (rather than books, which had hitherto been the main aid). Rural teaching institutes were built as centres for training rural converts to continue village teaching independently of their original urban Baha'i teachers. Perhaps above all, the Baha'i teachings were effectively presented in terms of the language and cultural symbols of Hinduism, Bahá'u'lláh being portrayed as the eschatological Vaishnavite figure of the *Kalkin avatar*. The results were impressive. At the beginning of 1961 there had been 850 Baha'is in India; just over two years later there were over 87,000; by 1973 there were close to 400,000, and there are now widely rumoured to be almost two million Baha'is in India, making India rather than Iran the largest Baha'i community. By 1983 of 25,014 Local Assemblies in the Baha'i world, 11,281, that is 45 per cent, were in India.[43]

CONCLUSION

It is a truism to say that we now live in one world. Since the late nineteenth century the productive forces of economic life have been increasingly integrated into a single world economy. Accompanying this integration, the world's states have been forced into a growing interdependence. Culturally a similar process has led to accelerating change and interaction. These processes of change have often been enormously disruptive and destructive of traditional ways of life. In terms of religious change the global integration of the modern world has occasioned a massive 'pluralization' of traditional world views. Traditional beliefs must now either be defended against the realities of external comparison and choice, or must be accommodated in some manner to the relativizing influences of modern thought. To the resultant tensions must be added those induced by the disestablishment of many state religions and the pervasive impact of modern scientific thinking on traditional religious ideas.

In this context of global integration and religious change, Bahaʾis claim a unique validity for their religion. For them the Bahaʾi Faith is, without equal, the religion for the modern world. For them its universalistic claims both fulfil the religious expectations of the past and provide the basis for a new and global religious unity. Its social teachings they regard as the God-given mandate for the betterment of humankind in an age which they believe must see the attainment of world unity or suffer the consequences of its own outdated enmities and divisions.

Certainly the context of world-historical integration and change supplies the backdrop against which the development of the Bahaʾi Faith may be seen. Isolated and traditionalistic, early nineteenth-century Iranian Shiʿism was subject to its own complex development, out of which emerged the religion of the Báb. Babism threw existing religious tensions into stark relief, but never transcended the world of its origin. By the time of the emergence of the Bahaʾi Faith much had changed. Traditional certainties had been eroded by the disintegrating impact of Western modernity, for 'when the eyes of the people of the East were captivated by the arts and wonders of the West, they roved distraught in the wilderness of material causes'.[1] More generally the whole 'prevailing order' of the world had been upset and 'the signs of impending convulsions and chaos' were now to be discerned.[2] Bahá'u'lláh and ʿAbdu'l-Bahá addressed these two clashing worlds. To the East they advocated 'modernization' and accommodative change. To the West they stressed the dangers of dominance and aggression. To both they raised a summons to religious renewal. Little heeded in the West, the Bahaʾi message was ultimately brought to the peoples of the Third World, the dominated periphery of the modern world. Here, for whatever reason, the response was enthusiastic, the new Third World Bahaʾis initiating what is likely to be a further far-reaching transformation of the Bahaʾi religion. Just as Bahaʾi expansion to the West marked the religion's effective break with the world of Iranian Shiʿism, so the expansion into the Third World makes Bahaʾi claims to the status of a world religion now plausible and suggestive.

As to the future, it seems likely that some of the most significant developments in the Bahaʾi religion will stem from its Third World expansion. Already constituting the major part of Bahaʾi membership, the Bahaʾi communities of the Third World are also experiencing the highest rate of numerical growth. Third World Bahaʾis are also becoming increasingly prominent in the international administration of their Faith. Whilst Iranian and Western Bahaʾis are likely to continue to play a disproportionately important role in the further progress of Bahaʾi, the religion's future is in all probability going to rest increasingly with their co-religionists of the 'South'. As a corollary of this, the new found emphasis on social and economic development will probably assume increasing importance. Again, as increasingly active participants in the work of the supporting institutions of the United Nations and as a genuine multi-racial and multi-cultural international community, the Bahaʾis may well come to play a role in the issues of dialogue between the world's rich 'North' and the poor 'South'.

Other developments are possible. The active promotion of Bahaʾi principles such as sexual equality and racial harmony will necessarily have wider repercussions and, in general, the tendency within the Bahaʾi community is likely to be towards greater social involvement as increasing emphasis is placed on the attainment as well as the simple advocacy of idealistic principles. Social involvement is also likely to involve increasing co-operation with those agencies and organizations with whose principles the Bahaʾis are sympathetic, a tendency which is already apparent in development and multi-faith activities. Again, in terms of community life, modern Western Baha'i communities are experiencing a 'familialization' comparable to that which earlier established the continuity and resilience of the Iranian Baha'i community. This may well continue, in which case the concept of membership in the Baha'i community is liable to change. As in Iran, so now amongst the Western Baha'is, children of Baha'i parents are increasingly assumed to be members of the community unless they opt out of membership, whereas formerly they were assumed only to be members of the community if they made a deliberate decision to join. Essentially, 'contracting-out' has replaced the earlier process of 'contracting-in'.

Some changes are more uncertain. There are undoubtedly pressures in some parts of the Baha'i world towards a greater emphasis on Baha'i legalism, a tendency which others would doubtless oppose. There is no inevitable dynamic involved here, however, and it is noticeable that the Universal House of Justice (as Shoghi Effendi before it) seems disinclined to add to the detailed corpus of Baha'i law, preferring to restate general moral principles and emphasize the importance of individual conscience and decision-making. Again, as in the time of Shoghi Effendi, there are undoubtedly those Baha'is who wish to emphasize and extend the prerogatives of the Baha'i administration, whilst there are others who would put more emphasis on the right of individual self-expression and stress the importance of individual initiative. As both individual rights and administrative prerogatives are upheld in the Baha'i writings, the difference between these views is one of emphasis, but, nevertheless, differences of practice would follow from changes in the exact balance between these principles. Similarly, at an intellectual level the balance between the authority claims of faith and reason (both upheld in the Baha'i writings) may be subject to variant interpretations, with varying results in the intellectual life of the Baha'i community.

The existence of these variant possibilities does not in itself imply any potential division. The Baha'i community is increasingly accommodative of diversity and there appears to be a distinct tendency towards increasing administrative flexibility. More than this, such administrative change as is apparent is in the direction of greater functional diversification. The establishment of the International Teaching Centre in Haifa is particularly significant in this regard, but there is also a steady proliferation of specialist international agencies concerned with particular aspects of Baha'i activity, as, for example, relations with the United Nations, social and economic development, and the promotion of Baha'i media work.

There is also an increase in the size of the administrative staff in several Baha'i communities, as well as at the Baha'i World Centre, but as much of this work is on a volunteer or under-remunerated basis, there is as yet no large-scale bureaucratic transformation.

Whatever the future, the present reality of the Baha'i Faith illustrates the force of religious change. Quite explicitly, however, Baha'is acknowledge the changing nature of their religion, interpreting such change as part of a process of progressive unfoldment by which the eternal message of God is mediated to an ever-changing human world. The external characteristics of religion are necessarily transformed in interaction with the changing realities of the social world. Claiming unique contemporary relevance, the Baha'is perceive themselves as being but part of a wider process of transformation. For them the implementation of their long-term goals is an objective that transcends the activities of their own religious community. The onward progress of mankind has a dynamic of its own, and whilst Baha'is believe themselves to have a unique and necessary role in that progress, they are themselves only part of that wider dynamic of human history and religious experience.

NOTES

INTRODUCTION

1. See Peter Smith, 'Motif research: Peter Berger and the Baháʾí faith', *Religion*, 8 (1978), 210–34; and Peter L. Berger, 'From Sect to Church: A Sociological Interpretation of the Bahaʾi Movement', PhD dissertation (New School for Social Research, New York, 1954).

I THE BABI MOVEMENT

1. For general references to this and subsequent chapters, see Appendix 3.
2. Seyyed Hossein Nasr, *Ideals and Realities of Islam* (London, Allen and Unwin, 1966), p. 166.
3. One of the innovations introduced by Shaykh Aḥmad into Shiʿi practice was a particular manner of visitation to the shrines of the Imams. Unlike other Shiʿis and as a mark of their extreme veneration for the Imams, Shaykhis stood at the foot of the graves of the Imams and would not circumambulate them. Thus the Shaykhis became known as *Pusht-i sarís* (lit. those 'behind the head'), whilst their opponents, who performed the traditional circumambulation, were called *Bálásarís* (lit. those 'above the head').
4. See Vahid Rafati, 'The Development of Shaykhi Thought in Shíʿí Islam', PhD dissertation (University of California, Los Angeles, 1979), p. 52.
5. Ḥájí Mullá Hádí Sabzivárí (1797/8–1878) later became the leading exponent of Shiʿi theosophy.
6. Denis MacEoin, 'From Shaykhism to Babism: A Study of Charismatic Renewal in Shiʿi Islam', PhD dissertation (University of Cambridge, 1979), p. 57.
7. *Ibid.*, p. 104.
8. Seyyèd Ali Mohammed dit le Bâb, *Le Livre des sept preuves*, trans. A.L.M. Nicolas (Paris, Maisonneuve, Librairie Orientale et Americaine, 1902), p. 58. See more generally Rafati, pp. 168–85.
9. MacEoin, 'From Shaykhism to Babism', p. 141; Muḥammad Zarandí Nabíl, *The Dawn-Breakers: Nabíl's Narrative of the Early Days of the Baháʾí Revelation* (Wilmette, Ill., Baháʾí Publishing Trust, 1932), p. 253.
10. MacEoin, *ibid.*, pp. 159–60, 173–4.
11. Thus the book's claims were discerned in this manner both by Karím Khán and by the ulama at the trial of Mullá ʿAlí Basṭámí. See Denis MacEoin, 'Early Shaykhi reactions to the Báb and his claims, *Studies in Bábí and Baháʾí History, vol. I*, ed. M. Momen (Los Angeles, Kalimat Press, 1982), pp. 1–47; and Moojan Momen, 'The trial of Mullá ʿAlí Basṭámí: a combined Sunní–Shíʿí *fatwá* against the Báb, *Iran*, 20 (1982), 113–43.
12. Momen, *ibid.*, p. 76.
13. MacEoin, 'Early Shaykhi reactions', p. 32.
14. *Ibid.*
15. Edward G. Browne (comp.), *Materials for the Study of the Bábí Religion* (Cambridge, Cambridge University Press, 1918), pp. 259, 261; Nabíl, *Dawn-Breakers*, p. 209.

16. See Denis MacEoin, 'The Babi concept of holy war', *Religion*, 12 (1982), 93–129; and Ruhullah Mehrabkhani, 'Some notes on fundamental principles: Western scholarship and the religion of the Báb', *Bahá'í Studies Bulletin*, 2, 4 (1984), 22–43 (mimeographed).
17. MacEoin, *ibid.*, pp. 102–4.
18. Mehrabkhani, p. 41.
19. Nabíl, *Dawn-Breakers*, p. 298.
20. Edward G. Browne (ed. and trans.), *The Táríkh-i-Jadíd, or New History of Mírzá ʿAlí Muḥammad the Báb, by Mírzá Ḥuseyn of Hamadán* (Cambridge, Cambridge University Press, 1893) pp. 357–9.
21. Edward G. Browne, (ed.), *Kitáb-i-Nuqṭatuʾl-Káf* (Leyden, Brill, and London, Luzac, 1910), pp. 61–2.
22. Berger, p. 161.
23. On these various claims, see Browne, *Táríkh-i-Jadíd*, pp. 335–6; Browne, *Nuqṭatuʾl-Káf*, pp. 154, 181; MacEoin, 'From Shaykhism to Babism', pp. 146, 206; MacEoin, 'The Babi concept of holy war', p. 115; and Shoghi Effendi, *God Passes By* (Wilmette, Ill., Baháʾí Publishing Trust, 1944), p. 49.
24. Browne, *Táríkh-i-Jadíd*, p. 359.
25. Robert Grant Watson, *A History of Persia from the Beginning of the Nineteenth Century to the Year 1858* (London, Smith, Elder, 1866), p. 367.
26. Nabíl, *Dawn-Breakers*, pp. 326, 329.
27. See, for example, Hamid Algar, *Religion and State in Iran, 1785–1906: The Role of the Ulama in the Qájár Period* (Berkeley and Los Angeles, University of California Press, 1969); Peter Avery, *Modern Iran* (London, Benn, 1965); Mangol Bayat, *Mysticism and Dissent: Socioreligious Thought in Qajar Iran* (Syracuse University Press, 1982); and M.S. Ivanov, *Babidski Vostanii i Irane, 1848–1852* (Moscow, Trudy Instituta Vostok-vedeniya, 1939).
28. Shoghi, *God Passes By*, p. 125.
29. Lady [Mary Leonora] Sheil, *Glimpses of Life and Manners in Persia* (London, Murray, 1856), p. 275.

2 BABI DOCTRINE AND DOMINANT MOTIFS

1. Khan Bahadur Agha Mirza Muhammad, 'Some new notes on Babiism', *Journal of the Royal Asiatic Society* (1927), p. 450.
2. Seyyèd Ali Mohammed dit le Bâb, *Le Béyân persan*, trans. A.L.M. Nicolas (Paris, Paul Geuthner, 1911–14), vol. I, p. 43; vol. III, p. 113.
3. Shoghi, *God Passes By*, p. 23.
4. The laws of the *Bayán* are summarized both by Browne (*Nuqṭatuʾl-Káf*, pp. liv-xcv); and by S.G. Wilson ('The Bayan of the Bab' *Princeton Theological Review*, 13 (1915), 633–54). Their ritualistic elements are discussed by Denis MacEoin, 'Ritual and semi-ritual observances in Babism and Bahaʾism', unpublished paper (1980).
5. MacEoin, 'From Shaykhism to Babism', pp. 165–6.
6. The Báb, *Selections from the Writings of the Báb*, trans. H. Taherzadeh (Haifa, Baháʾí World Centre, 1976), p. 119.
7. Denis MacEoin, 'Nineteenth-century Babi talismans', *Studia Islamica*, 14 (1985), 77–98.
8. Browne, *Táríkh-i-Jadíd*, pp. 226, 240, 351; Nabíl, *Dawn-Breakers*, pp. 201, 245–7, 302.
9. Browne, *ibid.*, p. 42.
10. See Edward G. Browne, *A Literary History of Persia* (Cambridge, Cambridge University Press, 1902–24; reprint, 1969), vol. IV, pp. 374–6.
11. Moojan Momen, *The Bábí and Bahá'í Religions, 1844–1944: Some Contemporary Western Accounts* (Oxford, George Ronald, 1981), pp. 111–12.
12. Smith, 'Motif research'.
13. Bâb, *Béyân persan*, vol. I, p. 39.
14. Edward G. Browne (ed. and trans.), *A Traveller's Narrative Written to Illustrate the Episode of the Báb* (Cambridge, Cambridge University Press), vol. II, p. 219.

15. Nabíl, *Dawn-Breakers*, pp. 61, 175, 202; see also Browne, *Táríkh-i-Jadíd*, p. 209.
16. Nabíl, *ibid.*, p. 61.
17. MacEoin, 'The Babi concept of holy war', pp. 109–10.
18. MacEoin, 'From Shaykhism to Babism', p. 146.
19. Nabíl, *Dawn-Breakers*, p. 57.
20. Bayat, *Mysticism and Dissent*; Mangol Bayat, 'Tradition, and change in Iranian socio-religious thought', in *Modern Iran*, ed. M.E. Bonine and N. Keddie (Albany, New York, State University of New York Press, 1981), pp. 37–58.
21. George N. Curzon, *Persia and the Persian Question* (London, Cass, 1892), vol. I, p. 502.
22. Browne, *Nuqṭatu'l-Káf*, pp. xlii, 62, 151–2; Browne, *Táríkh-i-Jadíd*, p. 361n.
23. Momen, *Bábí and Bahá'í Religions*, p. 7.

3 BABISM AS A SOCIO-RELIGIOUS MOVEMENT IN IRAN

1. Peter Smith, 'A note on Babi and Baha'i numbers in Iran, *Iranian Studies*, 17 (1984), 295–301.
2. Avery, *Modern Iran*, p. 53; cf. Abbas Amanat, 'The Early Years of the Babi Movement: Background and Development', D. Phil. dissertation (University of Oxford, 1981), p. 420.
3. Moojan Momen, 'The social basis of the Bábí upheavals in Iran (1848–53): a preliminary analysis', *International Journal of Middle East Studies*, 15 (1983), 157–83.
4. Ivanov, *Babidski Vostanii*. See also his 'Babism' and 'Babi uprisings', in the *Great Soviet Encyclopaedia*, 2 (1973), 521; V. Minorski, 'Review of M.S. Ivanov's, *Babidski Vostanii i Irane'*, *Bulletin of the School of Oriental and African Studies*, 11 (1946), 878–80; and Kurt Greussing, 'The Babi movement in Iran, 1844–52: from merchant protest to peasant revolution', in *Religion and Rural Revolt*, ed. J.M. Bak and G. Benecke (Manchester, Manchester University Press, 1984), pp. 256–69.
5. Bayat, *Mysticism and Dissent*, p. 167.
6. *Ibid.*, pp. 84–6.
7. Minorksi, 'Review of *Babidski Vostanii*'. If this was the case, then there is an interesting parallel with Emmanuel Le Roy Ladurie's observation concerning the link between resistance to the payment of tithes and the heretical movements of Occitania. See his *Montaillou: Cathars and Catholics in a French Village, 1294–1324*, trans. B. Bray (Harmondsworth, Penguin, 1978), pp. 21–3.
8. Max Weber, *From Max Weber: Essays in Sociology*, trans. and ed. H.H. Gerth and C.W. Mills (London, Routledge and Kegan Paul, 1948), pp. 281–5; Max Weber, *Economy and Society: An Outline of Interpretive Sociology*, ed. G. Roth and G. Wittich (Berkeley and Los Angeles, University of California Press, 1978), pp. 468–500.
9. See Peter Smith, 'Millenarianism in the Babi and Baha'i religions', in *Millennialism and Charisma*, ed. R. Wallis (Belfast, Queen's University, 1982), pp. 231–83; and Peter Smith, 'A Sociological Study of the Babi and Baha'i Religions', PhD dissertation (University of Lancaster, 1982), pp. 32–7, 251–62.
10. Cholera epidemics have had a particularly disturbing effect on religious expectations. See, for example, William H. McNeill, *Plagues and People* (Harmondsworth, Penguin, 1976), pp. 242–3.
11. Amanat, 'Babi Movement', pp. 71–86; MacEoin, 'From Shaykhism to Babism', p. 189.
12. Amanat, *ibid.*, pp. 342–78.

4 THE BABI RECOVERY AND THE EMERGENCE OF THE BAHA'I FAITH

1. Browne, *Materials*, p. 283.
2. Both brothers are referred to by their religious titles rather than by their names as it is by these titles that they are now generally known.

3. H.M. Balyuzi, *Bahá'u'lláh: The King of Glory* (Oxford, George Ronald, 1980), p. 66; Nabíl, *Dawn-Breakers*, p. 591.
4. Balyuzi, *ibid.*, p. 120; Lady [S.L.] Blomfield, *The Chosen Highway* (Wilmette, Ill., Bahá'í Publishing Trust, 1967), pp. 48, 50–2; Adib Taherzadeh, *The Revelation of Bahá'u'lláh* (Oxford, George Ronald, 1974–), vol. I, pp. 54, 246–8.
5. The authors of the Azali polemic *Hasht Bihisht* (*Eight Paradises*) later charged Bahá'u'lláh with responsibility for this murder (Browne, *Traveller's Narrative*, vol. II, p. 357), but there seems little doubt that it was Azal who had Dayyán murdered. Denouncing Dayyán in his *Mustayqiẓ* (*Sleeper Awakened*) as the 'father of iniquities', Azal asked why his followers 'sit silent in their places and do not transfix him with their spears', or 'rend his bowels with their hands' (Browne, *Materials*, p. 218). A later Azali tract, the *Risáli-yi ʿAmmih*, also readily admits and justifies the deed (see H.M. Balyuzi, *Edward Granville Browne and the Bahá'í Faith* (London, George Ronald, 1970), p. 43).
6. Momen, *Bábí and Bahá'í Religions*, pp. 180–3.
7. Browne, *Materials*, pp. 275–87.
8. Ḥájí Mírzá Ḥaydar-ʿAlí, *Stories from the Delight of Hearts: The Memoirs of Ḥájí Mírzá Ḥaydar-ʿAlí*, trans. and abridged by A.Q. Faizi (Los Angeles, Kalimat Press), p. 8.
9. Balyuzi, *Bahá'u'lláh*, pp. 112–13.
10. Shoghi, *God Passes By*, p. 138.
11. Balyuzi, *Bahá'u'lláh*, p. 113.
12. Bahá'u'lláh, *Long Healing Prayer* (London, Bahá'í Publishing Trust, 1980).
13. Taherzadeh, *Revelation*, vol. I, p. 219.
14. See Juan Cole, 'Bahá'u'lláh and the Naqshbandí Sufis in Iraq, 1854–1856', in *From Iran East and West: Studies in Bábí and Bahá'í History, vol. II*, ed. J.R. Cole and M. Momen (Los Angeles, Kalimat Press, 1984), pp. 1–28.
15. Momen, *Bábí and Bahá'í Religions*, p. 183; Hamid Algar, *Mírzá Malkum Khán: A Study in the History of Iranian Modernism* (Berkeley and Los Angeles, University of California Press, 1973), pp. 58–9.
16. Browne, *Materials*, p. 285. This is the famous verse written as a warning of Abú Muslim's revolt (AD 746–7). It continues:

    And if the wise ones of the people quench it not,
    its fuel will be corpses and skulls.
    Verily fire is kindled by two sticks,
    and verily words are the beginning of warfare.
    (Browne, *Literary History*, vol. I, p. 241)
17. The actual circumstances of this declaration are largely unknown (see Shoghi, *God Passes By*, p. 153), but according to a later account by either Bahá'u'lláh or his amanuensis, it was accompanied by statements forbidding *jihád* (holy war) and announcing that no further Manifestation of God would appear for a thousand years, and that all 'names and attributes' of God were now 'fully manifested within all created things' (Taherzadeh, *Revelation*, vol. I, pp. 278–80).
18. Balyuzi, *Bahá'u'lláh*, pp. 183-4, 190; Ustád Muḥammad-ʿAlí Salmání, *My Memories of Bahá'u'lláh*, trans. M. Gail (Los Angeles, Kalimat Press, 1982), pp. 26–9.
19. Taherzadeh, *Revelation*, vol. II, p. 69.
20. *Ibid.*, pp. 74, 114.
21. Momen, *Bábí and Bahá'í Religions*, pp. 198–9.
22. Browne, *Traveller's Narrative*, vol. II, pp. xxxix–xl.
23. Ḥaydar-ʿAlí, *Stories*, pp. 18–19, 69–70.
24. Bahá'u'lláh, *Tablets of Bahá'u'lláh, Revealed after the Kitáb-i-Aqdas*, trans. H. Taherzadeh *et al* (Haifa, Bahá'í World Centre, 1978), pp. 219–23. In Arabic, *akbar* and *aʿẓam* have the roughly equivalent meaning of 'greater' or 'greatest', but in the various Baha'i contexts in which the terms are used *aʿẓam* clearly has the higher status. Accordingly, Shoghi Effendi has translated *aʿẓam* as 'Most Great' and *akbar* as 'Greater', or in relationship to

the distinction between a spiritually based and a merely political peace (the *sulḥ-i aʿẓam* and *sulḥ-i akbar*), as 'Lesser'.

25. Eric Cohen, 'The Bahaʾi community of Acre', *Folklore Research Centre Studies* (Jerusalem), 3 (1972), 119–41.

5 DOMINANT MOTIFS IN THE BAHAʾI FAITH IN THE EAST

1. For example, E.G. Browne's own copy of the *Kitáb-i Íqán* was the 67th transcribed by just one copyist (Browne, *Traveller's Narrative*, vol. II, p. 413).
2. Baháʾuʾlláh, *Epistle to the Son of the Wolf*, trans. Shoghi Effendi, rev. edn (Wilmette, Ill., Baháʾí Publishing Trust, 1953), p. 165.
3. ʿAbduʾl-Bahá, *Will and Testament of ʿAbduʾl-Bahá* (Wilmette, Ill., Baháʾí Publishing Trust, 1944), p. 11.
4. Browne, *Traveller's Narrative*, vol. II, p. xl.
5. Shoghi Effendi, *World Order of Baháʾuʾlláh*, rev. edn (Wilmette Ill., Baháʾí Publishing Trust, 1955), pp. 162–3. See Chapter 4, note 24.
6. National Spiritual Assembly [NSA] of the Baháʾís of the British Isles (comp.), *The Baháʾí Revelation*, rev. edn (London, Baháʾí Publishing Trust, 1970), pp. 10–11. Emphasis added.
7. Compare Bayat's argument about the secularization of traditional progressivist concerns in Iran during the nineteenth century (*Mysticism and Dissent*).
8. ʿAbduʾl-Bahá, *The Secret of Divine Civilization*, trans. M. Gail (Wilmette, Ill., Baháʾí Publishing Trust, 1957), pp. 64–6; NSA of the British Isles, *Baháʾí Revelation*, pp. 9–12.
9. Baháʾuʾlláh, *Tablets*, p. 22.
10. Baháʾuʾlláh, *Gleanings from the Writings of Baháʾuʾlláh*, comp. and trans. Shoghi Effendi, rev. edn (London, Baháʾí Publishing Trust, 1978), pp. 249–52; Shoghi Effendi, *The Promised Day Is Come*, 2nd edn (Wilmette, Ill., Baháʾí Publishing Trust, 1961), pp. 20–3, 74–5.
11. Baháʾuʾlláh, *Tablets*, pp. 69, 144, 169.
12. ʿAbduʾl-Bahá, *Secret of Divine Civilization*, pp. 60–4.
13. Juan R. Cole, 'Muḥammad ʿAbduh and Ras̲h̲id Riḍá: a dialogue on the Baháʾí Faith', *World Order*, 15, 3/4 (1981), p. 10.
14. Baháʾuʾlláh, *Epistle*, p. 25; Edward G. Browne, 'Báb', 'Bábís', in *Encyclopaedia of Religion and Ethics*, ed. James Hastings (Edinburgh, T. and T. Clark), vol. II, p. 303.
15. Baháʾuʾlláh, *Epistle*, p. 91.
16. Baháʾuʾlláh, *Gleanings*, p. 240.
17. Denis MacEoin, 'From Babism to Bahaʾism: problems of militancy, quietism, and conflation in the construction of a religion', *Religion*, 13 (1983), p. 228.
18. ʿAbduʾl-Bahá, *Secret of Divine Civilization*, pp. 41–52.
19. Baháʾuʾlláh, *Tablets*, p. 24.
20. Baháʾuʾlláh, *Tablets*, pp. 60, 71; Baháʾuʾlláh, *Al-Kitáb al-Aqdas, or the Most Holy Book*, trans. and ed. E.E. Elder and W.M. Miller (London, Luzac, Royal Asiatic Society, 1961), pp. 32, 63.
21. Baháʾuʾlláh *Kitáb al-Aqdas*, pp. 30, 37, 50–1, 63; Baháʾuʾlláh, *Tablets*, pp. 71, 90, 128, 132–4.
22. Universal House of Justice, *A Synopsis and Codification of the Kitáb-i-Aqdas, the Most Holy Book of Baháʾuʾlláh* (Haifa, Baháʾí World Centre, 1973), p. 3.
23. Universal House of Justice, *Synopsis*, p. 12. On Islamic practice, see, for example, John A. Williams (ed.), *Islam* (London, Prentice-Hall, 1961), pp. 125–32.
24. Universal House of Justice, *Synopsis*, pp. 24–5.
25. *Ibid.*, pp. 25–6; Baháʾuʾlláh, *Kitáb al-Aqdas*, p. 66.
26. Baháʾuʾlláh, *Tablets*, p. 68.
27. Browne, *Materials*, p. 262.

28. MacEoin, 'From Babism to Bahaʾism', p. 228.
29. Baháʾuʾlláh, *Kitáb al-Aqdas*, p. 62; Baháʾuʾlláh, *Tablets*, pp. 22, 35–6, 72, 90–2, 94.
30. Baháʾuʾlláh, *The Kitáb-i Íqán: The Book of Certitude*, trans. Shoghi Effendi (London, Baháʾí Publishing Trust, 1946), p. 124.
31. Baháʾuʾlláh, *Gleanings*, p. 249.
32. *Ibid.*; Shoghi, *God Passes By*, p. 217; Shoghi Effendi, *The Advent of Divine Justice*, rev. edn (Wilmette, Ill., Baháʾí Publishing Trust, 1963), p. 31.
33. NSA of the British Isles, *Baháʾí Revelation*, p. 10; Shoghi, *God Passes By*, p. 217.
34. Edward G. Browne, *A Year amongst the Persians*, 3rd edn (London, A. and C. Black, 1950), pp. 431–2; Moojan Momen, 'Early relations between Christian missionaries and the Babi and Bahaʾi communities', in *Studies in Bábí and Baháʾí History, vol. I*, ed. M. Momen (Los Angeles, Kalimat Press, 1982), pp. 49–82.
35. Baháʾuʾlláh, *Long Healing Prayer.*
36. ʿAbduʾl-Bahá, *Some Answered Questions*, trans. L.C. Barney, rev. edn (Wilmette, Ill., Baháʾí Publishing Trust, 1981), pp. 100–2.
37. *Ibid.*, p. 34.
38. Most notably with reference to Sultan Abdulaziz, Napoleon III, and the twice-experienced 'lamentations of Berlin'. See Shoghi, *Promised Day.*

6 THE IRANIAN BAHAʾI COMMUNITY, C. 1866–1921

1. Ugo R. Giachery, 'An Italian scientist extols the Báb', *Baháʾí World*, vol. XII, p. 902.
2. Momen, *Bábí and Baháʾí Religions*, p. 244; Momen, 'Early relations', pp. 57–63.
3. Samuel G.E. Benjamin, *Persia and the Persians* (Boston, 1886) pp. 353–5. Europeans and Iranian Muslims commonly referred to Bahaʾis as Babis during this period.
4. Momen, *Bábí and Baháʾí Religions*, p. 28.
5. Browne, *Materials*, p. 293; Curzon, *Persia*, vol. I, p. 503.
6. Browne, *Traveller's Narrative*, vol. II, pp. 410–11; Denis MacEoin, 'Babism, Bahaʾism and the Iranian Constitutional Revolution', unpublished paper (1980); Momen, *Bábí and Baháʾí Religions*, pp. 268–89.
7. Smith, 'Babi and Bahaʾi numbers'.
8. Ḥaydar-ʿAlí, *Stories*, pp. 29–65; Momen, *Bábí and Baháʾí Religions*, pp. 257–67.
9. Anthony Lee, 'The rise of the Baháʾí community of ʿIshqábád', *Baháʾí Studies*, 5 (1979), 1–13; Momen, *Bábí and Baháʾí Religions*, pp. 296–300.
10. John D. Rees, 'The Bab and Babism', *Nineteenth Century* (London), 40 (1896), 65; Mary F. Wilson, 'The stoıy of the Bâb', *Contemporary Review*, 48 (1885), 829.
11. Susan J. Stiles, 'Zoroastrian Conversions to the Baháʾí Faith in Yazd, Irán', MA thesis (University of Arizona, 1983); Susan J. Stiles, 'The conversion of religious minorities to the Baháʾí Faith in Iran: some preliminary considerations', paper presented at the first Los Angeles Bahaʾi History Conference, UCLA, 5–7 August 1983; Susan J. Stiles, 'Early Zoroastrian conversions to the Baháʾí Faith in Yazd, Iran', in *From Iran East and West*, ed. Cole and Momen, pp. 67–93. On Jewish conversions, see also Walter J. Fischel, 'The Bahai movement and Persian Jewry', *The Jewish Review* (London), 7 (1934), 47–55; and Walter J. Fischel, 'The Jews of Persia', *Jewish Social Studies*, 12 (1950).
12. Bayat, *Mysticism and Dissent*, p. 85.
13. For example, see Bayat, *ibid.*, chapter 5; and Nikki R. Keddie, 'Religion and irreligion in early Iranian nationalism', *Comparative Studies in Society and History*, 4 (1962), 265–95.
14. Stiles, 'Zoroastrian Conversions', pp 40–1.
15. Vittorio Lanternari provides a classic statement of this argument. See his *The Religions of the Oppressed: A Study of Modern Messianic Cults*, trans. L. Sergio (London, MacGibbon and Kee, 1963).
16. Momen, *Bábí and Baháʾí Religions*, pp. 187–8, 194–5, 210–12; Momen, 'Early relations'.
17. Ivanov, 'Babism', 'Babi uprisings'; L.I. Klimovich, 'Bahaism', *Great Soviet Encyclopaedia*, 3 (1973), 10.

18. Ahmad Ashraf, 'Historical obstacles to the development of a bourgeoisie in Iran', *Iranian Studies*, 2 (1969), 54–79.
19. J.R. Richards, *The Religion of the Baha'is* (London, Society for Promoting Christian Knowledge, 1932) p. 207; see also Browne, *Materials*, p. xvi.
20. Balyuzi, *Bahá'u'lláh*, pp. 441–4.
21. Edward G. Browne, *The Persian Revolution of 1905–1909* (1910; reprint, London, Cass, 1966), pp. 426–9.
22. Iranian Jews were also subject to persecution at this time. See David Littman, 'Jews under Muslim rule: the case of Persia', *Wiener Library Bulletin*, NS 32, 49–50 (London, Institute of Contemporary History, 1979).
23. Browne, *Persian Revolution*, pp. 428–9; Momen, *Bábí and Bahá'í Religions*, p. 368.
24. Stiles, 'Zoroastrian Conversions'.
25. Browne, *Materials*, p. xix. More generally, see Bayat, *Mysticism and Dissent*; and Keddie, 'Religion and irreligion'.

7 THE EARLY AMERICAN BAHA'I COMMUNITY

1. This chapter represents a considerably condensed version of my 'The American Bahá'í community, 1894–1917: a preliminary survey', in *Studies in Bábí and Bahá'í History*, ed. Momen.
2. The Islamic tradition that there is a 'Greatest Name' of God is taken up by the Baha'is, who believe that this name is *Bahá* (glory, splendour), as in the title *Bahá'u'lláh*.
3. United States, Department of Commerce and Labour, Bureau of the Census, *Census of Religious Bodies, 1906* (Washington, DC, Government Printing Office, 1910), vol. II, pp. 41–2.
4. By 1911, 108 American Baha'is had made the pilgrimage (National Spiritual Assembly of the Bahá'ís of the United States and Canada (comp.), *The Bahá'í Centenary: 1844–1944* (Wilmette, Ill., Bahá'í Publishing Committee, 1944), pp. 139–42.
5. *Star of the West*, 3, 1 (1912), 8.
6. ʿAbdu'l-Bahá, *The Promulgation of Universal Peace*, comp. H. MacNutt, 2nd edn. (Wilmette, Ill., Bahá'í Publishing Trust, 1982), pp. 122, 317, 231–2, 376, 469; National Spiritual Assembly of the Bahá'ís of Canada, *ʿAbdu'l-Bahá in Canada* (Forest, Ontario, Forest Free Press, 1962), pp. 42, 48–51.
7. United States, Department of Commerce, Bureau of the Census, *Census of Religious Bodies, 1916* (Washington, DC, Government Printing Office, 1919), vol. II, pp. 43–5.
8. Roy Wallis, 'Ideology, authority and the development of cultic movements' *Social Research*, 41 (1974), pp. 299–327; Roy Wallis, 'The cult and its transformation', in *Sectarianism*, ed. R. Wallis (London, Peter Owen, 1975), pp. 35–49.
9. Marian Haney, in NSA of the United States and Canada, *Bahá'í Centenary*, p. 160.
10. See also Smith, 'Millenarianism', pp. 259–62.
11. Eric Adolphus Dime, 'Is the Millennium upon us?', *The Forum*, 58 (1917), pp. 167, 179–80.
12. *Star*, 13 (1922), 74.
13. Various listings of the 'Baha'i principles' were given by ʿAbdu'l-Bahá. For a summary, see Shoghi, *God Passes By*, pp. 281–2.
14. S. Neale Alter, *Studies in Bahaism* (Beirut, American Press, 1923), p. 69.
15. ʿAbdul'Bahá, in *Star*, 5 (1914), 67. This quotation was used by opponents of Baha'i organization in their efforts to restrict or prevent its development. For Shoghi Effendi's comment casting doubt on the reliability of the quotation, see his *World Order of Bahá'u'lláh*, p.4.
16. ʿAbdu'l-Bahá, cited in John E. Esslemont, *Bahá'u'lláh and the New Era* (London, Allen and Unwin, 1923), p. 70.
17. ʿAbdu'l-Bahá, in Eric Hammond (ed.), *Abdul Baha in London* (East Sheen, Surrey, Unity Press, for the Bahai Publishing Society, 1912), p. 109.

18. Albert R. Vail, 'Bahaism: a study of a contemporary movement', *Harvard Theological Review*, 7 (1914), 339.
19. Maude Holbach, 'The Bahai Movement, with some recollections of meetings with Abdul Baha', *Nineteenth Century* (February 1915), 453.
20. Gaius Glenn Atkins, *Modern Religious Cults and Movements* (1923; reprint, New York, AMS, 1971).
21. Charles Mason Remey, *The Bahai Movement: A Series of Nineteen Papers*, 2nd edn (Washington, DC, J.D. Milans, 1913), pp. 99–100; *Star*, 7 (1916), 51.
22. ʿAbduʾl-Bahá, *Promulgation*, p. 386.
23. Howard Colby Ives, *Portals to Freedom* (London, George Ronald, 1962), pp. 14–15.
24. On the Covenant doctrine, see John Ferraby, *All Things Made New: A Comprehensive Outline of the Baháʾí Faith*, rev. edn (London, Baháʾí Publishing Trust, 1975), pp. 241–55; and National Spiritual Assembly of the Baháʾís of Canada, *The Power of the Covenant* (3 vols., Thornhill, Ontario, Baháʾí Canada Publications).
25. J. Stillson Judah, *The History and Philosophy of the Metaphysical Movements in America* (Philadelphia, Westminster Press, 1967).
26. Vernon Elvin Johnson, 'An Historical Analysis of Critical Transformations in the Evolution of the Baháʾí World Faith', PhD dissertation (Baylor University, Texas, 1974), p. 392.
27. United States, *Census of Religious Bodies, 1916*, vol. II, p. 45.
28. *Ibid.*; Robert P. Richardson, 'The Persian rival to Jesus, and his American disciples', *Open Court*, 39 (1915), 460–83.
29. *Star*, 4 (1913), 135–6.
30. *Star*, 9 (1918), 55–8; Charles Mason Remey to 'The Friends of the Green Acre Fellowship regarding the development and maintenance of the constructive universal policy of Bahai teachings in Green Acre', 21 November 1919, cyclostyled letter (Wilmette, Ill., National Baháʾí Archives, Thornton Chase Papers).

8 INSTITUTIONALIZATION IN THE FORMATIVE AGE

1. Shoghi Effendi, *Citadel of Faith: Messages to America, 1947–1957* (Wilmette, Ill., Baháʾí Publishing Trust, 1965), pp. 4–6.
2. ʿAbduʾl-Bahá, *Will and Testament*, p. 11.
3. *Ibid.*, pp. 14, 19–20.
4. *Ibid.*, p. 11.
5. *Ibid.*, p. 26.
6. Shoghi Effendi, *Baháʾí Administration*, 5th edn (Wilmette, Ill., Baháʾí Publishing Trust, 1945), pp. 65–6; Shoghi Effendi, *The Unfolding Destiny of the British Baháʾí Community: The Messages of the Guardian of the Baháʾí Faith to the Baháʾís of the British Isles* (London, Baháʾí Publishing Trust, 1981), pp. 27–8.
7. *Baháʾí News*, 12, p. 5; *ibid.*, 13, p. 2.
8. ʿAbduʾl-Bahá, *Will and Testament*, pp. 5,9.
9. *Ibid.*, p. 20.
10. *Star*, 13 (1922), 25.
11. H.M. Balyuzi, *ʿAbduʾl-Bahá: The Centre of the Covenant of Baháʾuʾlláh* (London, George Ronald, 1971), p. 527.
12. Rúḥíyyih Rabbani, *The Priceless Pearl* (London, Baháʾí Publishing Trust, 1969), p. 47.
13. *Ibid.*, p. 56; *Star*, 13 (1922), 68.
14. Shoghi, *Baháʾí Administration*, pp. 17–25; *Star*, 13 (1922), 83–8.
15. Shoghi, *Baháʾí Administration*, pp. 34–43.
16. *Baháʾí Year Book*, vol. I (New York, Baháʾí Publishing Committee, 1926), pp. 101–3.
17. See *Baháʾí World*, vol. II, pp. 89–97.
18. Shoghi, *Baháʾí Administration*, p. 90.
19. *Ibid.*, p. 27.

20. *Star*, 13 (1922), 68.
21. Peter Smith, '*Reality* magazine: editorship and ownership of an American Bahá'í periodical', in *From Iran East and West*, ed. Cole and Momen (Los Angeles, Kalimat Press, 1984), pp. 135–55.
22. See Loni J. Bramson, 'Internal opposition to ʿAbdu'l-Bahá's Will and Testament and the establishment of the Guardianship', paper presented at the third Baha'i Studies Seminar, University of Lancaster, 7–8 April 1979.
23. Richards, *Religion of the Baha'is*, pp. 197–200.
24. Peter Smith, 'Emergence from the cultic milieu: the Baha'i movement in America, 1894–1936', paper presented at the first Los Angeles Baha'i History Conference, UCLA, 5–7 August 1983.
25. *Bahá'í News*, August 1930, p. 3; *ibid.*, September 1930, pp. 9–10.
26. *Bahá'í News* (Letter), December 1924, pp. 1,3; *ibid.*, February 1926, pp. 1–2; *ibid.*, June/July 1926, p. 1; *ibid.*, January 1928, pp. 1–3.
27. Rabbani, *Priceless Pearl*, pp. 247–50.
28. *Bahá'í World*, vol. XII, pp. 38–41, 373–90; *ibid.*, vol. XIII, pp. 333–8. Although the Hands of the Cause had been appointed by Bahá'u'lláh, they had not constituted a clearly defined administrative institution and they had not been replaced when they died. Until 1951 the appellation was retained only as an honorific title which was posthumously bestowed on various individuals.
29. Shoghi Effendi, *Messages to the Bahá'í World, 1950–1957*, 2nd edn (Wilmette, Ill., Bahá'í Publishing Trust, 1971), p. 127.
30. *Bahá'í World*, vol. XIII pp. 345–7.
31. *Ibid.*, pp. 347–53.
32. Johnson, 'Historical Analysis', p. 352.
33. *Ibid.*, pp. 364–5.
34. Universal House of Justice, *Wellspring of Guidance: Messages from the Universal House of Justice, 1963–1968* (Wilmette, Ill., Bahá'í Publishing Trust, 1969), p. 11; Universal House of Justice, *Messages from the Universal House of Justice, 1968–1973* (Wilmette, Ill., Bahá'í Publishing Trust, 1976), p. 41.
35. Weber, *Economy and Society*.
36. Universal House of Justice, *Messages, 1968–1973*, pp. 91–5.

9 MODERN BAHA'I MOTIFS

1. Eunice Braun, *Know Your Bahá'í Literature*, 2nd edn (Wilmette, Ill., Bahá'í Publishing Trust, 1968).
2. Universal House of Justice, *Wellspring*, pp. 88–9.
3. Shoghi Effendi's translations (with dates of first publication) include ʿAbdu'l-Bahá's *Will and Testament*, (1925); Bahá'u'lláh's *Hidden Words* (1924), *Book of Certitude* (1931) and *Epistle to the Son of the Wolf* (1941); one volume each of selections from the writings (*Gleanings*, 1935) and *Prayers and Meditations* (1938) of Bahá'u'lláh; and the history composed by Nabíl, *Dawn-Breakers* (1932).
4. See Johnson, 'Historical Analysis', pp. 279–87.
5. The subjects covered by these compilations include the Baha'i Fund, Local and National Spiritual Assemblies, the Continental Board of Counsellors, the Nineteen Day Feast, newsletters and Baha'i elections, summer schools and teaching institutes, consultation, prayer and meditation, teaching the Baha'i Faith, Baha'i education, the importance of textual study, morality and ethics, family life, divorce, the assurance of divine assistance, opposition, world peace, the status of women, spiritualism and reincarnation, and music.
6. Universal House of Justice, Department of Statistics, *The Seven Year Plan, 1979–1986: Statistical Report, 1983* (Haifa, Bahá'í World Centre, 1983), p. 22.
7. Universal House of Justice, *Synopsis*, pp. 4–5.

8. For example, Shoghi Effendi, *Dawn of a New Day*, (New Delhi, Bahá'í Publishing Trust, 1970), pp. 90, 123; Shoghi, *Unfolding Destiny*, p. 213.
9. Esslemont, *Bahá'u'lláh and the New Era*, pp. 209–12; *Star*, 13 (1922), 74.
10. *Bahá'í World*, vol. IV, p. 44; cf. Shoghi, *World Order of Bahá'u'lláh*, pp. 29–48.
11. See particularly his lengthy letters of 28 November 1931, 11 March 1936 and March 1941 (Shoghi, *World Order of Bahá'u'lláh*, pp. 29–48, 161–206; Shoghi, *Promised Day*).
12. Shoghi, *Messages to the Bahá'í World*, p. 103.
13. Shoghi, *World Order of Bahá'u'lláh*, pp. 203–4.
14. *Bahá'í World*, vol. V, p. 67.
15. Charles Mason Remey, 'The great global catastrophe', *Search Magazine*, 50 (December 1962), 34–40. On the continuation of apocalypticism amongst one group of Remey's followers, see Robert W. Balch, G. Farnsworth and S. Wilkins, 'When the bomb drops: reactions to disconfirmed prophecy in a millennial sect', *Sociological Perspective*, 26 (1983) 137–58.
16. Shoghi, *God Passes By*, pp. 57–8, 94–7.
17. Jamshed K. Fozdar, *Buddha Maitrya-Amitabha Has Appeared* (New Delhi, Bahá'í Publishing Trust, 1976); Shirin Fozdar, *Buddha and Amitabha* (Calcutta, n.p., n.d.); Howard Garey, '1260 AD or AH? Case of the mistaken date', *World Order*, 7,1 (1972), 4–20; Billy Rojas, 'The Saint-Simonians: messianic precursors of the Bahá'í Faith', *World Order*, 3,4 (1969), 29–37; Billy Rojas, 'The Millerites: millennialist precursors of the Bahá'í Faith', *World Order*, 4,1 (1969), 15–25; Kenneth D. Stephens, *So Great a Cause! A Surprising New Look at the Latter Day Saints* (Healdsburg, Cal., Naturegraph, 1973); George Townshend, *Christ and Bahá'u'lláh* (London, George Ronald, 1957), pp. 57–63; William Willoya and Vincent Brown, *Warriors of the Rainbow: Strange and Prophetic Dreams of the Indian People* (Healdsburg, Cal., Naturegraph, 1962).
18. William N. Garlington, 'Bahá'í *bhajans*,' *World Order*, 16,2 (1982), 43–9.
19. Shoghi, *Bahá'í Administration*, p. 90.
20. *Bahá'í World*, vol. VI, pp. 198–202.
21. See Shoghi, *World Order of Bahá'u'lláh*, pp. 64–7; Universal House of Justice, *Wellspring*, pp. 131–6; Universal House of Justice, *Messages, 1968–1973*, pp. 44–50.
22. *Bahá'í World*, vol. VIII, pp. 307–8; *ibid.*, vol. XII, pp. 316–18.
23. Universal House of Justice, in National Spiritual Assembly of the United States, 'War, government and conscience in this age of transition: the Bahá'í position on military service', *National Bahá'í Review* (August, 1969), reprint.
24. *Bahá'í World*, vol. VIII, p. 308.
25. *Reality* (New York) (September 1922), 55.
26. See Universal House of Justice, *The Promise of World Peace* (Haifa, Bahá'í World Centre, 1985). The campaign is linked to the United Nations International Year of Peace (1986).
27. *Star*, 3,1 (1912), 8; *Star*, 5 (1914), 67.
28. Shoghi, *Promised Day*, pp. 117–18.
29. Shoghi, *Citadel of Faith*, pp. 124–5.
30. *Bahá'í World*, vol. V, p. 567.
31. *Bahá'í World*, vol. XIII, pp. 795–9.
32. See the successive volumes of *Bahá'í World*, and also Wendy Heller's biography of the Baha'i daughter of Esperanto's founder, *Lidia: The Life of Lidia Zamenhof, Daughter of Esperanto* (Oxford, George Ronald, 1985).
33. See Marjorie Boulton, *Zamenhof, Creator of Esperanto* (London, Routledge and Kegan Paul, 1960), pp. 96–105.
34. Gayle Morrison, *To Move the World: Louis G. Gregory and the Advancement of* Racial *Unity in America* (Wilmette, Ill., Bahá'í Publishing Trust, 1982).
35. Shoghi, *Citadel of Faith*, p. 126.
36. Calculated from a handlist of 'Members of the National Spiritual Assembly of the United

States [and Canada], 1922–74' (Wilmette, Ill., National Bahá'í Archives). By comparison, in 1980, black Americans comprised some 11.7 per cent of the total US population. The 1985–6 membership of the American NSA consists of four blacks, two whites, one Russo-Persian, one Amerindian, and one Asian-American.

37. *Bahá'í World*, vol. XVII, p. 106.
38. Morrison, *To Move the World*.
39. *Bahá'í World*, vol. II, pp. 375–9.
40. Michael M.J. Fischer has noted a significant difference in marriage patterns between Baha'is and other groups in Yazd, with Baha'is being far more likely to marry non-kin than were the other religious groups considered (Muslims and Zoroastrians). See 'On changing the concept and position of Persian women', in *Women in the Muslim World*, ed. L. Beck and N. Keddie (Cambridge, Mass. and London, Harvard University Press, 1978), pp. 198, 211 n19.
41. For a recent account of Baha'i women's activities, see *Bahá'í World*, vol. XVII, pp. 202–14.
42. Smith, 'Sociological Study', p. 395.
43. Handlist of Members.
44. Bahá'í International Community, 'Documents concerning the rights of women', *World Order*, 9,3 (1975), 7–20.
45. On Baha'i educational principles, see H.T.D. Rost, *The Brilliant Stars: The Bahá'í Faith and the Education of Children* (Oxford, George Ronald, 1979); and Universal House of Justice, Research Department (comp.), *Bahá'í Education* (London, Bahá'í Publishing Trust, 1976). More generally, see Stephen Lambden, 'Baha'i', in *A Dictionary of Religious Education*, ed. J.M. Sutcliffe (London, SCM Press 1984), pp. 36–9.
46. For some initial statements on Baha'i views of developments, see *Bahá'í Studies Notebook*, 3, 3–4 (February 1984). See also the letter of the Universal House of Justice to the Baha'is of the world, 20 October 1983 (*Bahá'í News*, January 1984, pp. 1–2).
47. Universal House of Justice (comp.), *Bahá'í Institutions* (New Delhi, Bahá'í Publishing Trust, 1973), pp. 107–26.

10 WORLD-WIDE EXPANSION

1. *Bahá'í World*, vol. XVI, p. 130.
2. *Ibid*., pp. 572–3.
3. *Bahá'í World*, vol. XVII, p. 99; Universal House of Justice, *Seven Year Plan*, pp. 69–70.
4. Smith, 'Sociological Study', pp. 394–7.
5. *Bahá'í World*, vol. II, p. 37.
6. Walter Kolarz, *Religion in the Soviet Union* (London, Macmillan, 1961), p. 471.
7. *Bahá'í World*, vol. III, p. 49.
8. Mehri Samandari Jensen, 'The Impact of Religion, Socio-economic Status, and Degree of Religiosity on Family Planning among Moslems, and Baha'is in Iran: A Pilot Survey Research', EdD dissertation (University of Northern Colorado, 1981); Smith, 'Babi and Baha'i numbers'.
9. On this concept, see Michael Hill, *A Sociology of Religion* (London, Heinemann, 1973), pp. 50–1.
10. Patricia J. Higgins, 'Minority-state relations in contemporary Iran', *Iranian Studies*, 17 (1984), 37–71.
11. Fischer, 'On changing the concept', pp. 198, 211 n19; Richards, *Religion of the Baha'is*, p. 98.
12. See Nikki R. Keddie, *Roots of Revolution: An Interpretative History of Modern Iran* (New Haven and London, Yale University Press, 1981), pp. 215–25.
13. Shahrough Akhavi, *Religion and Politics in Contemporary Iran: Clergy–State Relations in the Pahlavi Period* (Albany, New York, State University of New York Press, 1980), pp. 76–82; Bahá'í International Community, 'BIC rebuts Iran's anti-Bahá'í document', *Bahá'í News*, May 1983, p. 4.

14. Roger Cooper, *The Baha'is of Iran*, 1st edn (London, Minority Rights Group, 1982), p. 11.
15. For a good example of such motivation in the 1955 persecution, see Muhammad Labíb, *The Seven Martyrs of Hurmuzak*, trans. M. Momen (Oxford, George Ronald, 1981). Will C. van den Hoonard refers to the looting of Baha'i property in Yazd as part of the present persecution ('Emerging from obscurity: the response of the Iranian Baha'i community to persecution, 1978–1982',*Conflict Quarterly*, 3 (1982), 9).
16. Harvey Cox, 'Deep structures in the study of new religions', in *Understanding the New Religions*, ed. J. Needleman and G. Baker (New York, Seabury Press, 1978), pp. 122–30.
17. Bayat, *Mysticism and Dissent*, p. 85.
18. Hoonard, 'Emerging from obscurity'.
19. Higgins, 'Minority-state relations'.
20. Smith, 'Emergence from the cultic milieu'.
21. *Bahá'í Year Book*, vol. I, pp. 101–3.
22. So successful were the Baha'is in gaining members from New Thought groups, that some groups later banned Baha'i speakers from their platforms (personal communication from Graham Hassall).
23. Florence E. Pinchon, *The Coming of the 'The Glory'* (London, Simpkin Marshall, 1928), p. 116.
24. *Bahá'í World*, vol. IV, p. 71; *Bahá'í News*, March 1932, p. 7.
25. On membership changes in the American Baha'i community, see Arthur Hampson, 'The Growth and Spread of the Baha'i Faith', PhD dissertation (University of Hawaii, 1980), pp. 218-46; and Smith, 'Sociological Study', pp. 375–8. The Canadian census figures for the Baha'is up to 1961 are listed in David Millett, 'A typology of religious organizations suggested by the Canadian census', *Sociological Analysis*, 30 (1969), 109.
26. National Spiritual Assembly of the Bahá'is of the British Isles, *World Development of the Faith* (London, Bahá'í Publishing Trust, 1952), p. 29.
27. *Bahá'í World*, vol. X, p. 29.
28. *Bahá'í World*, vol. VIII, pp. 688–92; *ibid.*, vol. XIV, pp. 133–5.
29. Millet, 'A typology', p. 109.
30. *Bahá'í News*, 193, p. 8; NSA of the British Isles, *World Development*, p. 29; *Baha'i Journal* (London), 69, p. 12.
31. Hampson, 'Growth and Spread', p. 229; Millet, 'A typology', p. 109. The British figure is estimated from a series of statistics compiled by the author.
32. Hampson, 'Growth and Spread', p. 229; James F. Nelson, 'Three years of horrors', *World Order*, 16,3 (1982), 14.
33. See Smith, 'Sociological Study', pp. 431–44. See also Berger, 'From Sect to Church', pp. 131–9; Marina Fischer-Kowalski and Josef Bucek, *Strukturen der sozialen Ungleichheit in Österreich, Teil II: Endbericht, Band 2* (Vienna, Bundesministerium für Wissenschaft und Forschung, 1978); Hampson, 'Growth and Spread', pp. 318–50; and Margaret J. Ross, 'Some Aspects of the Bahá'í Faith in New Zealand', MA thesis (University of Auckland, 1979).
34. All three surveys were conducted at second hand, through the intermediary of Local Spiritual Assembly officers, questionnaires being distributed and collected at regular Baha'i Nineteen Day Feasts, meetings usually attended by most religiously active Baha'is. Most or all of those present at the Feasts completed the questionnaires. Of the three surveys, Berger's survey in New York (N = 90) represented between one-third and one-half of the total Baha'i community; my British survey (N = 151) represented about 52 per cent of the adult and youth membership of the 19 communities which agreed to participate (of a sample of 29 contacted), and the Los Angeles survey (N = 118) only about 17 per cent of membership. In all cases respondents were asked to describe briefly what aspects of the Baha'i Faith most attracted them at first. As many gave multiple answers the frequency percentages in Table 4 do not add up to 100 per cent.

35. *Bahá'í World*, vol. XIII, p. 258.
36. *Bahá'í News*, November 1978, p. 9.
37. *Bahá'í News*, May 1978, p. 5.
38. That is Shaykh Sa'id Hindí, the Letter of the Living, and Sayyid Başír Hindí. On the latter, see Browne, *Táríkh-i-Jadíd*, pp. 244–7, 388–94.
39. *Bahá'í World*, vol. XIII, p. 299.
40. *Star*, 12 (1920), 20–6, 220.
41. *Bahá'í World*, vol. VIII, pp. 690–1; *ibid.*, vol. XIII, pp. 299–300.
42. Shoghi, *Dawn of a New Day*, p. 1.
43. *Bahá'í World*, vol. XIII, p. 299; William N. Garlington, 'The Baha'i Faith in Malwa', in *Religion in South Asia*, ed. G.A. Odie (London, Curzon Press, 1977), p. 104; Universal House of Justice, *Seven Year Plan*.

CONCLUSION

1. Bahá'u'lláh, *Tablets*, p. 144.
2. Shoghi, *World Order of Bahá'u'lláh*, p. 32.

APPENDIX 1 GLOSSARY

Afnán (twigs) the Báb's maternal uncles and their descendants

Aghṣán (branches) Baháʾuʾlláh's male descendants

Akhbárí 'traditionalist' school of Shiʿi jurisprudence

ʿAlíyuʾlláhí (or *Ahluʾl-Ḥaqq*) congeries of heterodox Shiʿi sects distinguished by their extreme veneration for ʿAlí

ʿAtabát (thresholds) the Shiʿi shrine cities of Iraq (Karbalá, Káẓimayn, Najaf and Sámarrá)

báb (pl. *abwáb*) (gate) Ithná-ʿAsharí intermediary between the Hidden Imam and the faithful

bábuʾl-imám the 'gate' of the Imam

Bálásarí (above-the-head) non-Shaykhi Shiʿi orthodoxy

baraka holiness, inherent spiritual power

bázárí merchant or craftsman of the bazaar

fatwá a legal ruling or expression of religio-legal opinion by a cleric

fiqh Islamic jurisprudence

Ghuṣn-i Akbar, Ghuṣn-i Aʿẓam the *akbar* and the *aʿẓam* branches – Bahaʾi titles applied to Muḥammad ʿAlí and to ʿAbduʾl-Bahá repectively

ḥadíth a tradition derived from the Prophet Muhammad or (for Shiʿis) the Imams

ḥajj the Islamic pilgrimage to Mecca

Ḥaẓíratuʾl-Quds (the Sacred Fold) Bahaʾi administrative building

ijáẓa (pl. *ijáẓát*) licence or diploma bestowed by higher-ranking members of the ulama on those they deem knowledgeable in particular aspects of the Islamic sciences

Imám in Shiʿism, the divinely appointed leaders of the community

Imám-Jumʿih state-appointed leader of the Friday prayers

Ithná-ʿAshariyya (Twelvers) those Shiʿis who follow the twelve Imams; Imámís

jihád Islamic holy war

Mahdí (the guided one) the messianic figure of Islam

Man-yuẓhiruhu'lláh (He whom God shall make manifest) the Divine Manifestation awaited by the Babis

Mashriqu'l-Adhkár (Dawning-place of the remembrance of God) the Baha'i House of Worship

maẓhar-i iláhí the Manifestation of God — term used by Baha'is to refer to most of the founders of the major religions and to certain other religious figures

Mírzá learned man (when used before a name); prince (when used after a name)

mubáhala 'mutual cursing' in a religious disputation

mujtahid a member of the ulama who is entitled to practise *ijtihád* (the making of independent legal judgements)

mullá lesser member of the ulama

Mu'tazala Islamic rationalist school of philosophy and theology

Náqiḍín (those who break agreements) Baha'i term for those regarded as having violated Bahá'u'lláh's Covenant with his followers

Qá'im (he who will arise) Shi'i term for the awaited Twelfth Imam

Riḍván (paradise) Baha'i name for the garden outside Baghdad in which Bahá'u'lláh first laid claim to be the expected one of Babism; the twelve-day Baha'i festival commemorating that declaration (21 April to 2 May), on the first day of which Baha'i Local Assemblies are elected

ruknu'r-rábi' the Shaykhi doctrine of the Fourth Support, the living source of authority

Sayyid descendant of the Prophet Muhammad

sharí'a Islamic holy law

takfír formal denunciation of an individual as an infidel

taqiyya (guarding oneself) the pious dissimulation of belief

'ulamá the 'learned' of Islam

Uṣulí the 'rationalist' school of Shi'i jurisprudence

APPENDIX 2 CHRONOLOGIES

Major public events are italicized

EARLY SHAYKHISM

early 1790s	Shaykh Aḥmad's migration to Iraq.
1796	*The Qajars establish a unitary state in Iran.*
1806–22	Shaykh Aḥmad's travels in Iran.
c. 1822	Muḥammad Taqí Baraghání accuses Shaykh Aḥmad of heresy.
1826	Death of Shaykh Aḥmad (27 June). Succession of Sayyid Káẓim Rashtí.
1834	*Accession of Muḥammad Sháh* (9 September).
1843/4	Death of Sayyid Káẓim (31 December/1 January).

THE BABI MOVEMENT, 1844–53

1819	Birth of Sayyid ᶜAlí Muḥammad Shírází (20 October).
c. 1839	ᶜAlí Muḥammad's visit to Karbalá.
1843	*The sack of Karbalá by the Ottomans.*
1843/4	Death of Sayyid Káẓim (31 December/1 January). ᶜAlí Muḥammad's initiatory visions.
1844	ᶜAlí Muḥammad declares his mission to Mullá Ḥusayn (22/23 May) and makes a claim to be the Báb of the Imam. He gathers his first disciples and disperses them throughout Iran as missionaries (summer). He himself leaves for Mecca (September).
1845	Crowds gather in Karbalá in response to the Báb's summons. Messianic expectation centres on the beginning of the new year, AH 1261 (10 January). The Báb's emissary is tried and convicted (13 January) and the Báb cancels his projected visit to Karbalá. The Báb

returns to Bushire (15 May) and proceeds to Shiraz, where he is placed under house arrest (July). Karím Khán Kirmání completes his first refutation of Babism (July). Important new disciples are gained.

1846 The Báb escapes from Shiraz (23 September) and proceeds to Isfahan. He is sympathetically received by the governor, Manúchihr Khán. Qurratu'l-ʿAyn provokes disturbances in Karbalá (December).

1847 *Manúchihr Khán's death* (February) leads to the Báb being transferred to the fortress of Mákú (March-July). Qurratu'l-ʿAyn makes a proclamatory progress through Western Iran (spring–summer) before returning to Qazvin. Her uncle, *Muḥammad Taqí Baraghání, is murdered* (late October) and a general persecution of the Qazvini Babis occurs.

1848 The Báb communicates his higher claims to his leading disciples. He is transferred to the fortress of Chihríq (April) and is later brought for trial in Tabriz, where he announces his higher claims (late July). These claims also announced to the Babis at Badasht (June-July). Mullá Ḥusayn and his companions leave Mashhad (21 July) and in the confused aftermath of *Muḥammad Sháh's death* (4 September) enter Mazandaran. They come into conflict with a mob in Bárfurúsh and retire to the nearby shrine of Shaykh Ṭabarsí (10 October). Fighting commences. *Náṣiri'd-Dín Sháh accedes to the throne.*

1849 The Babis at Ṭabarsí are offered a truce by their opponents (10 May) and are massacred.

1850 Seven leading Babis in Tehran are executed (19/20 February). Sayyid Yaḥyá Darábí becomes involved in a civil conflict in Yazd (January–February). He escapes and makes a missionary journey through Fars. At Nayríz fighting breaks out between the Babis under Darábí and their opponents (27 May to 21 June). The Babis are defeated and massacred. A larger Babi–Muslim conflict has already started in Zanján (*c.* 13 May). *The Báb is publicly executed in Tabriz* (8/9 July).

1851 The conflict in Zanján is finally ended and the Babi

survivors massacred (January). Áqá Khán Núrí succeeds Mírzá Taqí Khán as chief minister (November).

1852 *The attempt on the life of the Shah* (15 August) is followed by a general persecution of the Babis in Tehran and elsewhere. Most of the remaining Babi leaders are killed.

1853 Further fighting between the Babis and their opponents in Nayríz (October–November).

THE BABI RECOVERY AND THE EMERGENCE OF THE BAHAʾI FAITH, 1853–1921

1851 *Attempt on the life of Náṣiri ʾd-Dín Sháh* (15 August). General persecution of the Babis. Ṣubḥ-i Azal goes into hiding. Baháʾuʾlláh is imprisoned in the Black Pit, site of his initiatory visions.

1853 Baháʾuʾlláh is exiled to Baghdad (arrives 8 April). Ṣubḥ-i Azal later joins him but remains in seclusion.

1854 Baháʾuʾlláh withdraws to the mountains of Kurdistan (10 April), returning only in 1856 (19 March).

1856–63 Baháʾuʾlláh's increasing pre-eminence within the Babi community. His composition of the *Kalimát-i Maknúnih, Haft Vádí* and *Kitáb-i Íqán*.

1863 The order for Baháʾuʾlláh's removal from Baghdad. The gathering in the Najibiyya (Riḍván) garden and Baháʾuʾlláh's declaration of his mission to his disciples (21 April to 2 May). The journey to Istanbul (3 May to 16 August) and to Edirne (December).

1866 After increasing tension within the Babi colony in Edirne a division is made, in the spring, between the followers of Ṣubḥ-i Azal (Azalis) and those of Baháʾuʾlláh (Bahaʾis). Thereafter Baháʾuʾlláh's claim to be *Man-yuẓhiruhuʾlláh* is made known to the Babis in Iran, most of whom eventually become his followers.

1868 The Babis and Bahaʾis in Edirne are arrested. Ṣubḥ-i Azal is exiled to Famagusta and Baháʾuʾlláh is exiled to ʿAkká (12-31 August).

c. 1873 Composition of Baháʾuʾlláh's book of laws, the *Kitábuʾl-Aqdas*.

1877	Bahá'u'lláh is permitted to live outside the city of ʿAkká.
1892	*The death of Bahá'u'lláh* (29 May). He is succeeded by his eldest son, ʿAbdu'l-Bahá. Muḥammad ʿAlí challenges his leadership.
1908	ʿAbdu'l-Bahá is freed from Ottoman captivity (July) and moves to Haifa (1909).
1910–13	ʿAbdu'l-Bahá's travels: Egypt (August 1910 to August 1911), Europe (August–December 1911) and North America and Europe (March 1912 to June 1913).
1921	*Death of ʿAbdu'l-Bahá* (28 November).

THE BAHA'I COMMUNITY, 1866–1921
The Middle East

1850–3	Collapse of the Babi movement
1856–66	Gradual revival of Babism under Bahá'u'lláh's leadership.
1866–8	Split between the Azalis and the Baha'is (1866). Bahá'u'lláh's open claim to be *Man-yuẓhiruhu'lláh*. Baha'i missionaries in Iran. Bahá'u'lláh's exile to ʿAkká (1868). Persecutions in Iran (1867), Iraq and Egypt (1868).
1869	Bahá'u'lláh's emissary to the Shah is tortured and killed.
1871	Bahá'u'lláh despatches a missionary to India.
1870s on	Conversions amongst the Iranian Shiʿi population. Intermittent persecutions.
1880s on	Conversions amongst the Iranian Jews and Zoroastrians. Settlement of Baha'is in Russian Turkestan.
1889	Russian authorities convict Shiʿi murderers of a Baha'i: first instance of the opponents of Baha'is being punished.
1892	*Death of Bahá'u'lláh* (29 May) and *succession of ʿAbdu'l-Bahá*.
1894	Beginning of Baha'i missionary activity in the United States of America.
1896	*Assassination of Náṣiri'd-Dín Sháh by a follower of*

	Jamáluʾd-Dín Afghání (1 May). Several Bahaʾis are killed.
1897–1909	Establishment of Bahaʾi schools in Iran.
1902	Work commences on the Bahaʾi Temple in Russian Turkestan.
1903	Major persecutions of Bahaʾis in several Iranian cities
1905–11	*Constitutional Revolution in Iran.*
1910	Establishment of Bahaʾi hospital and clinic in Tehran.
1917	*Russian Revolutions.* Expansion of Bahaʾi activities in Asiatic Russia.
1921	*Death of ʿAbduʾl-Bahá* (28 November).
1925	*Formal abolition of the Qajar dynasty.*

The West

1894	The Bahaʾi Faith begins to be established in the West, I.G. Kheiralla gains his first converts in Chicago ('Truth-Seekers').
1898–9	First pilgrimage of Western Bahaʾis to visit ʿAbduʾl-Bahá in ʿAkká. Returning pilgrims establish Bahaʾi groups in Paris and London.
1900	Public split between the American supporters of ʿAbduʾl-Bahá and those of Kheiralla and Muḥammad ʿAli (March). Arrival of the first of four Persian Bahaʾi teachers (April).
1905	Beginning of Bahaʾi activities in Germany.
1909	Establishment of the Chicago-based Bahai Temple Unity.
1911–13	ʿAbduʾl-Bahá's visits to the West (Europe, August–December 1911; North America, April–December 1912; Europe again, December 1912 to June 1913).
1915 on	Subsidization of itinerant Bahaʾi 'missionary' teachers in North America.
1916	Receipt of the first of ʿAbduʾl-Bahá's general letters on teaching, the *Tablets of the Divine Plan*.
1917	*The entry of the United States into the First World War*, Kheiralla's prophesied year of the millennium. The Chicago Reading Room controversy.
1919	The 'unveiling' of ʿAbduʾl-Bahá's general letters on teaching.

India and Japan

1872–8	Jamál Effendi's missionary work in India.
1911	First systematic teaching campaign in India
1914	Beginning of Baha'i activity in Japan.
1920	First All-India Baha'i Convention.

INSTITUTIONALIZATION IN THE FORMATIVE AGE, 1922–85

1921	*The death of ʿAbdu'l-Bahá* (28 November). Shoghi Effendi is summoned from England.

1922–c. 1935. Initial development of the Administrative Order

1922	The public reading of ʿAbdu'l-Bahá's Will (3 January). Shoghi Effendi is named as Guardian of the Cause. Leading group of Baha'is gather in Haifa for consultations with Shoghi (March). Shoghi Effendi's first general letter on Baha'i administration (April). His first departure from Haifa (April–December).
early 1920s	Short-lived Baha'i 'Scientific Society' in Egypt opposes Shoghi Effendi. H.G. Dyar opposes Baha'i administration in the New York *Reality* magazine (1922–5).
1923	Shoghi's second general letter on administration (March). National Spiritual Assemblies (NSAs) are established in England, Germany and India. Shoghi's second departure from Haifa (June–November).
1924	NSA established in Egypt.
1925	Shoghi Effendi introduces definite qualifications for Baha'i membership.
1926	Ruth White begins her campaign of opposition to Shoghi Effendi and the Baha'i administration.
1927	North American NSA adopts a Declaration of Trust preparatory to legal incorporation (May 1929).
1929	Conflict between Ahmad Sohrab and the New York Baha'i Assembly. Sohrab forms the New History Society and is excommunicated (1930).
1931	NSA established in Iraq.
1934	NSAs established in Iran and Australia–New Zealand.

1935 Baha'is prohibited from membership of other religious bodies.

1939–41 Public dispute between the North American NSA and Ahmad Sohrab concerning the use of the name 'Baha'i'.

1941–2 Excommunication of dissident members of Shoghi Effendi's family.

1951–7. The establishment of appointed institutions

1951 Shoghi Effendi announces the formation of the International Baha'i Council (9 January) and his appointment of the first contingent of 12 Hands of the Cause (24 December).

1952 A second contingent of Hands of the Cause is appointed (29 February)

1954 Appointment of the first Auxiliary Boards.

1957 Appointment of a third contingent of Hands of the Cause and the Auxiliary Boards for Protection. The Hands are designated 'Chief Stewards' (October). *Shoghi Effendi dies in London* (4 November). The Hands gather in conclave in Haifa. In the absence of any Will, and pending the formation of the Universal House of Justice, the Hands assume supreme authority (25 November).

1960 Charles Mason Remey proclaims himself to be the Second Guardian and is declared a Covenant-breaker by his fellow Hands (October).

1961 Election of the second International Baha'i Council (April).

1963 on. Developments under the Universal House of Justice

1963 *Election of the Universal House of Justice* (April). Celebration of the Most Great Jubilee in London (28 April to 2 May).

1968 Establishment of the Continental Boards of Counsellors.

1972	Constitution of the Universal House of Justice adopted.
1973	Establishment of the International Teaching Centre.

THE BAHA'I COMMUNITY, 1922–85

Global

1948	Establishment of the 'Baha'i International Community' affiliated with the United Nations.
1948–53	Construction of the superstructure of the Shrine of the Báb.
1951–7	Appointment of the Hands of the Cause (1951–7), Auxiliary Boards (1954 on) and the first International Baha'i Council (1951).
1955–7	Construction of the International Archives Building in Haifa.
1957–64	Construction of Baha'i temples in Uganda, Australia and West Germany.
1964 on	International Baha'i Plans: Nine Year (1964–73), Five Year (1974–9), Seven Year (1979–86), Six Year (1986–92).
1967	Initiation of a world-wide proclamation campaign.
1967–86	Construction of Baha'i temples in Panama, Western Samoa and India.
1973	Establishment of the International Teaching Centre.
1975–83	Construction of the Seat of the Universal House of Justice.
1983	Establishment of the Baha'i Office of Social and Economic Development in Haifa.
1985	Universal House of Justice issues its general letter on peace to 'the peoples of the world'.

The Middle East

1921–5	*Establishment of Pahlavi rule in Iran.*
1922	Seizure of Bahá'u'lláh's house in Iraq.
1924	NSA established in Egypt.
1925	Baha'is in Egypt proclaimed non-Muslims.
1928 on	Suppression of the Baha'i community in Asiatic Russia.

1931	NSA established in Iraq.
1934	NSA established in Iran. Baha'i schools closed. Purge of Baha'is in government employment.
1946–53	Post-war plans: Iran (1946–50), Iraq (1947–50), Egypt (1949–53).
1955	Major persecution of Baha'is in Iran.
1960 on	Banning of all Baha'i activities in Egypt.
1962	Persecution of Baha'is in Morocco.
1970 on	Banning of all Baha'i activities in Iraq.
1979 on	*Islamic revolution in Iran.* Major persecution of Baha'is.

The West

1922–5	Transformation of the American Bahai Temple Unity into the National Spiritual Assembly.
1923	NSAs established in England and Germany.
1926 on	Ruth White's campaign of opposition to 'Baha'i organization'.
1929–30	Conflict between the American Baha'i administration and Ahmad Sohrab.
1930–1	Construction of the superstructure of the Baha'i temple at Wilmette.
1930–7	Wilhelm Herrigel's 'Bahai World Union'.
1931	First German Baha'i summer school.
1934	NSA established for Australia and New Zealand.
1937	First American Seven Year Plan (1937–44). Establishment of the British Baha'i Publishing Trust and the commencement of regular British summer schools. The Baha'i Faith is banned in Germany by the Gestapo (May).
1944	British Six Year Plan (1944–50).
1945–6	German Baha'is reorganize.
1946–53	Post-war plans: North America (1946–53), Australia–New Zealand (1947–53), Canada (1948–53), Germany (1948–53), Britain (1951–3).
1953	Final completion of the Wilmette temple.
1957	Work starts on the Baha'i temple in Sydney (1957–61) and the Baha'i Home for the Aged in Wilmette (1957–9).
1960–4	Construction of the Baha'i temple at Frankfurt.

late 1960s on	Large-scale conversion of youth and minority groups in various Western countries.

The Third World

1923	NSA established for India and Burma.
1937–44	First American Seven Year Plan: Bahaʾi expansion in Latin America.
1938–53	Indian Plans (1938–44, 1946–50, 1951–3) direct attention to South and South-East Asia.
1951–3	British Two Year Plan and the international 'Africa project'.
late 1950s on	Beginning of large-scale conversions in Latin America, Africa and Southern Asia.
1957–61	Construction of Bahaʾi temple at Kampala.
1967–72	Construction of Bahaʾi temple at Panama City.
1973 on	Establishment of Bahaʾi radio station in Latin America.
1977–86	Construction of Bahaʾi temple at New Delhi.
1979–84	Construction of Bahaʾi temple at Apia, Western Samoa.

APPENDIX 3 A NOTE ON THE SOURCES AND A GUIDE TO FURTHER READING

GENERAL

Babi and Bahaʾi Studies

The academic study of the Babi and Bahaʾi religions is in its infancy. Much valuable work was accomplished during the period from the 1880s to the 1910s by scholars such as Browne and Nicolas, but inevitably many of their observations are now dated. Western scholarly interest in the two movements only revived during the 1970s and whilst many useful works have been produced in the past fifteen years or so, they have served more to define basic research questions than to establish a common research tradition (or traditions). Many issues remain controversial. Again, whilst certain areas of Babi and Bahaʾi Studies have received detailed attention, others, often quite crucial, remain more or less obscure. Thus, whilst we now have a substantial scholarly base for a general work of synthesis such as this present book, the next fifteen years or so will undoubtedly see much new research and the clarification of issues that for the present are unclear or which can only be described in general outline.

Bibliographies

There is as yet no comprehensive bibliography of Babi and Bahaʾi literature, although such a work is in preparation by William P. Collins, the chief librarian at the Bahaʾi World Centre in Haifa. An existing bibliographic guide by Joel Bjorline, *The Bahaʾi Faith* (Garland, 1985), is highly uneven in quality and is not comprehensive. The successive volumes of the *Baháʾí World* (vols. II–XII (Wilmette, Ill., Baháʾí Publishing Trust, 1928–56); vols. XIII– (Haifa, Baháʾí World Centre, 1970–)) provide much useful bibliographic information, but this is mostly related to the Bahaʾi Faith rather than to Babism. Denis MacEoin, 'A Revised Survey of the Sources for Early Bábí Doctrine and History',

Fellowship dissertation (King's College, Cambridge, 1977), provides the most detailed guide to the sources for the earlier movement.

General works

There are a number of works which are concerned with the development of both the Babi and the Baha'i religions. Several of these are written quite clearly from a Baha'i vantage point, and focus their attention on the development of the Baha'i Faith, discussing the Babi movement as an integral part of that later development. For Baha'is, the most important of these works is Shoghi Effendi's *God Passes By* (Wilmette, Ill., Bahá'í Publishing Trust, 1944), a forceful work of interpretation which reviews the main events of the 'first century of the Bahá'í Era' (1844–1944, that is incorporating Babism) with a view to identifying the patterns and correlations which are of significance to Baha'is. Another work of great significance for Baha'is is ᶜAbdu'l-Bahá's *Maqáli-yi shakhṣi sayyaḥ*, translated into English and edited with considerable supplementary material by Edward G. Browne as *A Traveller's Narrative, Written to Illustrate the Episode of the Báb* (2 vols., Cambridge, Cambridge University Press, 1891).

There are several general accounts of the Babi and Baha'i movements written by (former) Christian missionaries in Iran. Vernon Elvin Johnson, 'An Historical Analysis of Critical Transformations in the Evolution of the Bahá'í World Faith', PhD dissertation (Baylor University, Texas, 1974), pp. 93–100, makes a useful comparison of these works. All of them are extremely hostile in tone. The earliest, by Samuel Graham Wilson, *Bahaism and its Claims: A Study of the Religion Promulgated by Baha Ullah and Abdu'l-Baha* (New York, Fleming Revel, 1915; reprinted 1970, New York, AMS Press), is primarily concerned with mounting a wide-ranging critique of Baha'i claims and doctrine. More comprehensive accounts are provided by William S. Miller, *Bahaism: Its Origin, History and Teachings* (New York, Fleming Revel, 1931) and *The Baha'i Faith: Its History and Teachings* (South Pasadena, Cal., William Carey Library, 1974), but these need to be used with caution. See J. Douglas Martin, 'The missionary as historian', *Bahá'í Studies*, 4 (1978), 1–29, for a critique. Far more satisfactory is the work by J.R. Richards, *The Religion of the Baha'is* (London, Society for Promoting Christian Knowledge, 1932), which, although now dated, makes a number of important points.

There are also several doctoral dissertations which deal with both the Babi and Baha'i movements. Of these, the following may be mentioned:

Peter L. Berger, 'From Sect to Church: A Sociological Interpretation of the Bahaʾi Movement' (New School for Social Research, New York, 1954); Arthur Hampson, 'The Growth and Spread of the Bahaʾi Faith' (University of Hawaii, 1980); V.E. Johnson, 'Historical Analysis'; and Peter Smith, 'A Sociological Study of the Babi and Bahaʾi Religions' (University of Lancaster, 1982).

Finally, note should be made of the periodical *Baháʾí Studies*, published by the Association for Baháʾí Studies (Ottawa, Ontario); of the series, *Studies in Bábí and Baháʾí History* (Los Angeles, Cal., Kalimat Press) – *SBBH, vol. I*, ed. Moojan Momen (1982), *From Iran East and West, SBBH, vol. II*, ed. Juan R. Cole and Moojan Momen (1984), and *In Iran, SBBH, vol. III*, ed. Peter Smith (1986) (further volumes forthcoming); and of the collection of source materials collected by Moojan Momen, *The Bábí and Baháʾí Religions, 1844–1944: Some Contemporary Western Accounts* (Oxford, George Ronald, 1981).

BABISM

The Iranian and Shiʿi background

The study of Shiʿi Islam – a topic long neglected in the West – is well served by the recent publication of Moojan Momen's *An Introduction to Shiʿi Islam: The History and Doctrines of Twelver Shiʿism* (New Haven and London, Yale University Press, 1985). This book also provides a guide to the literature. On the Islamic tradition and Islamic history in general, see Marshall G.S. Hodgson, *The Venture of Islam: Conscience and History in a World Civilization* (3 vols., Chicago and London, University of Chicago Press, 1974).

As to nineteenth-century Iranian history, again an area of relative scholarly neglect, a useful general introduction is provided by Nikki R. Keddie, *Roots of Revolution: An Interpretive History of Modern Iran* (New Haven and London, Yale University Press, 1981). On religious and intellectual developments during the period, see Hamid Algar, *Religion and State in Iran, 1785–1906: The Role of the Ulama in the Qajar Period* (Berkeley and Los Angeles, University of California Press, 1969); Said Amir Arjomand, *The Shadow of God and the Hidden Imam* (Chicago, Chicago University Press, 1984); Mangol Bayat, *Mysticism and Dissent: Socioreligious Thought in Qajar Iran* (Syracuse, New York, Syracuse University Press, 1982); and Edward G. Browne, *A Literary History of Persia* (4 vols., Cambridge, Cambridge University Press, 1902–24; reprint 1969), vol. IV, pp. 353–411.

The Shaykhi movement

The most detailed modern account of the development of the Shaykhi movement up to the 1840s is provided by Denis MacEoin, 'From Shaykhism to Babism: A Study in Charismatic Renewal in Shiʿi Islam', PhD dissertation (University of Cambridge, 1979), pp. 51–124. Detailed accounts of Shaykhi doctrine are provided by Henri Corbin, *En islam iranien: Aspects spirituels et philosophiques* (4 vols., Paris, Gallimard, 1971–2), vol. IV, pp. 205–300; and Vahid Rafati, 'The Development of Shaykhí Thought in Shíʿí Islam', PhD dissertation (University of California, Los Angeles, 1979). These two works differ considerably in emphasis, and whilst Corbin stresses the continuity of early Shaykhism with the later Shaykhi tradition of Karím Khán, Rafati stresses the movement's linkages with the Babi–Bahaʾi tradition. The older work by A.L.M. Nicolas, *Essai sur le Chéikisme* (4 vols., Paris, Librairie Paul Geuthner and Ernest Leroux, 1910–14) remains useful. Bayat, *Mysticism and Dissent*, pp. 37–58, places the movement in the wider context of Shiʿi dissent.

Babi history

The Babi movement remains under-researched. Two recent dissertations provide the best modern accounts: Abbas Amanat, 'The Early Years of the Babi Movement: Background and Development' D. Phil dissertation (University of Oxford, 1981), from the standpoint of social history; and MacEoin's 'From Shaykhism to Babism', in terms of the movement's logistical and doctrinal emergence from Shaykhism. MacEoin discusses sources in 'Revised Survey'.

Of other work, that by Edward Granville Browne is particularly noteworthy. This includes two translations of Bahaʾi histories of the Babi movement (both with copious notes and appendices), *A Traveller's Narrative*, by ʿAbduʾl-Bahá, and the *Táríkh-i-Jadíd, or New History of Mírzá ʿAlí Muḥammad the Báb* (Cambridge, Cambridge University Press, 1893); the Persian text of the controversial Babi text, *Kitáb-i-Nuqṭatuʾl-Káf* (Leyden, Brill, and London, Luzac, 1910); and the rather uneven *Materials for the Study of the Bábí Religion* (Cambridge, Cambridge University Press, 1918). Of Browne's articles, mention should be made of 'The Bábís of Persia', *Journal of the Royal Asiatic Society*, 21 (1889), 485–526, 881–1009; and 'Personal reminiscences of the Bábí insurrection at Zanjan in 1850, by Áqá ʿAbduʾl-Aḥad-i-Zanjání, *Journal of the Royal Asiatic Society*, 29 (1897),

761–827. For an assessment of Browne's work by a leading Bahaʾi scholar, see Hasan M. Balyuzi, *Edward Granville Browne and the Baháʾí Faith* (London, George Ronald, 1970).

Other works of particular value are the collection of diplomatic reports assembled by Momen, *Bábí and Baháʾí Religions*, pp. 69–179; (see also 'Excerpts from despatches written during 1848–1852, by Prince Dolgorukov, Russian minister to Persia', *World Order*, 1,1 (1966), 17–27); the early Bahaʾi history by Muḥammad Zarandí Nabíl, *The Dawn-Breakers: Nabíl's Narrative of the Early Days of the Baháʾí Revelation*, trans. and ed. Shoghi Effendi (Wilmette, Ill., Baháʾí Publishing Trust, 1932) and A.L.M. Nicolas, *Seyyèd Ali Mohammed dit le Bâb* (Paris, Dujarric, 1905). In addition, H.M. Balyuzi has provided a convenient general account of Babism from a Bahaʾi perspective in *The Báb: The Herald of the Day of Days* (Oxford, George Ronald, 1973), and a short biographical study, *Khadíjih Bagum: The Wife of the Báb* (Oxford, George Ronald, 1981). Mikhail S. Ivanov, *Babidski Vostanii i Irane, 1848–1852* (Moscow, Trudy Instituta Vostok-vedeniya, 1939) provides a Marxist interpretation of the movement.

The Báb's writings

There are general accounts of the Báb's writings in the works of Browne, MacEoin and Nicolas. Nicolas has also published French translations of three of the Báb's later works: The *Daláʾil-i sabʿa*, as *Le Livre des sept preuves* (Paris, Maisonneuve, Librairie Orientale et Americaine, 1902;) and the Arabic and Persian *Bayáns*, as *Le Béyân arabe* (Paris, Ernest Leroux, 1905), and *Le Béyân persan* (4 vols., Paris, Librairie Paul Geuthner, 1911–14). There is also a recent Bahaʾi translation of selected passages from some of the Báb's writings, *Selections from the Writings of the Báb*, comp. Research Department of the Universal House of Justice, trans. H. Taherzadeh (Haifa, Baháʾí World Centre, 1976).

THE BAHAʾI FAITH IN THE EAST

There is as yet little material available in any Western language concerning the emergence and early development of the Bahaʾi community in the East. Most of the research has focused on the lives of Baháʾuʾlláh and ʿAbduʾl-Báha, though in passing this work often illuminates the wider Bahaʾi milieu.

Baháʾuʾlláh

We now have a full-length biography by H.M. Balyuzi, *Baháʾuʾlláh: The King of Glory* (Oxford, George Ronald, 1980). There is also a memoir by one of Baháʾuʾlláh's attendants, Ustád Muḥammad-ʿAlí Salmání, *My Memories of Baháʾuʾlláh*, trans. M. Gail (Los Angeles, Kalimat Press, 1982). More generally, Ḥájí Mírzá Ḥaydar-ʿAlí, *Stories from the Delight of Hearts*, trans. and abridged by A.Q. Faizi (Los Angeles, Kalimat Press, 1980) contains interesting reminiscences of both Baháʾuʾlláh and the Bahaʾi community of the time, whilst Adib Taherzadeh, *The Revelation of Baháʾuʾlláh* (3 vols. to date, Oxford, George Ronald, 1974–), and H.M. Balyuzi, *Eminent Baháʾís in the Time of Baháʾuʾlláh* (Oxford, George Ronald, 1985), provide additional material on the early Bahaʾis of the East. E.G. Browne, *A Year amongst the Persians* (1893; 3rd edn, London, A. and C. Black, 1950), includes many observations on the Bahaʾi community of the 1880s. Shoghi Effendi, *God Passes By* (Wilmette, Ill., Baháʾí Publishing Trust, 1944), and Moojan Momen, *The Bábí and Baháʾí Religions, 1844–1944: Some Contemporary Western Accounts* (Oxford, George Ronald, 1981), also deal with this period and that of ʿAbduʾl-Bahá's leadership at length.

ʿAbduʾl-Bahá

We again have a full-length biography by H.M. Balyuzi, *ʿAbduʾl-Bahá: The Centre of the Covenant of Baháʾuʾlláh* (London, George Ronald, 1971), although this concentrates on the three-year period of his travels in the West. For diary accounts of his life in the East by two of his close associates, see Yúnis Khán Afrúkhtih, *Khátirát-i nuh sálih*, rev. edn (Los Angeles, Kalimat Press, 1983); and Mirza Ahmad Sohrab, *Abdul Baha in Egypt* (New York, New History Foundation, 1929; London, Rider, n.d.). There is also an account derived from ʿAbduʾl-Bahá's sister, Bahiyyih Khánum, in Myron P. Phelps, *The Life and Teachings of Abbas Effendi* (New York, G.P. Putnams, 1904); see also the recent abridged edition, *The Master in ʿAkká* (Los Angeles, Kalimat Press, 1985).

The most detailed account of ʿAbduʾl-Bahá's travels in Europe and America is that of his secretary, Mírzá Maḥmúd Zarqání, *Kitáb-i badáyiʿuʾl-áthár* (2 vols., Bombay, 1914–21; reprint, Hofheim-Langenhain, Baháʾí-Verlag, 1982). A translation of the American section of this work is forthcoming, as *ʿAbduʾl-Bahá in America: Maḥmúd's diary*, trans. Abbas Ali of Rangoon and Sayyid Mustafa of Mandalay, edited and annotated by Sammireh A. Smith (Los Angeles, Kalimat Press). Several Americans have left memoirs of the visit: Ramona Allen Brown, *Memories of ᶜAbduʾl-Bahá: Recollections of the Early Days of the Baháʾí Faith in California* (Wilmette, Ill., Baháʾí Publishing Trust, 1980); Howard Colby Ives, *Portals to Freedom* (London, George Ronald, 1962); and Juliet Thompson, *The Diary of Juliet Thompson* (Los Angeles, Kalimat Press, 1982). Overall accounts of the North American visit have been provided by Alan Lucius Ward, 'An Historical Study of the North American Speaking Tour of ᶜAbduʾl-Bahá and a Rhetorical Analysis of his Addresses', PhD dissertation (Ohio University, 1960) and *239 Days: ᶜAbduʾl-Bahá's Journey in America* (Wilmette, Ill., Baháʾí Publishing Trust, 1979). On the visit to Canada, see also National Spiritual Assembly of the Baháʾís of Canada, *ᶜAbduʾl-Bahá in Canada* (Forest, Ontario, Forest Free Press, 1962). On the visits to Britain and France, see Lady [S.L.] Blomfield, *The Chosen Highway* (Wilmette, Ill., Baháʾí Publishing Trust, 1967); Eric Hammond, *Abdul Baha in London* (East Sheen, Surrey, Unity Press, for the Bahai Publishing Society, 1912); and National Spiritual Assembly of the Baháʾís of the British Isles, *ᶜAbduʾl-Bahá in Edinburgh* (London, 1963).

There are numerous accounts of visits to ᶜAbduʾl-Bahá by Western pilgrims. These include Thornton Chase, *In Galilee* (Chicago, Bahai Publishing Society, 1908; rev. edn, Los Angeles, Kalimat Press, 1985); Helen S. Goodall and Ella Goodall Cooper, *Daily Lessons Received at Acca, January 1908* (Chicago, Bahai Publishing Society, 1908; rev. edn, Wilmette, Ill., Baháʾí Publishing Trust, 1979); Louis G. Gregory, *A Heavenly Vista* (Washington, DC, 1912?); Julia M. Grundy, *Ten Days in the Light of Acca* (Chicago, Bahai Publishing Society, 1907; rev. edn, Wilmette, Ill., Baháʾí Publishing Trust, 1979); George Orr Latimer, *The Light of the World* (Boston, Mass., 1920); May Maxwell, *An Early Pilgrimage* (Oxford, George Ronald, 1953); and Corinne True, *Table Talks by Abdul Baha* (Chicago, Bahai Publishing Society, 1907).

The writings of Baháʾuʾlláh

Extensive collections of Bahaʾi scripture in the original Persian and Arabic have been published at various times in Iran, but given the difficulties of the present Bahaʾi situation in that country, these are not readily accessible. It is to be welcomed, then, that Bahaʾi publishers elsewhere have recently published a number of Baháʾuʾlláh's works in Persian, notably the *Kitáb-i mustaṭáb-i íqán* (1934; reprint, Hofheim-Langenhain, Baháʾí-Verlag, 1980); the *Lawḥ-i mubárak khaṭáb bih Shaykh Muḥammad Táqí Mujtahid Isfahání maᶜrúf bih Najafí* (the *Lawḥ-i ibn-i dhiᶜb*)

(Hofheim-Langenhain, Bahá'í-Verlag, 1982); and the major writings of the late ʿAkká period, *Majmúʿi'í az alwáḥ-i jamál-i aqdas-i abhá kih baʿad az kitáb-i aqdas názil shudih* (Hofheim-Langenhain, Bahá'í-Verlag, 1980).

In English, there are authorised Baha'i translations of most of Bahá'u'lláh's major works. Of the writings of the Baghdad period (1853–63), there are *The Hidden Words*, trans. Shoghi Effendi with the assistance of some English friends, rev. edn (London, National Spiritual Assembly of the Bahá'ís of the British Isles, 1932); *The Seven Valleys and the Four Valleys*, trans. Ali Kuli Khan and Marzieh Gail (Wilmette, Ill., Bahá'í Publishing Trust, 1952); and *The Kitáb-i Íqán: The Book of Certitude*, trans. Shoghi Effendi (London, Bahá'í Publishing Trust, 1946). Of the later writings, there are some of the 'Letters to the Kings', *The Proclamation of Bahá'u'lláh to the Kings and Leaders of the World* (Haifa, Bahá'í World Centre, 1967); *Epistle to the Son of the Wolf*, trans. Shoghi Effendi, rev. edn (Wilmette, Ill., Bahá'í Publishing Trust, 1946); and *Tablets of Bahá'u'lláh, Revealed after the Kitáb-i Aqdas*, trans. H. Taherzadeh and others (Haifa, Bahá'í World Centre, 1978). There are also two general compilations of his writings and prayers: *Gleanings from the Writings of Bahá'u'lláh*, [comp. and] trans. Shoghi Effendi, rev. edn (London, Bahá'í Publishing Trust, 1978); and *Prayers and Meditations by Bahá'u'lláh*, comp. and trans. Shoghi Effendi, rev. edn (London, Bahá'í Publishing Trust, 1978), together with a non-Baha'i edition of *Al-Kitáb al-Aqdas, or the Most Holy Book*, trans. and ed. E.E. Elder and W.M. Miller (London, Luzac, Royal Asiatic Society, 1961). A Baha'i edition of the *Aqdas* and its supplementary texts is in preparation.

The writings of ʿAbdu'l-Bahá

Editions of ʿAbdu'l-Bahá's writings in Persian include: *Mufávaḍát*, 2nd edn (Cairo, 1920; reprint, New Delhi, Bahá'í Publishing Trust, 1983); the *Risáli-yi madaniyyih* (Hofheim-Langenhain, Bahá'í-Verlag, 1984); and a collection of his letters, *Majmúʿi-yi khaṭábát-i haḍrat-i ʿAbdu'l-Bahá* (Hofheim-Langenhain, Bahá'í-Verlag, 1984).

In English, there are translations of several of his writings: *The Secret of Divine Civilization*, trans. M. Gail (Wilmette, Ill., Bahá'í Publishing Trust, 1957); the *Maqáli-yi shakhṣí sayyáḥ* (Browne, *Traveller's Narrative*); his letters to the North American Baha'is regarding teaching, the *Tablets of the Divine Plan*, rev. edn (Wilmette, Ill., Bahá'í Publishing Trust, 1977); and the *Will and Testament of ʿAbdu'l-Bahá* (Wilmette, Ill., Bahá'í Publishing Trust, 1944). There are also several volumes of his letters, *Tablets of Abdul*

Baha Abbas (3 vols., Chicago, Bahai Publishing Society, 1909–16); and *Selections from the Writings of ᶜAbdul-Bahá*, trans. M. Gail and others (Haifa, Bahá'í World Centre, 1978).

As to ᶜAbdu'l-Bahá's talks, many of these have been recorded verbatim in Persian and, in the case of *Some Answered Questions*, collected and trans. L.C. Barney (1908; rev. edn, Wilmette, Ill., Bahá'í Publishing Trust, 1981) and *Memorials of the Faithful*, trans. M. Gail (Wilmette, Ill., Bahá'í Publishing Trust, 1971), the English translations have been made from these transcripts. In the case of ᶜAbdu'l-Bahá's talks in the West, however, the translations generally represent the original rendering by the interpreter, as with *Paris Talks: Addresses Given by ᶜAbdu'l-Bahá in Paris in 1911–1912*, 11th edn (London, Bahá'í Publishing Trust, 1969); *The Promulgation of Universal Peace*, comp. Howard MacNutt (1922–5; 2nd edn, Wilmette, Ill., Bahá'í Publishing Trust, 1982); Hammond, *Abdul Baha in London*; and Soraya Chamberlain (comp.), *Abdul Baha on Divine Philosophy* (Boston, Mass., Tudor Press, 1918). Consequently, these later works are regarded as less authoritative.

THE BAHA'I FAITH AS A WORLD RELIGION

The early American Baha'i community

For an overview of early American Baha'i history, see Peter Smith, 'The American Bahá'í community, 1894–1917: a preliminary survey, in *Studies in Bábí and Bahá'í History, vol. I*, ed. M. Momen (Los Angeles, Kalimat Press, 1982), pp. 85–223. For detailed studies of the Kheiralla period, see Robert H. Stockman, *The Bahá'í Faith in America, vol. I: Origins, 1892–1900* (Wilmette, Ill., Bahá'í Publishing Trust, 1985); and a forthcoming study by Richard Hollinger, *Covenant and Crisis: Studies in Babi and Baha'i History, vol. IV* (Los Angeles, Kalimat Press). The recently reprinted volumes of the periodical *Bahai News/Star of the West* (Chicago, 1910–22) are an invaluable general resource for the period.

Shoghi Effendi and the Administrative Order

The only full-length biography of Shoghi Effendi is the memorial volume by his widow, Rúḥíyyih Rabbani, *The Priceless Pearl* (London, Bahá'í Publishing Trust, 1969). There are also memoirs by Ugo Giachery, *Shoghi Effendi: Recollections* (Oxford, George Ronald, 1973), and the non-Baha'i writer, Marcus Bach, *Shoghi Effendi: An Appreciation* (New York, Hawthorne Books, 1958).

An overview of the early development of the Administrative Order is provided by Shoghi Effendi, *God Passes By* (Wilmette, Ill., Bahá'í Publishing Trust, 1944), pp. 323–53, and more generally up to the present day by Eunice Braun, *The March of the Institutions* (Oxford, George Ronald, 1984). The letters of Shoghi Effendi and of the Universal House of Justice provide more detailed references. Many of the more significant documents are reproduced in the successive volumes of *Bahá'í World*. For details of administrative practice, see the handbooks published by various National Spiritual Assemblies, for example NSA of the Bahá'ís of the United Kingdom, *Principles of Bahá'í Administration*, 3rd edn (London, Bahá'í Publishing Trust, 1973); NSA of the Bahá'ís of the United Kingdom, *Notes for Guidance for Local Spiritual Assemblies*, mimeographed (London, 1981); and NSA of the Bahá'ís of the United States (comp.), *Guidelines for Local Spiritual Assemblies* (Wilmette, Ill., Bahá'í Publishing Trust, 1975).

The most detailed overview of opposition to the administration is provided by Vernon Elvin Johnson, 'An Historical Analysis of Critical Transformations in the Evolution of the Bahá'í World Faith', PhD dissertation (Baylor University, Texas, 1974), pp. 306–21. See also National Spiritual Assembly of the Bahá'ís of Canada, *The Power of the Covenant* (3 vols., Thornhill, Ontario, Baha'i Canada Publications, 1976–7).

The writings of Shoghi Effendi

Apart from his book, *God Passes By*, Shoghi Effendi's voluminous writings consist almost entirely of letters, written either by him, or on his behalf by one of his secretaries. His letters in English include a number of lengthy general letters: see *The Advent of Divine Justice* (1939; rev. edn, Wilmette, Ill, Bahá'í Publishing Trust, 1963); *The Promised Day is Come* (1941, 2nd edn, Wilmette, Ill., Bahá'í Publishing Trust, 1961); and *The World Order of Bahá'u'lláh* (1938; rev. edn, Wilmette, Ill., Bahá'í Publishing Trust, 1955). There is also his *Messages to the Bahá'í World, 1950–1957* (1958; 2nd edn, Wilmette, Ill., Bahá'í Publishing Trust, 1971), and volumes of letters to various national Baha'i communities, to date: *Bahá'í Administration* (1928; 5th edn, Wilmette, Ill., Bahá'í Publishing Trust, 1945) (to the American Baha'is); *Messages to America: Selected Letters and Cablegrams addressed to the Bahá'ís of North America, 1932–1946* (Wilmette, Ill., Bahá'í Publishing Committee, 1947); *Citadel of Faith: Messages to America, 1947–1957* (Wilmette, Ill., Bahá'í Publishing Trust, 1965); *Messages to Canada*

(Toronto, National Spiritual Assembly of the Bahá'ís of Canada, 1965); *High Endeavours: Messages to Alaska* ([Anchorage], National Spiritual Assembly of the Bahá'ís of Alaska, 1976); *The Unfolding Destiny of the British Bahá'í Community: The Messages of the Guardian of the Bahá'í Faith to the Bahá'ís of the British Isles* (London, Bahá'í Publishing Trust, 1981); *The Light of Divine Guidance: The Messages from the Guardian of the Bahá'í Faith to the Bahá'ís of Germany and Austria* (2 vols., Hofheim-Langenhain, Bahá'í-Verlag, 1982–5); *Dawn of a New Day* (New Delhi, Bahá'í Publishing Trust, 1970) (to the Baha'is of the Indian subcontinent and Burma); *Letters from the Guardian to Australia and New Zealand 1923–1957* (Sydney, National Spiritual Assembly of the Bahá'ís of Australia, 1970); and *Arohanui: Letters from Shoghi Effendi to New Zealand* (Suva, Bahá'í Publishing Trust, 1982). For his letters to Japan, see B.R Sims, *Japan Will Turn Ablaze: Tablets of ᶜAbdu'l-Bahá, Letters of Shoghi Effendi, and Historical Notes about Japan* ([Tokyo], Bahá'í Publishing Trust, 1974). Additionally there are several volumes of letters in Persian.

The writings of the Universal House of Justice

To date there have been two volumes of collected letters of the Universal House of Justice: *Wellspring of Guidance: Messages from the Universal House of Justice, 1963–1968* (Wilmette, Ill., Bahá'í Publishing Trust, 1969); and *Messages from the Universal House of Justice, 1968–1973* (Wilmette, Ill., Bahá'í Publishing Trust, 1976). For more recent letters, see Baha'i periodicals such as the American *Bahá'í News*. Other major publications are: *The Constitution of the Universal House of Justice* (Haifa, Bahá'í World Centre, 1972); *The Promise of World Peace* (Haifa, Bahá'í World Centre, 1985); and *A Synopsis and Codification of the Kitáb-i-Aqdas, the Most Holy Book of Bahá'u'lláh* (Haifa, Bahá'í World Centre, 1973). The Research Department of the House has also produced a series of compilations of writings from Bahá'u'lláh, ᶜAbdu'l-Bahá, Shoghi Effendi and the Universal House of Justice on various aspects of Baha'i belief and practice (see Chapter 9, note 5).

Modern Baha'i belief and practice

There are a number of useful introductions to the main elements of modern Baha'i belief and practice, notably John E. Esslemont, *Bahá'u'lláh and the New Era* (London, Allen and Unwin, 1923; 4th edn, London, Bahá'í Publishing Trust, 1974); John Ferraby, *All Things Made New: A*

Comprehensive Outline of the Bahá'í Faith (1957; rev. edn, London, Bahá'í Publishing Trust, 1975); William S. Hatcher and J. Douglas Martin, *The Bahá'í Faith: The Emerging Global Religion* (New York, Harper and Row, 1984); and John Huddleston, *The Earth Is But One Country* (London, Bahá'í Publishing Trust, 1976). The books by Esslemont and Ferraby have both been posthumously revised from the original editions.

Some indication of contemporary Baha'i thinking in the West can be gained from the periodicals *Bahá'í Studies* and *Bahá'í Studies Notebook* (Ottawa), *Dialogue* (Los Angeles), and *World Order* (Wilmette, Ill.). There is also a wide range of literature on a variety of topics produced by the independent Baha'i publishers George Ronald (Oxford) and Kalimat Press (Los Angeles). With the exception of Juan R. Cole, 'The concept of manifestation in the Bahá'í writings', *Bahá'í Studies* (1982), there is little in the way of systematic theology.

World-wide expansion

For a general account of Baha'i expansion up to 1944, see Shoghi Effendi, *God Passes By*. The volumes of the *Bahá'í Yearbook*, vol. I (New York, Bahá'í Publishing Committee, 1926) and the *Bahá'í World* provide detailed information on most Baha'i national communities from 1925 until 1953, thereafter becoming increasingly general in nature as the range and complexity of Baha'i activity increased. The various national Baha'i periodicals are also a major source of information, particularly the American *Bahá'í News*. Reference should also be made to the *Bahá'í International News Service* (Haifa). Statistics of Baha'i expansion are provided in the *Bahá'í World* volumes and the occasional statistical digests produced by the Baha'i World Centre.

The Middle East. There is little material on the development of the Iranian Baha'i community during the Pahlavi period. Peter L. Berger, 'From Sect to Church: A Sociological Interpretation of the Baha'i Movement', PhD dissertation (New School for Social Research, New York, 1954), pp. 124–30, provides a brief account. On the persecutions, see Douglas Martin, 'The persecution of the Bahá'ís of Iran, 1844–1984', *Bahá'í Studies*, 12–13 (1984); and Moojan Momen, *The Bábí and Bahá'í Religions, 1844–1944: Some Contemporary Western Accounts* (Oxford, George Ronald, 1981), pp. 462–81. On the 1955 persecution, see also Shahrough Akhavi, *Religion and Politics in Contemporary Iran: Clergy–State Relations in the Pahlaví Period* (Albany, New York, State University of New York Press, 1980), pp. 76–

80. On the current persecutions, see Bahá'í International Community, *The Bahá'ís of Iran: A Report on the Persecution of a Religious Minority*, rev. edn (New York, Bahá'í International Community, 1982); and Roger Cooper, *The Baha'is of Iran*, rev. edn (London, Minority Rights Group, 1985). On developments in Soviet Asia, see Walter Kolarz, *Religion in the Soviet Union* (London, Macmillan, 1961), pp. 470–3.

The West. On North America, see Berger, 'From Sect to Church', pp. 131–9; Loni J. Bramson, 'The Baha'i Faith and its Evolution in the United States and Canada from 1922 to 1936', PhD dissertation (Université Catholique de Louvain, 1981); Arthur Hampson, 'The Growth and Spread of the Baha'i Faith', PhD dissertation (University of Hawaii, 1980), pp. 218–35; Sandra S. Kahn, 'Encounter of Two Myths, Baha'i and Christian, in the Rural American South: A Study in Transmythicization', PhD dissertation (University of California at Santa Barbara, 1977); and National Spiritual Assembly of the Bahá'ís of the United States and Canada (comp.) *The Bahá'í Centenary: 1844–1944* (Wilmette, Ill., Bahá'í Publishing Committee, 1944). See also Gayle Morrison, *To Move the World: Louis G. Gregory and the Advancement of Racial Unity in America* (Wilmette, Ill., Bahá'í Publishing Trust, 1982).

On Europe and the 'Anglo-Pacific', see Rainer Flasche, 'Die Religion der Einheit und Selbstverwirklichung der Menschheit: Geschichte und Mission der Baha'i in Deutschland', *Zeitschrift für Missionswissenschaft und Religion*, 61,3 (1977), 188–213; National Spiritual Assembly of the Bahá'ís of the British Isles, *The Centenary of a World Faith: The History of the Bahá'í Faith and its Development in the British Isles* (London, Bahá'í Publishing Trust, 1944); NSA of the Bahá'ís of the British Isles, *World Development of the Faith* (London, Bahá'í Publishing Trust, 1952); Margaret J. Ross, 'Some Aspects of the Bahá'í Faith in New Zealand', MA thesis (University of Auckland, 1979); and Agnes B. Alexander, *Forty Years of the Bahá'í Cause in Hawaii, 1902–1942* (Honolulu, National Spiritual Assembly of the Bahá'ís of the Hawaiian Islands, 1974). A volume of essays on Baha'i history in various Western countries, Peter Smith (ed.), *Bahá'ís in the West: Studies in Bábí and Bahá'í History, vol. V* (Los Angeles, Kalimat Press), is in preparation.

The Third World. The only parts of the Baha'i Third World to have received detailed attention are India and Japan. On India, see William N. Garlington, 'The Baha'i Faith in Malwa: A Study of a Contemporary Religious Movement'. PhD dissertation (Australian National University,

1975), 'The Baha'i Faith in Malwa' in *Religion in South Asia*, ed. G.A. Odie (London, Curzon Press, 1977), pp. 101–17, and 'Baha'i conversions in Malwa, Central India', in *From Iran East and West: Studies in Bábí and Bahá'í History, vol. II*, ed. J.R. Cole and M. Momen (Los Angeles, Kalimat Press, 1984), pp. 157–85; and Steve L. Garrigues, 'The Baha'is of Malwa: Identity and Change among the Urban Baha'is of Central India', PhD dissertation (University of Lucknow, 1976). On Japan, see Agnes B. Alexander, *History of the Bahá'í Faith in Japan, 1914–1938* ([Tokyo], Japanese Bahá'í Publishing Trust, 1977).

INDEX

31; doctrines and motifs of, 31–47; growth and social composition of, 48–51, 53; Bahá'u'lláh's transformation of, 57, 59–62; schism within, 66
Badasht, 23–4, 46, 47, 54
Baha'i Faith, Baha'is, 1–2; contrast with Babism, 2, 47, 56, 82; emergence of, 66–8; initial consolidation of, 69–71, 73, 87–8, 89, 90; scripture and literature of, 72, 136–8, 160 (*see also* ʿAbdu'l-Bahá, the Báb, Bahá'u'lláh, Shoghi Effendi, Universal House of Justice); expansion of, 87–91, 100, 157–62 (*see also under individual countries and regions*); distribution of, 162–71
Baha'i International Community, 149
Bahai Temple Unity, 106, 120–1
Baha'i World Centre (Haifa–ʿAkká), 127, 162, 199
Baha'i World Federation, 139
Baha'i World Union, 184
Bahá'u'lláh, Mírzá Ḥusayn ʿAlí Núrí, 30, 41, 58; and the revival of Babism, 57, 59–62; leadership in Baghdad, 59–66; contrast with Ṣubḥ-i Azal, 59–60; attempted *rapprochement* with the Iranian government, 60, 79, 97; contacts with Sufism, 60–1, 64; in Edirne, 66–8; in ʿAkká, 69–70; proclamation of his cause, 83
Bahá'u'lláh, writings and teachings of, 62–5, 72, 138, 231–2; *Haft Vádí*, 64, 81; *Kitáb-i ʿAhdí*, 70; *al-Kitábu'l-Aqdas*, 80–1; *Kitáb-i Íqán*, 63, 64–5; *Long Healing Prayer*, 63, 84; on the Most Great Peace, 75–6; on the duties of the world's rulers, 76–7; on the impact of the West, 78, 196–7; his abrogation of *jihád*, 79; on liberty, 81
Bahiyyih Khánum, 70, 116
Bahjí, 69, 70, 162
Bálásarís, 9, 200n3
Baraghání, Fáṭimih Bigum, *see* Qurratu'l-ʿAyn
Baraghání, Ḥájí Mullá Muḥammad Taqí, 9, 22, 52
baraka (holiness), 11, 84, 213
Bárfurúsh, 26, 52
Bárfurúshí, Mullá Muḥammad ʿAlí, *see* Quddús
Bible, the: the Báb's reading of, 47, 82; Baha'i use of, 79, 83–4, 96
Boards of Counsel, 101, 106
Britain, 106, 121, 158, 161, 181, 182–3, 184–5, 186, 188; sample survey, 188–90
Bushrú'í, Mullá Ḥusayn, *see* Ḥusayn Bushrú'í
Burma, 91, 193–4
Burújirdí, Áqá Jamál, 71, 74

Canada, 106–7, 154, 158, 184, 186; *see also* North America
'charismatic field', 24, 29, 41
Chicago, 100, 104, 106
Chicago Reading Room, 113–14, 125, 154
Christians, Christianity: in Iran, 49, 84, 92, 94, 95–6; ʿAbdu'l-Bahá's view of their missionary success, 79; Baha'i proclamation to, 83; *see also* Bible
communism, 148
Counsellors, and Continental Boards, 132–3, 134–5, 152, 172
Covenant-breakers, violators (*Náqiḍín*), 71, 73–4, 111, 113, 119, 120, 124–5, 130–1
Covenant doctrine, 73–4, 111, 113–14

Darábí, Sayyid Yaḥyá Vaḥíd (Peerless), 21, 28, 41, 52, 54
Dayyán, Mírzá Asadu'lláh (of Khuy), 60, 203n5
Dyar, Harrison Gray, 124

East Asia, 100, 167, 169, 171, 190
Edirne, 66–8
education, 80, 152–3; in Baha'i schools, 90, 153, 173
Egypt, 68–9, 71, 72, 90, 91, 119, 120, 121, 158, 173–4
esotericism: as motif, 3, 33; in Shaykhism, 10–11, 35; in Babism, 35–8; in Baha'i, 84, 111–12, 154–5
Esperanto, 149–50, 182, 191
Europe, 100, 106–7, 161, 166, 168, 171, 182, 184–6, 187

'familialization', 92–3, 198
Fourth Support (*ruknu'r-rábiʿ*), 11, 25, 35
France, 106, 182
Furútan, ʿAlí Akbar, 153

Germany, 107, 121, 158, 162, 181–2, 183, 184, 185, 186
Green Acre, 104, 114, 182
Guardian of the Cause of God (*Valí-amru'lláh*), the Guardianship, 115, 130,